BILL HOOLE
Engineman Extraordinary

P. W. B. SEMMENS, M.A., F.R.I.C.

A Goodall paperback
from
Crécy Publishing Limited

First published in 1966 by Ian Allan LTD

A CIP record for this book is available from the British Library

This edition published in 2024

ISBN 9781800353183

A Goodall paperback

Printed in Malta by Gutenberg Press

published by

Crécy Publishing Limited

1a Ringway Trading Estate, Shadowmoss Road, Manchester M22 5LH

www.crecy.co.uk

BILL HOOLE

Contents

Foreword

By Gerard Fiennes
General Manager, Eastern Region, British Railways

Railway historians often write about railways as things: Great Western, Great Central, Great Northern. Railways are not things. They are the sum of people: designers of engines and timetables, maintainers, inspectors and drivers. Gresley; the faceless men in Great Northern House; Palmer; Dixon; and Hoole. This book is about railways in terms of people and that is as it should be.

Mr. Semmens tells me a lot about William Hoole that I did not know but suspected. Indeed I approached the whole subject of Bill with deep suspicion having arrived at King's Cross at the time of that put up job, the bomb hoax. I made it my business to take a look at him at King's Cross. A foul, thick night of fog on the main line: Drivers, their eyes bright slits in raw faces, clambered wearily from their engines. Then one who "alighted". He padded off into the murk with the brief economical movements of perfect balance. Driver Hoole.

Thereafter whenever the temptation came to repress Bill-and it came now and again-I said to myself "perfect balance; he knows". I yielded to the temptation once only when he wanted to go after Mallard's record. Then, for reasons unconnected with Bill or '7' I threatened Cyril Palmer and him that if they wouldn't be good we would hang on another 300 tons behind him at Grantham.

Bill did a great deal for railways beyond his duty. One of the most silent of men; devoted to the "no paper" war (thanks a million) he wrote to me in a tiny corner of a tiny sheet) he yet communicated the magic of railways to thousands.

I wish we had him over again and more like him-but not in the Top Link at the same time. The Race to the North on the same day on the same metals would not endear us to the Management.

Acknowledgements

My grateful acknowledgements are due to the following people who have very kindly acted as sources of information:

A. J. Boston	Mr. & Mrs. W. Mather
F. Boughey	F. Mayes
W. Carter	The late C. Palmer
P. J. Coster	A. F. Pegler
A. G. W. Garraway	A. B. Quick
N. Harvey	T. G. Rushton
Mrs. A. Hatherill	C. P. Walker
A. E. Leech	F. T. Wayne
K. Leech	

The following bodies or officials have also provided considerable assistance:

The Cunard Steam-Ship Co. Limited
The Editor, The Barnet Press
The Libraries of Co. Durham and Middlesbrough
The Liverpool Records Office
The City of Liverpool Museums
The Mersey Docks and Harbour Board
The Royal Mint

In addition, I am grateful to all those who have lent me illustrations, which are acknowledged individually. Mr. G. F. Fiennes has most kindly written the Foreword, and my thanks are also due to Mr. E. S. Knee for his assistance with reading the proofs.

P. W. B. Semmens.
Middlesbrough, December, 1965.

Preface

Many books have been written in recent years about railways, railway locomotives, or railway locomotive performance, but comparatively little has been published about the lives of those who had the task of battling through summer heat and wintry chills on the footplate of a steam locomotive. When I was offered the chance of writing the biography of Bill Hoole, I decided that it would be an excellent opportunity to try and record, before it was too late, something of what it was like to have one's whole life centre around the steam locomotive. Dirt was inevitably the lot of the cleaner, and when he graduated to become a fireman, there would often be a wet shirt and blistered hands to put up with in addition. For the driver there was the thrill of fast running, but set against that was the arduous task of feeling one's way down the line in thick fog or falling snow, with an engine whose steaming was proving troublesome. All these aspects I have tried to capture in this book, set against the background of the technical, managerial, and union developments that took place on the Railways during the first half of this century. I have tried to be as objective as possible throughout the book, but our nearness to the later events has necessitated a certain amount of reticence about some of the incidents, and in 20 years' time it will probably be possible to write an even more lively account of Bill's last years on British Railways.

Other main-line drivers have undoubtedly been equally as capable of time-recovery as Bill, and Norman McKillop has already ably described some of these "Ace Enginemen" and "Enginemen Elite". Other locomo tive men have also risen to far greater eminence than Bill did in Union or Civic affairs, but few have made so many friends, inside as well as outside the railways. It is the very number of those who know Bill or who have heard of some of his exploits that has justified the publication of a full-length book on this out-of-the-ordinary or extraordinary engineman, whose life has been more than usually eventful. Bill retired from British Railways just before the diesel era came in with a rush, and readers must be very careful not to equate conditions as they were in the years before 1959 with those on British Rail today. Fundamental managerial changes have resulted from a thorough assessment of the true cost of all the various railway operations, which has now shown up the weaknesses and advan tages that the railways possess in the second half of the twentieth century. In the course of this, however, the steam locomotive has been all but swept away, and far less scope now remains for the individually-minded engineman to improve on contemporary standards of train running.

My thanks are due to many people for their assistance during the preparation of this book, and whose names can be found in the list of acknowledgements. A special word of thanks must be recorded, however, to the subject of the biography, Bill himself, for his very patient replies to my numerous spoken and written questions which have sallied back and forth between Middlesbrough and Boston Lodge over a period of 18 months.

I would like to make it quite clear that, throughout the book, the opinions expressed are entirely my own, unless they are specifically ascribed to a particular individual.

P. W. B. Semmens, M.A.

"Airdrie",
34 Harrow Road, Linthorpe,
Middlesbrough,
Yorkshire
December, 1965.

Preface to Paperback Edition

In the eight years since this book was written much has happened. In August 1968, British Rail retired their last standard-gauge steam locomotives, the final rail tour being a sell-out at £15 per head. Since then "Inter-City" services have shot ahead in popularity, speed and frequency, as the full potentialities of the existing diesel and electric locomotives have been realised, aided by improvements in the track. No longer, for instance, is it necessary for East Coast expresses to slow to 20 mph to thread the tortuous curves of Peterborough station, and nearly 80% of the main line between King's Cross and Newcastle has been cleared for 100 mph running. Already the next generation of motive power is at work, with the appearance of new electric locomotives for the extension of the electrification to Glasgow, and the High Speed Train, with diesel quasi-locomotives, which reached 143 mph during trials.

The railway preservation movement, which had got under way with the formation of the Talyllyn Preservation Society in 1950, celebrated its coming of age in 1971, by which time the pioneer North Wales lines had been joined by many standard-gauge societies, situated throughout thewhole country. On top of these preserved railways, appreciable numbers of main-line locomotives had been purchased and were maintained in running condition at depots such as Tyseley and Dinting. British Rail, with the understandable object of displaying as modern an image to the world as possible, stopped the running of any steam-hauled trains on their lines until 1972, when a relaxation of the ban saw certain of the locomotives at work on rail tours again over specified routes.

One of the first locomotives to be involved in this "Return to Steam" was Bill's old engine, Sir Nigel Gresley, now restored to full LNER garter-blue livery by the A4 Society as No. 4498. After withdrawal by British Rail, she had been thoroughly overhauled at Crewe, and had worked a few rail tours for the

Society, before the ban on steam specials. She was kept in the National Coal Board's sheds at Philadelphia, County Durham, venturing out to trundle up and down some 200 yards of track on a couple of steaming week-ends each year. It seemed akin to exercising a thoroughbred horse in a tennis-court, but we could nevertheless admire her immaculate appearance, and be grateful for the knowledge that she was ready for a come-back as soon as British Rail gave the word.

The Festiniog Railway too has changed, to an almost unbelievable extent, since this book was first written. From what was then thought to be a staggering total of 150,000 passenger journeys in 1964, it is now handling no less than 400,000 a year. During the peak season, 3 separate trains work on 45-minute regular interval services, their coaches, now in cherry-red livery, being hauled by oil burning locomotives, some of them new to the Festiniog, and all extensively modernised. No longer is Tan-y-Bwlch the upper terminus, as trains continue to Dduallt or even beyond, where an army of "Deviationalists" has been at work since 1965 to build a new alignment for the railway to replace the section flooded by the CEGB pumped storage scheme. This work was, initially, all carried out by volunteers. However, following the Festiniog's final success in the courts, with their £106,000 award for compensation, contractors could be called in for the construction of the new Moelwyn Tunnel, to supplement the continuing voluntary labour. The target is for the line to Blaenau Ffestiniog to be completed for the summer of 1978. There have been other changes on the Festiniog too, amongst the volunteers, with a new generation acting as firemen on the locomotives, while the majority of those with whom Bill used to work are now married and bringing up families that are as yet too young to be able·to join in the activities of running one of the "Great Little Trains of Wales".

During all these developments, Bill had, unfortunately, to play a passive role, as at Easter 1967, in his 73rd year, he suffered a stroke, which made him very much less mobile, and meant he was no longer able to drive Prince. After the initial period, though, he was still able to potter about the sheds at Boston·Lodge. Encouraged by Dolly, who would accompany him on his regular visits to the physiotherapist at Blaenau Ffestiniog, he quickly learnt to write and shave himself with his left hand, but because he was less active, he tended to find the winters were more troublesome. The Festiniog Management kept a kindly, if unobtrusive, eye on them throughout, and their daughter's move to Birmingham meant they had relatives within fairly close range. On special occasions, too, one of the trains would be stopped outside No. 1 Boston Lodge, for Bill to climb aboard for Tan-y-Bwlch or Dduallt. Other friends would, by arrangement, call to take Bill and Dolly for a car ride on suitable occasions, perhaps to a place of new railway interest such as the Llyn Padarn Railway at Llanberis.

During Sir Nigel Gresley's forced sojourn at Philadelphia, the directors of the A4 Society were most anxious that Bill should, if at all possible, manage to visit the locomotive during one of its week-ends in steam. I was drawn into the arrangements, and after much behind-the-scenes activity, Gerard Fiennes collected Bill and Dolly in his car one Friday in April 1972 to bring them part way to Middlesbrough where I could meet them for the remainder of the distance. This was much the furthest journey Bill had undertaken since his illness, and we had arranged for a rest day for him on the Saturday, but such was his interest that we finished up taking him and Dolly on a tour of Whitby and the North Yorkshire Moors. Another urgent problem presented itself, however, as Bill no longer possessed any overalls, but I was able to lend him mine, and he was delighted to be back in uniform again, with the prospect of seeing Sir Nigel Gresley the following day.

On the Sunday we journeyed north to Philadelphia, after lunch, where the usual crowds had gathered to watch the locomotive at work. Bill was received like royalty, installed in the left seat and then, before setting off, Dolly was also escorted on to the footplate. As it turned out, this was the first time in her life she had been on a locomotive with Bill. With a cab-full of other dignitaries, including one of the Directors of the Canadian Railroad Historical Association, Bill eased open the regulator and "No. 7" responded once more to his touch after a gap of nearly 13 years since he had retired from King's Cross. I forget how many times we ran up and down the few hundred yards of track, but Bill was enjoying himself, and it was like old times when the press came and asked him to pose for a photograph. Finally he left the footplate, and, in the warm spring sunshine, spent the next half hour leaning against the shed office wall, watching other, less expert, drivers at work with Sir Nigel. Copies of this book were produced for him to autograph, and the Society members presented him with a miniature cast nameplate of the locomotive. It was delightful to see Bill at the centre of interest once again, and as Dolly put it in a later letter, "Words cannot express what a wonderful week-end we have had; such kind Folk to make Bill's day. To drive Sir Nigel was a real treat for Bill with no effects on his health".

Bill and Dolly still live at No. 1 Boston Lodge, and although unable to keep up their correspondence as they did previously, they are still glad to hear from friends old and new about railway happenings, while those who do manage to get to North Wales are always welcome to call. And Bill's influence is still having its effect on the preservation scene, since it was his advice that finally decided Ken Saunders, one of his former firemen, to emulate his example and take up the post of regular driver on the North Yorkhire Moors Railway.

Since first writing this book, I have received numerous letters, many of them from complete strangers, telling me their stories about Bill, supplying some new item of information, or enquiring after his health. Perhaps the most interesting of these was from Miss Adeline Skinner, the daughter of Driver Charlie Skinner whose locomotive Bill used to clean at Neasden. She lent me her father's note books, including the one in which he was recording the timings of the "Coronation" express up to a few minutes before he was killed, just north of Northallerton, as recorded on page 75. During recent months, the predominant question in these letters has been "How can I get hold of a copy of the book". I was consequently delighted when Ian Allan Ltd. suggested the possibility of a paperback edition, and I was able to bring up to date this story of a great character and railwayman at work among the steam locomotives that provided the background to his life.

P. W. B. Semmens, MA. FRIG.

Middlesbrough
November, 1973.

CHAPTER ONE

A Liverpool Lad

Liverpool, during the opening years of this century, must have been one of the most interesting cities in the world in which a mechanically minded youngster could hope to grow up. Historians have argued about the origins of the port and even of the derivation of its name, but in the first 700 years that had elapsed since the borough was founded by King John in 1207, Liverpool had developed into one of the world's foremost ports, and will always be associated with the first railway that was steam worked from its inception.

Like so many of the cities in this small island, with its long, indented coastline, Liverpool owed much of its prosperity to the geographical features of the Mersey, its wide, well-protected estuary stretching for more than a dozen paunch-like miles south-eastwards between the Cheshire plains and the mosses of South Lancashire. In days of sail, however, the difficulties of beating very far up-river against adverse winds or tides could easily make a port less attractive, as Stockton-on-Tees found to its cost when the railways reached Port Clarence and Middlesbrough. On the north bank of the Mersey, however, there was a small side creek, swinging back northwards, and known as the "Pool" of Liverpool, offering welcome protection to the small vessel from the fierce currents as the tides rushed in and out to cover or expose the wide acres of mudflats that lay up-river. On the northern promontory formed by the Mersey and the Pool of Liverpool, on the site now occupied by Queen Victoria's monument, King John built his castle as the first stage in the conversion of the existing port into a naval base from which he could conquer Wales and Ireland.

Our island adventurers have always tended to look westward, rather than towards the mainland of Europe, and with the foundation of our colonies in North America, Liverpool was excellently situated to handle the steadily-growing traffic. In the latter half of the 18th century, Liverpool became the centre of the slave trade, the ships working a triangular route from the Mersey to Africa, and then the West Indies, returning with sugar, tobacco, and cotton to be processed in the rapidly expanding city. The Great Reform Bill of 1835, sweeping away the rotten boroughs throughout the country, provided Liverpool with a civic body better suited for rapid expansion to match the rise of industry. So much so, that during the 19th century, its boundaries had been thrice enlarged, the last addition taking in the ancient township of Walton-on-the-Hill, which could claim greater antiquity than Liverpool itself. The population rose from 77,000 to over 700,000, the total being swelled by immigrants from Ireland, many of whom did not have the money to continue their way across the Atlantic to America. In their wake came slums, chronic unemployment, and labour unrest, all of which contributed to Liverpool's distinctive and cosmopolitan character, while the ocean liners of the Cunard and White Star Lines brought back to Pierhead those who had made the grade in the New World.

It was against this background that William (always to be known as Bill) Hoole was born on 27th July 1894, the second son of William and Martha Hoole. Their home, where Bill and all his brothers and sisters were born, was in Luther Street, one of the side streets that opens off Great Homer Street, which lies one block away to the west of Scotland Road. Before his marriage, William Hoole senior had been a seaman, and had made two trips round the world on windjammers. After settling on dry land, however, until 1904 he kept a lock-up greengrocer's shop in Great Homer Street, some 10 minutes' walk away from his home. Jim, the eldest son, was five years older than Bill, and so grew up "way out" from the rest of the family, and after Bill came Christopher, Ethel, Frank, Tom and Martha. In their younger days, Christopher and Bill had good fun together, in spite of the former's short temper which was well associated with his nickname and hair colouring, "Ginger". These two brothers were both to become enginemen, Christopher working as a driver on the inter-Island trains in New Zealand, which, needless to say, necessitated spending most of his time on the train ferries. Here his father once joined him for a journey, but although he also hoped to ride with Bill, he was never able to achieve this ambition before his death in the early 1930s.

2

As a member of a large family brought up in a time when the working week was anything in the range of 55 to 72 hours, and paid holidays were rare, Bill was very much left to himself to find his own amusements, and from an early age took to exploring Liverpool at weekends and during the school holidays. First amongst the attractions was the bustle of the port itself, spread along both banks of the Mersey as defined by the Surveyor General of the Customs as long ago as 1660. Second only to London in size, Liverpool's exports were 30 per cent greater in value than those leaving the Thames, while the tonnage of vessels handled in the year ending on lst July 1905 was 32 million, being only eclipsed by one other port in the world-London. Great civic pride was taken in the port installations, 63 wet docks and basins enclosing 569 acres of water and providing more than 35 miles of quayside. Some 260 cranes with lifting capacities of up to 100 tons transferred cargoes between freighters and the shed accommodation on the dock-side. There were more than 200 acres of covered storage area, pride of place being taken by the Tobacco Warehouse at Stanley Dock, believed to be the largest building of its sort in the world; 125 feet high, with a floor area of 36 acres, it provided storage for over 60,000 casks of tobacco in a single tier spread over the 13 floors. Besides tobacco, there were granaries, such as those at East Waterloo Dock and at East Float, Birkenhead, both capable of taking more than 35,000 tons of corn. Visitors to the city were enjoined to make a special effort to see the elevators at work, scooping the golden grain out of the ships' holds. The modern generation, used to the arrival of frozen and tinned meat from overseas, does not appreciate the vast quantities of livestock that were imported "on the hoof" to supply the "red meat" made so well known half a century later by Lord Woolton, one of the city's most famous sons, renowned both as politician and businessman. This trade was mainly handled at Birkenhead, where the Foreign Animals Wharf had pens for 6,000 cattle and no less than 16,000 sheep. Slaughter-houses nearby could handle 3,000 sheep a day, and even more cattle, while the chill rooms dealt with 2,800 carcases in 24 hours. During 1905, over a quarter of a million oxen were landed at Birkenhead, together with 160,000 sheep. Oil and petroleum products were already playing a part in the business of the port as long ago as 1905, when the Anglo American Oil Company boasted storage facilities for 18,000 tons of petrol at Birkenhead. As a contrast, during the year ending in July 1964, nearly 7 million tons of petroleum products were imported through the Mersey, much of the total being made up of crude oil discharged at Tranmere Oil Terminal for the Shell refinery at Stanlow.

Tramp steamers and sailing vessels have never captured the glamour that has surrounded the ocean liner, Kipling's eulogies on the subject notwithstanding, and in the 1900s Liverpool could boast a virtual monopoly of the transatlantic traffic. Constant dredging at the mouth of the Mersey in the 16 years since 1890 had removed nearly 100 million tons of sand, increasing the minimum depth of water over the bar from 11 to 27 feet, so that the last knot squeezed out of the turbines of an ocean greyhound would not be frittered away waiting for the tide. The range between high and low water in the Mersey is no less than 35 feet, and to combat the effects of this, a floating structure, St. George's Landing Stage, was opened in 1847. 29 years later it was followed by a larger down-river extension, Prince's Stage, the largest floating structure of its kind in the world. Known locally as "The Stick", it is half a mile long by approximately 80 feet wide, deriving its support from 200 pontoons, and having eight bridges connecting it to the quayside. Alongside the northern, seaward, end of this, the liners would berth, assisted by paddle tugs, while an official of the Mersey Docks and Harbour Board stood by ready to start his stop-watch as soon as the first mooring rope was secured. So intensive was the use of the stage that very high dues were exacted for its use, the ships casting off again after the passengers had gone ashore, and making their way to the then most-recently constructed berths at the north end of the Dock Estate at Bootle, or to a buoy in the Sloyne the deep-water channel upstream of Cammell Laird's shipyard. While the Harbour Board watch was ticking off the minutes, however, many would be the reunions on the stage as returning immigrants who had made their fortunes in the Americas walked down the gangways. Interspersed among them would be the financiers and industrialists, impatient to catch their London-bound train from the adjoining London and North Western Riverside station, its name emblazoned across its roof to catch the eyes of potential passengers while their ship was still in mid-river. The Midland Railway also sought their share of these passengers, in addition to the bullion traffic which was later to concern Bill. Advertise ments over the name of John Mathieson, their General Manager, pro claimed that "the Midland Railway of England was the best route in the Old Country for comfortable travel and picturesque scenery". Passen gers on the Atlantic liners were enjoined to ask the Purser for a MIDLAND timetable and travel brochure entitled "The Picturesque Route in the Old Country". Against these blandishments the L.N.W.R. was boasting the "Quickest, Shortest, and Smoothest Route between Liverpool, Birmingham (2 hours 15 minutes) and London (3 hours 35 minutes)". In the summer of 1964, 41 years after Derby and Euston had both been grouped into the London, Midland and Scottish Railway and converted 25 years later into one of the six Regions of British Railways, the best time from Lime Street to London was 3 hours 40 minutes.

What were the ships that Bill saw arrive and depart, when, with the other watching crowds, he made his way down to Pierhead? Early in this century competition for passenger traffic across the Atlantic was fierce. The Cunard and White Star Companies both sought to outbid each other with larger and more luxurious vessels. Patronage was sufficient to attract foreigners like Norddeutscher Lloyd, as well as the two great British lines, who were only to be amalgamated in the depression of the early 1930s, when No. 542 lay motionless on John Brown's Clyde side stocks for 2½ long years before being named Queen Mary at her 1933 launching. In 1899, the pride of the White Star fleet was the 704- foot Oceanic, the first vessel to exceed in length Brunel's Great Eastern, that great masterpiece conceived by the builder of the G.W.R. 40 years ahead of her time. Never a commercial success on the Atlantic run, the Great Eastern had spun the first telegraphic cables across that stormy ocean, only to return in 1889 to the Mersey, where during the ensuing two years the crash of the ship-breakers' ball reverberated across Liverpool as the double wrought iron hull was smashed into manageable portions. Over in Luther Street, Martha Hoole may well have had occasion to curse the noise as it woke a fretful Jim, but by the time that Bill was born the last of the Great Eastern had disappeared, together with the two skeletons that she had carried in her double bottom since she first entered the water at the Isle of Dogs, 32 years previously. Although the 1899 Oceanic exceeded the Great Eastern in length, she was some 6,000 tons lighter, and it was not until 1906 that Cunard launched a vessel with a greater displacement-the Lusitania. After making her record-breaking maiden voyage from Liverpool the following year, she became a well known sight on the Mersey, her four red and black funnels regularly tower ing above the quayside buildings until they appeared in the periscope of a U-Boat Commander, and her sinking helped bring the United States into World War I. And if the name Lusitania strikes a chord of terror into all those who have read of the vessel's fate, in 1907 her speed and luxury were shortly to be challenged by the pride of the White Star line, the Titanic. Next to the ocean greyhounds in fascination for a youngster came the shorter-distance passenger boats sailing between Liverpool and Ireland, the Isle of Man, or on day cruises along the Lancashire and North Wales coasts. Paddle steamers mainly, they were a joy to behold, their ornate paddleboxes echoing to the thrash of the wheels, while rivulets of water ran down and splashed over the rotating spokes as the vessels cast off and made down-river in response to the pings of the engine-room tele graph. In a city that depended so much on the sea for its economic well-being, there were many other sights that attracted a youngster down to the water's edge. Bill remembers seeing the equipment for one of the polar expeditions laid out for exhibition in the dock shed alongside the ship, the takings helping to meet the cost of the enterprise. He also recalls the visit of the Australian prison ship connected with the Ned Kelly Gang, and seeing in dry dock another vessel with notorious associa tions, the Brazilian Dreadnought Sao Paulo, whose first crew mutinied. Other vessels sailed to and from the Prince's Stage, as well as the ocean-going liners and those voyaging across the Irish Sea. As far back as 1817, steam ferry boats had started to ply across the Mersey to the town of Birkenhead, which by the turn of the century had a population of over 100,000. At the time Bill used to make his way down to Pierhead, paddle ferries were still in service, their twin funnels surmounting their rather ungainly superstructure, while the ever-open bars below decks kept up a continuous trade. The two most famous vessels associated with this service came into operation in 1906-the Iris and Daffodil, which per formed such epic feats during the raid on Zeebrugge during World War I. Fogs crept in from the Irish Sea at times, and the conurbation haze spreading out from both sides of the Mersey would, on occasions, lengthen the normal 15-minute crossing into a far longer siren-hooting journey, while ship's hooters and bells came echoing faintly through the murk. In spite of these obstacles, some 30 million passengers a year used the ferries across the Mersey, so that there were always footsteps echoing across the southern end of the landing stage.

I

3

The ferries did not have a monopoly of the cross-river passengers, however, as the Mersey Railway had driven its twin-track tunnel from below Liverpool Central Station under the Mersey to just short of Birkenhead Park, in 1886. Steadily increasing traffic and difficulties of operating on gradients as steep as 1 in 27 with steam posed a considerable problem to the directors, and in 1903 electrification of the 4¾ route miles was completed at a cost of £386,000. The railway, which was to remain independent until Nationalisation in 1948, was thus the first urban under ground line to see the disappearance of steam and smoke, beating London's Inner Circle by 2 years. By 1906, they were cheerfully advertising their service of 750 trains per day, "Free from Fogs, Gales, and Tides", taking "4½ minutes from the heart of Liverpool to the centre of Birkenhead". Trains ran every 3 minutes, the actual passage under the Mersey from James Street station to Hamilton Square only requiring 2¼ minutes. The original Mersey Railway electric stock lasted into British Railways days, so that Southern green ultimately replaced the former Indian red livery with its gold-lined matchboard panels, and the name of the company in shaded lettering between the cant-rail and the tops of the numerous small rectangular windows. Clerestory roofs were provided, with domed ends leading down to the fussy front with its recessed central door, so that the units had a strong resemblance to the early Pullman cars. The driving position was on the left, and the other side of the front compartment was occupied with electric contactors which would emit blinding flashes in the semi-gloom of the Central Station, as the trains were set back into the shunting neck before running into the departure side of the Low Level's single island platform.

The Mersey Railway's electrified tracks ultimately formed a "Y", running to Birkenhead Park and Rock Ferry, with a very busy flat junction at the western end of Hamilton Square. Rock Ferry formed an exchange point with the G.W.R./L.N.

W.R. joint line running up to Birkenhead from Chester. It was these metals, leading down through the tunnel to Woodside, that carried the emigrant trains run every Thursday by the G.W.R. to the cavernous variegated-brick terminus from as far away as Penzance. The author's father, born 7½ months before Bill, always used to recall a journey he made by train through Cornwall as a young boy. In the mining area around Camborne and Redruth, the up platforms were packed with miners waiting for this train, en route for the Yukon, half a world away, where the lure of gold was brighter than the dulling fortunes of my native Cornish copper and tin mines.

The right-hand junction at Hamilton Square led to Birkenhead Park, the exchange station with the Wirral Railway, whose tank engines used to shuttle their loads backwards and forwards to the resorts and residential areas of New Brighton and West Kirby. In 1938 these lines too were electrified by the LMS, their maroon multiple-units with air-operated doors working through to Liverpool Central over the Mersey Railway, and contrasting strangely with the original Mersey Railway stock.

4

New Brighton was made much of on Merseyside as a resort, the 1906 Official Handbook waxing eloquent about the "capital sands with safe bathing", the pier nearly 600 feet in length, and the 560 foot tower set in the pleasure gardens, which was a smaller edition of the famous Blackpool landmark. There was a direct ferry service to Liverpool, and the promenade formed an ideal vantage point from which to watch the numerous ships passing in and out of the Mersey. At the turn of the century sailing vessels were more common than steamers, and a full-rigged ship was by no means an unusual sight for Bill, as she broke out her canvas to begin her ocean voyage. The Handbook contains a half-tone block of the sands, fairly crowded, even by modern standards, with holidaymakers. But where today pink skin would be seen in abundance, rapidly tanning in the sunshine, 60 years ago there was almost a complete absence of any exposed flesh other than hands and faces, blue serge dresses or knicker bockers continuing down to ankle level, with the occasional starched white cotton dress to set off the straw hats being worn by nearly everyone. It certainly looked far less comfortable for the children, but to youngsters of those days it was a welcome change from the cramped living conditions of Liverpool and the other Lancashire towns.

Holidays for Liverpool children were not always seaside ones, however. Bill remembers enjoying a farm holiday at Nannerch in North Wales during the summer of 1903, which was arranged by the Liverpool Education Committee. He spent the 2 weeks in the company of three other boys under the kindly care of the farmer's wife, Mrs. Griffiths, and on Bill's ninth birthday, as a treat, they were entertained to a picnic on Snowdon, travelling there by pony and trap. This was Bill's first visit to North Wales, and his second was two years later, when Jim took him and Christopher for a day trip on the popular paddle steamer La Marguerite. Her owners, the Liverpool and North Wales Steamship Company, had acquired her from the Victoria Steamship Association a few years previously to help meet the demand for day trips to and from Liverpool, and she looked very smart in their house livery of yellow funnels, with their flag proudly waving from the masthead. This consisted of a gold Prince of Wales plume mounted in the centre of a blue cross on a white ground, and the thought never crossed Bill's mind that 55 years later he would be wearing the same badge in his railway cap on the Festiniog.

Going ashore at Llandudno, the three lads made their way to the top of the Great Orme. After enjoying the view across the Irish Sea and the thrill of looking down the 500 feet near-vertical drop to the rocks below, they made their way back to the pier through Happy Valley. Jim, who had visited Llandudno before, suddenly put his fingers to his mouth and gave a shrill whistle, the resulting repeated echo startling his two brothers. They were so taken with the effect that Jim was pressed for numerous encores, and finally had to give up as the repeated whistling made him really thirsty. Some of the enjoyment that Bill now gets out of sounding Prince's chime whistle on the Festiniog may well stem from the fun the three Hoole brothers had in Happy Valley in 1905.

5

Pierhead was not only the centre of the passenger shipping on the Mersey, but from it radiated no less than 12 out of the 21 routes that comprised Liverpool's tramway system. They had been taken over by the Corporation for a sum of over £-½ m. in 1897, the year after the city had acquired the electricity undertaking with its power station at Trafalgar Dock. Not surprisingly, therefore, electrification of the tramways began the following year with German-built single-decker cars and trailers, their route being shown by letters painted on three-foot high vertical boards mounted on the roof in front of the clerestory. In December 1900 the horse cars ceased running, and by 1905 the electric trams were carrying 119 million passengers a year. With fares as low as two miles a penny, this vast total only brought in a revenue of £550,000. Operating expenses were low, however, and it is worth recalling that it was only in 1897 that the working hours of busmen and tramwaymen were reduced to 72 hours per week.

The Liverpool Tramways were laid to standard gauge, most of the streets being wide enough to take double track, set in the cobblestones with, in many cases, central supports for the overhead wires. Elsewhere, as in Ranelagh Street outside Central Station, the road was not sufficiently wide for this arrangement, and there was only a single line of rails. At busy junctions, round-capped pointsmen routed trams on to their correct routes by means of pinch bars which were inserted into the toe of the turnout to move them in the appropriate direction. Down at Pierhead, the main terminus, there were some turning loops and a maze of intersecting tracks, over which the cars would squeal and clank before passing under the arched bridges that carried the Liverpool Overhead Railway. Even as late as 1943, Liverpool was extending its tram routes, when the line to the Kirkby Industrial Estate was completed. This gave a 9-mile ride from Pierhead, two thirds of the distance being over reserved track provided with cross-sleepers. In 1939 their fleet of trams numbered 788, and nearly half this total was made up from new modern vehicles built or acquired during the previous five years. 1958, however, saw the start of the replacement of the trams by buses, the first of which had been brought into use by the Corporation in 1912.

In 1906, the City was advertising "Excursions by Electric Car" from Pierhead as a tourist attraction for visitors, and these were remarkably cheap by modern standards. Excursion No. 1 by the Garston Car covered 23½ miles in 2½ hours at a fare of 1 ld., while if this was too expensive or too long a time to spend, taking the Knotty Ash Car on Excursion No. 3 occupied only 40 minutes, and cost 2d. for the 5 miles 223 yards. The accuracy with which the distances were quoted makes one wonder whether due allowance was made for the differences caused by the varying radii between the outer and inner tracks on curves, nor is it known whether any visitor complained when the Cars stopped a yard or two short of the large square notices that indicated the tram stops! On some of these excursions, use was made of the vast interconnecting network of tram routes that used to exist in South Lancashire. At one time it was possible to travel 40 miles as the crow flies from Seaforth, at the north end of Bootle, to Roaches, a mile or so east of Stalybridge, over physically continuous 4' 8½" tramway track. There were numerous ways of completing the journey, of course, but even the shortest involved numerous detours from the most direct route, and frequent changes of vehicles. Sightseeing trips of this sort were often publicised, and even as late as 1920 it was possible to travel from Manchester to Liverpool by Electric Car for 2/3d. single. The journey involved five changes, and the average time for the 37½ miles was 4½ hours.

6

Early in this century, passenger traffic between Manchester and Liver pool was sufficient to set the three competing railway companies straining to outbid each other for the greatest share of it, all of them offering the same non-stop time of 40 minutes for their principal expresses. Out of Central Station, the Cheshire Lines ("The Punctual Service-Best Route") ran hourly express trains over their 34-mile fairly easily-graded route to Manchester Central, leaving Liverpool at half past every hour from 8.30 a.m. until 9.30 p.m., but only one train in each direction achieved a 40-minute timing. In most cases the Sacre 4-4-0s with their trains of 12-wheeled coaches were content with a 45-minute schedule, inclusive of a stop at Warrington. The L.N.W.R. from Lime Street had inherited the route of Stephenson's 1830 Liverpool and Manchester Railway, with its gentle gradients apart from the immediate climb out of the terminus and the Rainhill hump. Over this route of 31 miles, now so effortlessly traversed by the Trans-Pennine diesels with one intermediate stop in 39 minutes, the L.N.W.R. ran their 40-minute service, but this was no sinecure for the fireman, as Prof. Tuplin has so graphically described in "North Western Steam". Not to be outdone, the L. & Y. introduced a similar timing in 1901 over their far harder 36½ mile route out of Exchange station, and by the end of 1902 were running 29 trains at this schedule, the eastbound ones being the only service to miss out a call at Salford for ticket-collecting purposes. It is significant, perhaps, that their whole page advertisement in the 1906 Handbook, over the name of John A. F. Aspinall as General Manager, gave pride of place to their freight services, claiming that they were "General Carriers between Liverpool and Manchester". They were on the telephone (which had come to Liverpool in 1877, two months after it was introduced in London), and their telegraphic address was "Promptitude".

Since Liverpool was the main port for incoming passengers

I

from the Americas, there was considerable competition, too, for the traffic between there and the ports on the East Coast that provided steamer links with the mainland of Europe. The L. & Y., for instance, ran through express trains between Liverpool Exchange and Riverside Quay, Hull (connecting with their own steamship Duke of Clarence) and Parkeston Quay, Harwich, for Zeebrugge. Sam Fay, General Manager of the Great Central ("Rapid Travel in Luxury"), could offer a direct route off the Cheshire lines to the Continent via their own port of Grimsby, only adding reference to the Great Eastern's shorter sea route via Harwich as an afterthought. "Great Central Company's representatives meet all Steamers arriving at Liverpool, and will assist American Passengers in clearing their baggage through the Customs, make arrangements for their travelling comfort, and afford them all information required". Trans-Atlantic passengers landing at Prince's Stage in the early n1900s might well have had considerable difficulty in choosing between the offers being made by the rival companies. In Edwardian days, however, our railways were perhaps at their most attractive from a passenger's point of view, bearing in mind that general standards of comfort everywhere were not then up to those we take for granted today. As complete masters of the inland passenger travel scene, the railways were only competing between themselves, and could afford to be lavish with their blandishments at a time when there were no private cars and C licence lorries, both of which are now often run for prestige purposes and frequently regardless of their true cost.

7

For a youngster like Bill, the railway scene in Liverpool at the turn of the century also provided much that was of interest. Nowadays we often tend to think that the cult of the loco spotter was born of Ian Allan's enterprise in publishing his "ABCs" during World War II, but the absence of these booklets did not stop Bill enjoying the sight and sounds of spotless steam locomotives from the platform ends of the great Liverpool termini 40 years earlier. The most northern of these was the Lancashire and Yorkshire Railway's Exchange Station, built on the site of the mediaeval Stutts and Higher Sea Shute. Its 10 platforms underneath the overall roof were opened in 1888, replacing the older Tithebarn Street station. To work their principal expresses, Aspinall introduced his "1400" Class Atlantics, the class ultimately numbering 40, built in two equal-sized batches during 1899 and 1902. They were extremely impressive machines, their parallel boilers with Belpaire fireboxes being the largest fitted to any engine in Great Britain when they were constructed. They were pitched high to clear the 7' 3" drivers, which were the largest coupled wheels to be fitted to an engine in this country, with the exception of the two N.E.R. "Q1" Class. These two machines were built at Gateshead in 1896 as an aftermath of the previous year's race to the north. They were designed as racers to impress the L.N.W.R. with the speed capabilities of the East Coast Route in case Euston had any ideas about restarting the competition. The "Lanky Highfliers", however, had to compete with the L.N.W.R. day-in and day-out in Lancashire and parts of Yorkshire, and were consequently far more robust machines. A straight running plate emphasised the length of the "1400" Class and the top half of the driving wheels was covered by the massive splashers picked out with brass beading, lining, and the company's painted coat of arms, contrasting with the oval numberplates on the cab sides. An unusual feature of these locomotives was the small door in the cab front at each side of the boiler, which enabled the crew to go out on to the foot-framing to attend to the lu brication, even when they were under way. Bill used to admire these loco motives very much, commenting to me that they had lovely legs for sprin ting. Besides seeing them in Exchange, there was a low wall giving a view of the main line at Bank Hall, where he used to pause on his errands of taking greengrocery orders out on evenings and Saturdays. The nearby shed was at that time known as Sandhills, only being renamed Bank Hall in the

1920s, and seven of the "Highfliers" were shedded there when built. However, most of the other members of the class from as far afield as Newton Heath and Low Moor regularly worked into Liverpool, as did the one shedded at Hull for working the boat train services already mentioned. The "Lanky" shared with the Midland in the working of Anglo Scottish traffic from Liverpool out of Exchange, and Bill would wait "an awful long time" by his Bank Hall wall to catch a glimpse of the beauty and grace of a Midland single en route to Hellifield, hauling its train of Midland stock with a solitary L. & Y. 2nd class carriage sandwiched among the crimson-liveried vehicles.

Liverpool Exchange was also the terminus of the electrified line to Southport which was completed in October 1904, the original stock having wedge-shaped driving compartments. In general style they were quite different from the Mersey stock of the previous year, being fitted with larger windows for the passenger compartments. There were two large glass windows spanning the front end, one of them being fitted with a clear-view panel reminiscent of those now fitted to the London Midland 25kV electric locomotives. The Southport electric service was, of course, to cause one of the greatest surprises of the Beeching Report in 1963, when it appeared in the list of services scheduled for withdrawal in spite of its modern stock and 100,000 weekly passengers. Wider considerations of the transport requirements of Merseyside are likely to ensure its retention, possibly coupled with its integration into a central underground terminal loop serving Lime Street and Central Stations. Such a scheme, coupled with the rationalisation of the Liverpool-Manchester services, would, however, in all probability see the end of the present Exchange Station on whose platforms Bill used to wander 50 years ago.

Three quarters of a mile from Exchange, across the centre of Liverpool, lies Central Station, where in Bill's young days, Great Central and Midland single-wheelers could be seen, shuttling in and out with their trains over the Cheshire lines. A few hundred yards further on was Lime Street Station, the terminus of the Premier Line, as the L.N.W.R. liked to style itself, at that time undergoing a major upheaval with its motive power. May 1903 had seen the retirement of Webb after 32 years as Chief Mechanical Engineer, during which time he had multiplied his compound classes to the detriment of those who had to operate them. When George Whale took over the reins at Crewe, he immediately set about modernising the motive power. Ten months later saw the first of his simple 4-4-0s, Precursor, making dynamometer car runs between Crewe and Rugby, and demonstrating that it was capable of producing indicated horsepowers of 1,000 indefinitely at speeds of a mile-a-minute. So successful was the class that Whale set about building more with the relish of a modern manufacturer receiving an order for diesels, and in 26 months Crewe turned out 110 of them, while the scrapyard cut up the similarly named locomotives of the "Lady" and compound classes. We do not know whether railway enthusiasts of those days were equally sentimental about the way in which the Webb engines were withdrawn after a very short life. The devastation that has occurred among our steam locomotive classes since the advent of the diesels had, however, a very similar, one might say, precursor, on the L.N.W.R. in the early 1900s. So simple and rugged were the Whale designs and those that followed, that they were able to stand up to the unmerciful flogging they received, a thing which we cannot perhaps as yet say about the modern generation of diesels.

The Premier Line believed in naming its express locomotives, the small neat brass plates arcing round the tops of the curved splashers, which, like the rest of the locomotive, were lined out in the livery we now associate with the remaining British Railways' mixed-traffic steam stock. But whereas we now usually have difficulty in detecting the colour of the locomotive below the layers of grime, when Bill used to visit Lime Street, every engine he saw would be gleaming, its bright black boiler picking up the sunlight that filtered through the arched overall roof, or pierced the smoke lying in the tunnels and rocky cutting leading up the 1 in 93 incline to Edge Hill. The names of the "Nor' West" locomotives were noted for their catholic nature, but looking through the list one is immediately struck with the high proportion that were associated with Liverpool, thus indicating the importance that railway attached to their Merseyside traffic. This tradition still survives, of course, in the modern naming of the L.M.R. Type 4 diesel-electrics after liners that ply from the Mersey. In L.N.W.R. days, the launch of a new White Star liner, with its name ending in "-ic", was quickly followed by the appearance of the same name on a locomotive. However, until 1910, none of the great Cunard liner names ever graced one of the engines of the Premier Line, but the explanation may have been no more subtle than that the L.N.W.R. shared more directors with the White Star Line than it did with Cunard. Behind the locomotives that Bill saw would be trains of coaches in spotless plum and spilt milk livery, which also had a brief revival immediately after Nationalisation, only to succumb to the more garish crimson lake and cream that has helped to make the present Corporate Identity Programme so vitally necessary.

Bill's greatest thrill at Lime Street came on 19th July 1904, when King Edward and Queen Alexandra visited Liverpool to lay the foundation stone of Gilbert Scott's new cathedral, whose pink stone tower now rises so prominently above the city. After the long, slow closing years of the Victorian age, England was now responding to a monarch who liked travelling, luxury, and punctuality. In 1903 Wolverton had turned out the superb pair of Royal saloons which were to be used for the most important Royal journeys for all of 40 years. The spaciousness of their Edwardian splendour can still be seen by visiting the Clapham Transport Museum, where they are on display, we hope for posterity. It was these two clerestory vehicles in their plum and spilt milk livery, with each panel lined in gold, that formed the nucleus of the Royal Train that Bill saw brake slowly to a halt in Lime Street at 1.30 p.m. after a 3¾ hour non stop run from Euston. The train consisted of 7 coaches altogether, the Royal saloons being accompanied by two other carriages, the Director's inspection coach, and a brake van at each end. In charge of the 250- ton load was No. 1419 Tamerlane, the third of Whale's "Precursors", turned out from Crewe four months previously, and carrying the name of the scrapped Webb "Dreadnought" dating from 1886. It must have been a wonderful sight for a young boy within a few days of his 10th birthday, having stood since early morning amongst the crowd, which in Lime Street itself, outside the station, numbered 100,000. The weather was scorchingly hot, and by way of air conditioning, a large block of ice had been placed in Queen Alexandra's saloon at the start of the journey among the pink carnations and lilies of the valley that decorated the tables, filling the interior of both graceful Royal saloons with their scent. Liverpool was treating the occasion as a bank holiday, and the L.N.W.R. took no chances, the Locomotive Superintendent of the Southern Division travelling on the footplate from London. This was none other than Bowen-Cooke who was to succeed Whale as Chief Mechanical Engineer in 1909, and his presence on the engine at such a time is perhaps a fitting testimony to the detailed knowledge of the line that even such an elevated railway officer would be expected to possess in those days.

From his vantage point on the platform, Bill was able to see for the first time the introductions and ceremonial that follow a Royal arrival. These complete, the King, together with the Queen in her heliotrope dress and parasol, walked down the platform into the Station Hotel. The L.N.W.R. were very proud of this building, which was lighted through out by electricity and was "by far the largest and most comfortable in Liverpool", being "patronised by the Elite of American travellers". The Royal party made their way out into Lime Street, where the vast crowd joined in the singing of the national anthem, the sound clearly carrying to Bill in the station itself. Cheering marked the start of the procession of five carriages to the Town Hall for luncheon, passing under the garlands, streamers and triumphal arches en route, while the Conservative Club was decorated with festoons of electric lights. After a typically Edwardian repast came addresses of welcome by the Lord Mayor (who was promptly knighted by the King), and by the Vice Chancellor of the University which had achieved its present status in the previous year. After this came the service at the cathedral and the laying of the foundation stone. Fine though the building is now, boasting as it does in the central tower the heaviest peal of bells in the world hung for ringing, the original plans showed two additional towers, one either side of the west end.

The Royal party left Liverpool by sea, embarking on the Royal Yacht "Victoria and Albert" at Pierhead at 5.30, a Royal salute being fired as she cast off by the gunboats in the Sloyne. As The Times correspondent describing the events put it, "The scene presented by the Mersey was extremely beautiful, many vessels being anchored in the stream decked from stem to stern and making an effective marine display". The King was due to sail round to Swansea to open a new dock there next day, but later in the evening word reached Liverpool that the Royal Yacht had put in to Holyhead as there was a gale blowing in the Irish Channel, the journey being completed by train. One wonders just how much notice the L.N.W.R. received of this change of plan. They may have already worked the Royal train over the 140 miles to Holyhead via Chester just in case of such an eventuality, but the alternatives would have involved using ordinary stock, or they would have had to send word along the line to intercept the Royal train on its way back to Wolverton. The Premier Line could, of course, reach Swansea over its own metals by the Central Wales line; a route now suffering the indignity of being reduced to light railway status.

9

There was one unique railway in Liverpool with which Bill was familiar the Liverpool Overhead. The central 5½-mile portion of this line between Herculaneum and the original

Seaforth station had been opened in March 1893, and a later extension took it underground to Dingle at the southern end, while in 1905 connections were made at the north end with the L. & Y. lines to Southport and Aintree. Carried on a continuous wrought iron viaduct some 16 feet above the roadway, the wooden stations were reached by stairs. At Seaforth, however, an escalator, the second in this country, was installed between 1903 and 1906, and Bill enjoyed the novelty of riding on it, as well as walking against it, as was the custom of the young lads on the grain and coal elevators in the docks. The L.O.R. soon earned the nickname of the "Dockers' Umbrella", its watertight decking forming a useful shelter from the rain during breaks in an arduous manual occupation which is still, 60 years later, entirely carried out in the open. For much of the distance, goods lines serving the docks ran underneath the viaduct, the various "pugs" using them being fitted with a flat metal deflector-plate above the chimney to stop the blast damaging the structure. These locomotives were fitted with bells, but even their clanging was not at times sufficient warning, as Bill found out when he was about 17. A friend of his used to fire one of the L. & Y. "pugs", and Bill used to go down and join him in the evening, his old mates being good types and not objecting to the youngster riding with them. On the last trip coming back, Bill used to go along with the man in front, helping to lift the legs of the sleeping tramps clear of the line! Each of the railway companies serving Liverpool had their own dock shunters. The "Nor' West", G.C., and Midland stuck to 0-4-0s, the Midland ones being of a design that struck Bill as queer, but the "Lanky" went in for 0-6-0s as well as three separate classes of 0-4-0, the bigger engines being very strong. It was only in 1895 that locomotives came into use on the line between the L. & Y. South Docks station and North Docks station adjoining Stanley Dock. Originally five horses were required to draw six wagons, but on the level line one engine was capable of hauling 40 coal wagons. The locomotives then burnt shale oil, so that no sparks were emitted in the intervening tunnel.

It should be mentioned that all the lines leading down to the docks in Liverpool are on steep gradients. Not only does adequate motive power have to be provided to lift trains up the banks but considerable caution has to be observed when working loads down the inclines. One of Bill's early railway memories is tarrying on his greengrocery round to watch the "Nor' West" guards pinning down the brakes·on coal trains before they descended Walton incline to the docks. This was on the line from Edge Hill through Stanley which passed under the L. & Y. main-line tunnel just south of Kirkdale station. A lot of the coal was to bunker the ocean-going liners, which swallowed a vast tonnage on each voyage, Cunarders such as the Lusitania and Mauritania requiring as much as 7,000 tons, which was put aboard them by elevator from barges at Cunard Buoy. On a round voyage to New York, their stokers were faced with the task of feeding approximately 11,600 tons into the boilers, an average of more than 1,000 tons per day.

10

As 1907 wore on, Bill's thoughts turned more and more to what sort of job he would take when he left school in July. Railways, ships, tram ways, and many other possibilities passed through his mind, but over and above all was the ever-present threat of unemployment. In the final event, the choice did not turn out to be his, and it was another who guided him into the career that forms the subject of this book.

CHAPTER TWO

Early Days on the Railways

Although, as a schoolboy, Bill had been attracted to locomotives, it was purely by chance that he commenced his working life on the railways in 1907. Up to the age of 13 he had attended Kirkdale Day Industrial School in Liverpool, and when he was due to leave, his headmaster there, Mr. William Corrie, sent for him, and told him that a friend of his, Mr. Charles Flint, Goods Agent at Huskisson, had a job for him. Bill duly made his way down to the Goods Depot, and discovered that the post was with the Traffic Department of the Midland Railway as a Dock Messenger.

In and around the docks there have always been many jobs of this sort for young boys, with the romance of the comings and goings of the liners between Liverpool and other ports throughout the world. Bill's duties took him around many of these ships, and later on he visited Belfast, where his elder brother, Jim, showed him the two crack transatlantic liners Olympic and her ill-fated sister ship Titanic under construction. Jim, who was later to emigrate to Melbourne, started as a shipwright at Harland and Wolff in Belfast, and was one of the 22,000 workmen that were employed on these two "unsinkable" ships. He was able to take Bill aboard the Titanic, and showed him some of his deck caulking, and from her they looked across at the hull of the Olympic on the next slipway. In spite of the lure of the sea, however, Bill still found railways had far more of a pull with him.

It was the first medical examination, however, that finally decided him. This fairly informal affair was conducted at Manchester Central station, and as a 13-year-old, Bill found himself with a free pass and a day to spend on his own in Manchester. It was marvellous; he felt most important being away by himself, and there and then he was sold the idea of a railway career.

As a Dock Messenger, Bill worked a 12-hour day from

Mondays to Fridays, with a further 6 hours on Saturday morning. Starting time was 6 a.m., and as the family was by then living out at Aintree he had over four miles to go to work every morning. Like many boys, however, Bill discovered there was an easier way, by walking to Walton-on-the-Hill locomotive sheds, which were owned jointly by the Great Central and the Cheshire Lines Committee, and cadging a lift on one of the Great Central dock pilots that made its way down to Huskisson in time for him to clock on each morning. This was much quicker than walking, and not as expensive as taking the tram, cheap though these were. Moreover, it enabled him to ride on the engine, and, knowing Bill, it is not surprising that he was soon giving the firemen a hand with the shovel, and then, in considerably less time than it usually takes to pass up through the links by the normal route, was being allowed to take over the regulator. Bill still recalls the thrill as a boy of handling the regulator of a small dock engine, and from then on steam was just what he wanted. One wonders if those crews who encouraged Bill's youthful enthusiasm on the G.C. four coupled tanks had any inkling that their protege would, 50 years later, achieve the second fastest speed attained by a steam locomotive in this country. Although the Dock Messengers worked a 12-hour day, they had two breaks of an hour for meals, between 9 and 10 in the morning and from 3 to 4 in the afternoon. The lads took their meals in the mess-room down below the dock offices, and with a number of young boys together, they were on occasions up to mischief of one sort or another. Inland of Huskisson Goods Station is the Leeds and Liverpool Canal, linked with the Mersey by a chain of locks rising out of Stanley Dock. Some of the lads used to bathe in the canal, and one of their tricks was to swim in front of a barge, where, by bracing their feet against its bow, they could get the vessel to push them through the water as far as the next lock.

After Bill had completed his first 12 months on the railway, he became entitled to one free third class pass per year. London naturally attracted him, and he was able to persuade a friend to accompany him there for a long weekend. They thoroughly enjoyed themselves, and were especially impressed with the gaiety of Sunday in the capital. They went to Rotten Row and Kensington Gardens, later taking a rowing boat on the Serpentine, after which they finished up at a cinematograph show in the evening. It was an exciting day that was more like a bank holiday, in marked contrast to a Sunday in Liverpool, which was just dull.

2

When he was 15, Bill left the job of Dock Messenger, and became a Guard Caller-up, still attached to the Traffic Department at Huskisson. The majority of the 25 guards stationed there were not on regular rostered turns, because of their irregular workings that depended on the time ships arrived and departed. When a guard booked off in the morning, therefore, it was unlikely that he could be told the time of his next turn. When the diagrams had been worked out, it was Bill's job to go round and inform the men of their booking-on times, while if someone had to be called out at short notice, Bill would be knocking on his door an hour before the train was booked to start.

Since the job of caller-up did not occupy the whole of Bill's day, he had to sweep out the guards' brakes and fill the tail lamp cisterns. The Midland Railway was the first to organise a central system of control for freight trains. As part of this, the guards on certain long-distance freights were provided with six foot-square metal sheets on which they stuck code letters, before sliding them into runners on the sides of the brake vans where signalmen and number-takers could see them. Bill also had the job of tidying up these number plates, and looking after the canvas satchels that contained them.

In his free time, he was able to earn some "Bonce" by repairing guard's lamps for 6d. a time. These lamps might have been dropped accidentally, or had been, perhaps, standing on the floor in a van when the train buffered up unexpectedly.

They mainly needed new coloured shades putting in them, although soldering was required with some of them. Bill admits that occasionally, when pocket money was short, he had been known to trip over a lamp accidentally-on-purpose, and then find it had to be repaired.

In 1911, there was a considerable amount of industrial unrest in Liverpool, culminating in the Transport Strike in August, which included the guards at Huskisson. Bill, a lifelong union man, joined them, but the extent of the stoppage on the railway was uncertain as the men were very badly organised, it being their first strike. After they had been out two days, the guards began to get worried that, without the services of their caller-up, they might never be able to get back to work again, so Bill was told to report back for duty in order to keep them informed of what was going on. This strike culminated in a mass meeting of railwaymen on St. George's Plateau, on August 11th 1911, which was dispersed by the. police after the Riot Act had been read. 12 policemen and over 100 strikers were injured in this incident, and that night the mob erected barricades in Christian Street. This resulted in the military being summoned and the Riot Act read again, and two days later came "Bloody Sunday" when the Scots Greys clashed with the strikers. Like many of the other labour disputes in Liverpool during the late nineteenth and early twentieth centuries, the real cause of the trouble lay in the large amount of unemployment in the city, which in turn was aggravated by the wholesale immigration from Ireland.

3

As part of his new duties, Bill had to hold himself available on alternate week-ends to act as Bullion Messenger, a post of remarkable responsibility for a boy of 16. The regular arrival time of the liners from Australia, South America, or Africa, was at the week-end, the actual time depending somewhat on the state of the tides in the Mersey. Many of these vessels had gold or silver aboard, which was wanted in London in the shortest possible time. The Midland seemed to have secured this traffic, which they usually worked from Liverpool Central to St. Pancras with, at the most, one intermediate stop at Derby to change the engine crew. A load of 3, 4 or 5 non-bogie parcels vans made light work for one of the Johnson "Spinners", and no doubt quite high speeds were put up along the excellent Midland main line. There would be an appreciable financial incentive to fast running on such a train, as someone, no doubt, would be paying interest on the value of the bullion until it was actually lodged in the vaults of the Bank of England.

When a ship containing bullion was due, Control would notify Bill, who would make his way down to Pierhead and board the tender that was going out to meet the incoming liner. As well as a rise in wages, the job of Caller-up and Bullion Messenger carried with it a uniform, which appropriately had a line of gold braid on the peak of the cap, setting off the metal hat badge in the shape of the Midland wyvern. The tender came alongside the liner in mid-stream and the valuables were transferred, together with the urgent mails and dispatches, as well as any V.I.P.s. Gold came in bullion chests which required two men to lift them, but the silver ingots were carried unboxed, being cast with hand-grips at each end for lifting purposes. Arriving back at Pierhead, the bullion was transferred to horse drays and sheeted for the short run through the cobbled streets to Central Station. Here the train would be already waiting, in Midland crimson livery throughout, with the locomotive's huge brass axle-boxes on the driving wheels gleaming below the upswept curve of the foot-framing, which was itself clean enough to eat a meal off. The bullion had to be stowed carefully, the 60 lb. silver ingots being placed across 3 boards to ensure that a weak one did not lead to the Midland permanent way becoming accidentally silver-plated. Care was also taken to see that the boxes of bullion were similarly placed across four or five boards. Typically, a load might comprise between 130 and 160 bars of silver, and a maximum of 6 bullion chests, each containing two 28 lb. bars.

A check was made that everything was aboard, and Bill would then be locked into the leading van together with a substantial proportion of the £50,000 under his control. A wave from the guard before he climbed aboard the last vehicle, and the light train was away up the 1 in 96 through Great George Street Tunnel, the arch over the three tracks being fitfully illuminated as the fireman built up the fire of the "Spinner" for its 220-mile run to London. The load varied between three and five vans, usually 6-wheelers, and the riding could be quite lively as they bucketed down from Peak Forest, or bounced over the numerous junctions that bespatter the Midland main line in the Derby area.

Normally these bullion specials worked non-stop to St. Pancras, but were sometimes booked to stop at Derby to change the locomotive crew. There was usually a policeman about on such occasions, and if the halt was in one of the platform roads, Bill would put down the latest episode about Billy Bunter in favour of a short conversation until the guard's whistle blew again and they were off on the second stage of the run. On arrival in London, Bill would receive a clear signature as a receipt for the gold and silver, which was then handed into Headquarters at Derby on his way home. The trip was a lodging turn, however, and to someone with the curiosity of Bill, the chance to spend one night a month in London must have been wonderful. Even at 16 he accepted it automatically, and from then on, never minded the prospect of regularly spending the night in a strange bed, hundreds of miles from home.

Their destination in London was not always St. Pancras, as on occasions they worked through to Mint Street station, the Midland outpost just outside Fenchurch Street station, that served the Royal Mint. Although less than 3 miles as the crow flies separate St. Pancras from Mint Street, the route that Bill used to follow by rail took him via Tottenham, Stratford and Stepney, a distance of something like 15 miles by rail. Their train did not go into St. Pancras, however, but would stop north of Kentish Town Locomotive Shed on the west-to-east spur. After changing engines, they continued through Highgate Road on to the Tottenham and Hampstead Joint Railway, following the route formerly taken by Tilbury boat trains from St. Pancras. After passing under the Great Northern main line, and the Great Eastern Churchbury Loop, they swung right at south Tottenham around the 7-chain-radius spur on to the G.E. Lea Valley line, which brought them in to Stratford from the north. The maze of lines hereabouts completely baffled Bill, with the royal blue G.E. locomotives flashing by during the run along the main line to Fenchurch Street Line Junction, where the special diverged southwards on to the branch leading to Stepney. Just over half a mile further on, after passing through Bow Road station, they joined, at Gas Factory Junction, the route used by the Midland's subsidiary, the London, Tilbury, and Southend Railway. The latter's green 4-4-2 tanks could be seen bustling past, their names emblazoned on the tank sides.

Mint Street station was one of a number of Midland outposts in the East End of London. Nowadays, it is often not realised that several of the northern railways had numerous isolated goods depots dotted about the Metropolis, on both sides of the Thames, which were reached by various half-forgotten, but jealously preserved, running powers over some other company's metals. The Great Eastern had a depot at New Cross, for instance, and the L.N.W.R. numerous similar outposts, as far afield as Clapham, Knight's Hill and East Ham. Coming up to Fenchurch Street from Stepney, the first of the foreign branches swung off northwards at Commercial Road Junction to serve the L.T. & S. goods depot. Eleven chains further on came Leman Street station, 30 yards beyond which was London Docks Junction. This box controlled the entrance to two branches on the south side of the main line. The parent company's London Docks Line swung away left in a semicircle, and one chain clear of the junction with the main line was the right-hand facing connection for Midland Mint Street. For some reason the G.E. property extended for one chain beyond this second junction, a fact which the

Railway Clearing House maps have solemnly recorded. The Midland line was only 12 chains long and the bullion trains worked in behind a row of iron railings on the arrival side, with every appearance of going inside a prison. Like much of East London, this area was very badly bombed during the Blitz, and many of the landmarks that became familiar to Bill disappeared during the holocausts of 1940 and 1941. Frank Mayes, who at one time fired for Bill on the G.N. main line, recalls, however, that even after his transfer to Stratford in 1956, on certain turns from Temple Mills, he would take a J69 to shunt Cable Street coal depot, just outside Fenchurch Street. The empties having been duly cut out and made up into a train, they would briefly adjourn to Mint Street or Fenchurch Street to take water before the return journey.

To a generation that has seen £2,500,000 disappear from a well manned train in a matter of minutes, the responsibility that rested on a young lad of 16 taking £50,000 to London might seem overwhelming, particularly when his weekly wage, inclusive of his other duties, was only 10s. By present-day standards too, the value of the bullion in terms of spending power was 4 times what it is today. However, the Midland Railway and its insurance agents were not as foolhardy as they may at first sight appear. First and foremost was the fact that the railways were then the only fast means of inland transport, and in consequence there was no possibility of spiriting the bullion any distance away by road while the defence was rallying its forces. As late as 1912, even the Al through the North Riding consisted of no more than a narrow strip of water-laid gravel. A farmer who had lived for 50 years beside the road once told me that, in the Boroughbridge area, there was even grass growing through the surface. Also, in a countryside where rapid communication had not yet brought about the anonymity that clings to the present day traveller, any strangers would have been noted by numerous pairs of curious, and, often idle, eyes! Disposing of bullion is no easy matter, either then or now, especially when it would probably have had to be got out of the country without any possible aid from aircraft or frogmen's outfits. Coupled with the fact that there had been no large-scale robberies in those days, the responsibility did not weigh unduly on Bill's shoulders, and the prospect of a monthly spin up to London became something to look forward to with pleasure. To begin with, he spent his hours in the capital in his lodgings, but later took to sight-seeing, visiting Buckingham Palace, the Tower of London, and Tower Bridge. He was able to take one of the four lifts to the upper walkway at the last-named landmark and view the shipping on the Thames from this vantage point, before it was closed to sightseers in 1909.

4

With Bill's appetite whetted by his footplate experiences, he wanted to take the first opportunity of transferring to the locomotive side as a cleaner. None of his former messenger mates were interested, as jobs were fairly plentiful in Liverpool at this time, many of the lads leaving the railway to go to sea or work in the paper or flour mills, where there was the lure of piecework. So Bill, now aged 17½, approached his inspector at Huskisson, Tom Cherry, and asked him if he could arrange a transfer. After Inspector Cherry had had a chat with the Midland Shedmaster at Walton-on-the-Hill, however, Bill was told there were no vacancies there, but if he were interested, a job might be going on the Great Central which shared the shed. Mr. James Ogden, the G.C. shed boss (Bill thinks that the title of Shedmaster was not used by the G.C. in those days), said he wanted some lads as cleaners and Bill could start the following Monday.

The Hoole family had moved again from Walton, and were now living in a house that backed on to the "Lanky" line to Preston near Aintree station. They had no back garden, but from Bill's bedroom, which he shared with Chris, he was able to see the tracks, and the trains passing over them. On the Monday morning he was up early, and made his way down to the sheds for 6 a.m. When he arrived, Bill drew a numbered brass check from the timekeeper and went to meet the shed foreman, Jack Greenwood, who told him he would have to go to Gorton for a medical and eyesight test on the Wednesday. These formalities over, Bill was taken to be introduced to the senior cleaner, Mike Hunt, whose cauliflower ear and split nose belied his gentle disposition, although he could use his fists when necessary. Bill got on very well with him, and was soon being shown the art of removing filth from a locomotive using as few sponge cloths as possible and not much oil.

At noon the timekeeper swung on the bell outside the stores, and Bill and Mike made their way into the messroom for lunch. This gave Bill his first chance of meeting the rest of the shed staff. The cleaners were barred from the messroom except at meal breaks, and this rule landed Bill in trouble on his first day there. At 3 o'clock in the middle of the afternoon, Mike told Bill he felt hungry, and asked him to slip inside to collect the home-made cakes he had left on the messroom table. Anxious to oblige, Bill went off, and much to his surprise found the foreman, Jack Greenwood, fast asleep. He tiptoed in, collected the cakes and turned to make his way out again, only to discover Jack glaring at him out of one eye. Bill immediately began to explain what he was doing, which caused the foreman to jump to his feet in confusion and start swearing at Bill. It turned out that he had a glass eye and in consequence slept with it open, so that when Bill had spoken, it woke him up with a start. In no uncertain terms, Bill was well and truly told off about going into the mess room when he was not supposed to, as well as waking him up. The story naturally got round the sheds, and Bill's embarrassment was thoroughly enjoyed by the other lads.

Walton sheds, which were closed in December 1963, comprised six roads, three of them used by the Midland, and the other three by the Great Central. Bill does not remember the detailed locomotive allocation at the time he worked there, but has the impression that the "Derby" people kept 10 or

12 Johnson 0-6-0s for freight at Walton, in addition to half a dozen small 0-4-0 saddle tanks, and several Johnson 0-6-0 side tanks. On the G.C. they had approximately the same number of 0-6-0 freight engines, up to eight "Humpies" (saddle tank shunters), and two 2-4-2 tanks for local passenger turns on the Southport line. The Great Northern, the third of the partners in the Cheshire Lines Committee, also used to allocate an 0-6-0 there, which lived on the G.C. side. Each of the roads, which would take four tender engines apiece, had a pit outside for use during preparation. The two owning companies each provided their own coaling plant, stores, offices and so on.

On the Wednesday after he started, Bill travelled by himself to Gorton for his medical, which was a more severe one than he had had when he first joined the Midland 2½ years earlier. He travelled from Central Station on the Cheshire Lines Committee, changing in Manchester, to London Road station for the short run to the locomotive works of the Great Central. There were about 10 others waiting when Bill arrived, and after his introductory note had been checked, he was told to loosen his clothing and await the doctor's pleasure. When his turn came to go into the consulting room, he had a thorough examination, covering his toes, teeth, and lungs, as well as a check on any previous ailments he had had. The medical part of the examination over, he was passed on to an assistant who conducted Bill's first eyesight test. This consisted of getting him to read the usual letter card with alternate eyes covered, and then as a test of his colour vision, he was given a pile of loose ends of wool on a fair-sized table. The bits were of every possible hue, and he was told to sort them out into colours and match them up. Bill had no difficulty, but was surprised to find out how many people suffered from colour blindness to a smaller or greater extent. This simple test with bits of wool was employed extensively by the railways in the early days, but it could get a bit awkward when the wool became soiled after being handled by numerous pairs of none-too-clean hands. Needless to say Bill passed the medical satisfactorily, and from then on he could be used as a fireman if required, since the Great Central in those days did not examine cleaners on their knowledge of the rules and so on before allowing them to fire.

Bill's prospects of regular firing were several years off, however, and he had first to learn the job of cleaning locomotives. To those who are now accustomed to more than a quarter of a century of grimy steam locomo tives, the condition of even the smallest dock pilot in Liverpool in 1912 would have come as a surprise. The Great Central goods locomotives were painted black, lined out in red even on the underframing. When one had been disposed of by its crew at the end of their turn, the cleaners' first job was to wipe off any dust. Cleaning proper then started from the dome downwards using Russian tallow or rape oil to give a protective film over the paintwork. All the spare grease was removed from the wheels and motion, and finally the foot-framing was wiped clean. This left it in a semi-bright condition like a frying pan, so much so that anyone leaning on it in clean overalls would not get them dirty. The boiler hand-rails and side rods were burnished bright, and the trick with these was to use rope impregnated with brick dust. If the locomotive had been laid up, however, and had collected some rust, it was necessary to resort to emery cloth in the first instance, and then keep up the finish with brick dust and plenty of elbow grease.

The final appearance of one of their locomotives was something the cleaners were proud of, and they developed their own individual styles of finishing, known as "gimp". The final strokes of the cloth that they applied left a grained surface in the thin oil film, which showed up, especially in reflected light, enhancing the colour scheme, particularly on the passenger engines with their more ornate livery. Each cleaner adopted his own pattern for the gimp on the splashers or tank sides and on the smoke-box door, so that the shed foreman knew, when he saw the gimp on an engine, not only that it was ready for duty again, but which cleaner had been working on it. Looking through some old photographs of G.C. locomotives while this biography was in preparation, Bill was able to point out to me one of No. 4341 Earl of Kerry after it had been cleaned by him, simply by the pattern of the gimp on the splashers. All the brass and copper was thoroughly polished too, and the foot-framing could be seen reflected in the curve of the boiler.

If there was any serious neglect by one of the cleaners, he was liable to be severely disciplined, and could easily be fined a whole week's pay. The foreman would recommend the punishment, which would then be confirmed by the shedmaster. Even for a slight misdemeanour, a day's pay could be deducted from their pay packet. As Bill put it, this discipline was really harsh, as nothing hits harder than "a smack in the pocket". It was not only the foreman at the shed who was on the look-out for bad workmanship in those days when there was so much unemployment. At Exchange Station, the Midland representative would often come out of his office with a white cloth in his hand when a locomotive was due to depart on one of their Carlisle workings. He would rub the cloth over various parts of the locomotive and then inspect it. If it picked up any dirt, especially any thick oil, a wire would be sent to Bank Hall sheds and the cleaner concerned would be on the carpet.

This harsh discipline was not confined to locomotive cleaners either, and could even be applied to someone as exalted as an inspector. Every year a considerable number of live quails was imported through Liverpool for a feast held by the Egyptian colony in London. The birds arrived in baskets, and required plenty of air in order to survive the journey. Accordingly it was necessary to use cattle vans to contain the baskets, and these were drawn from the considerable stock of this type of vehicle that was normally kept in the Liverpool area for handling the Irish traffic. One year, two unexpected cattle boats docked the day before the quails arrived, so that when the baskets were swung ashore, there were no cattle wagons available. The Cheshire Lines Traffic Inspector at

Huskisson therefore decided to make use of some horseboxes instead, and the birds were duly loaded and sent off to St. Pancras. Unfortunately, on arrival in London, nearly half of them were found to be dead through lack of air, and after the usual company inquiry, the Inspector was given the sack for making the wrong decision.

The young cleaners did not have much opportunity of getting to places of entertainment, and could probably not afford to go very often, anyway, by the time they had handed over most of their wage packet to their mothers. When Bill was getting seven shillings a week as caller-up, he was only allowed 6d. a week pocket money, and although his weekly wage as a cleaner was now 10 shillings, his spending money did not increase a lot. In contrast to our modern teenagers with their large "uncommitted" incomes, the lads at Walton 60 years ago had to provide their own amusements, which more often than not ended up as horseplay. They did, however, often constitute their own courts of honour and awarded punishments to any of their members who had transgressed their local code of behaviour. The ceremony was taken seriously, with the "Crown Counsel" addressing the "Judge" who wore a wig made out of the flax used for cleaning boiler tubes. Bill remembers one cleaner being "convicted" of cadging cigarettes off his mates when he had plenty of his own in his pockets. The "Judge", who was quite a character, ordered him to be "tightened". This involved each member of the "jury" taking hold of a lock of the victim's hair and pulling it at the agreed intervals while the "Judge" spoke the "sentence" :

"0 Brother,0 Brother, thou has transgressed (pull);
Broken the law before our very eyes. (pull)
If you do not mend your manners, (pull)
You will be skinned and sent to the tanners (pull), (pull), (pull)"

It was quite an ordeal for the culprit, but his mates had no further occasion to complain of his cadging, so it was evidently an effective punishment. Bill was involved in one amusing incident which shows the fascination that steam engines had for him. Every year a travelling fair came to Walton on a site next to the shed, and like many lads, Bill was very taken with the steam-operated roundabout with its organ. He and Harry Marsden Edwards decided one night that they would have a go at driving this, and after the fair had closed down at midnight, crept under the sheets to see what they could do. The little Foden engine with its cylinder and fly-wheel on top of the boiler was still warm, and with the aid of some kindling lying about, they soon had the fire going. After what seemed an age, there was at last sufficient pressure showing on the gauge to try opening the regulator to see what happened, and this Bill gingerly did. The roundabout started to rotate, slowly at first, and then picking up speed. However, what they had overlooked was the fact that the steam organ was also connected, and the quietness of the night was suddenly shattered by "When you wore a tulip, a big yellow tulip, and I wore a big red rose" being played fortissimo. There was only one course open to the two miscreants, who dodged out under the sheets and were away into the darkness, pursued by the sounds of the organ and the waking fairground owners. They successfully made their escape, however, largely due to the foresight of Jim Murray, another of Bill's friends, in slipping bolts through the hasps on the outsides of those caravans nearest the roundabout.

No uniforms were provided for the cleaners or enginemen on the Great Central in those days, and the lads were called on to do some very filthy jobs on occasions. If a fitter's labourer did not turn up, one of the cleaners would be told to go and assist him. Being of slight build, however, Bill never got called on to help the blacksmith, unlike some of his heftier mates. There was little in the way of machinery about the sheds in 1912, many jobs requiring considerable brute strength by those called on to carry them out. Washing out the boilers was a filthy occupation too, and if coal supplies came along quicker than they were using them, a squad of lads would be put on the job of stacking the surplus on a convenient site for subsequent loading on to tenders.

5

Liverpool, and Aintree in particular, is well known for its sporting tradition. Horse racing in the area dates back nearly 400 years to the first recorded one at Crosby in 1577, and the Aintree flat races began as long ago as 1828. Nine years later they started going "over the sticks", and in 1847 William Lynn introduced the Grand National, that most exacting of all steeplechases. Historians have recorded that in the first year it was run, "at an early hour the road to the Ground was crowded by vehicles of all descriptions conveying human cargoes to the scene of the race, while the pedestrians formed a complete tide". Not surprisingly the railways quickly realised the profitability of race specials, and even now Grand National Day still produces considerable activity on the lines in the Aintree area, although the intensity of working is far less than when it concerned Bill in the years 1912 and 1913, giving him his first two days firing.

The race course at Aintree lies between two railway lines. To the south, the goods branch to Alexandra Dock branches off the L. & Y. line from Manchester at Fazakerley Junction, and, for use on race days, a platform was built just before the line crosses the main road and the parallel L. & Y. and C.L.C. routes which pass to the west of the course. Each of the latter two lines used to boast an Aintree station, known latterly as Aintree Sefton Arms and Aintree Central respectively. The owning companies naturally ran an intensive local service from Liverpool itself, there being typically 24 additional "Lanky" trains from Exchange to Sefton Arms. These ran over the electrified line to Ormskirk, and the L. & Y. used special trains consisting of old stock marshalled between motor coaches, this flexibility considerably assisting the smooth operation of the traffic. On the occasion of the Grand National too, the Liverpool Overhead spread its wings, and at

15-minute intervals throughout the day forsook Seaforth and Litherland as its northern terminus in favour of Sefton Arms, their diminutive 3-coach trains removing from the conductor rails the rust that had accumulated during the intervening 12 months on the 2¼-mile connection. In addition to these local services, there were numerous long-distance specials into Aintree from many different parts of the country.

Brunswick and Walton-on-the-Hill sheds used to play a vital part in the operation of the race traffic on Grand National Day, with local crews relieving the long-distance men and preparing the locomotives for their return journey. Every available man was needed, so the young cleaners joined the exalted ranks of firemen on this·one day in the year, and the normal 20 or so engines at Walton would be swelled by numerous strangers, many of which made a great impression on Bill. After relieving the main-line men, the disposal crew would usually take the locomotive round the triangle on their way to Walton sheds, thus turning it without occupying the turntable. Bill was very struck by the North Eastern engines with the protection from their generous side-window cabs, which compared very markedly with the 9" roofs on their own old 0-6-0s. The Hull & Barnsley too, provided fair-sized cabs, and in addition to the locomotives from these two foreign companies, Bill recalls seeing North Staffordshire, and Great Northern passenger engines. One of the engines Bill and his mate handled was a Great Central Pollitt single-wheeler, but although this was the only occasion he ever worked a single, its appearance did not come up to the standard of the Johnson "Spinners" in Bill's opinion. By now he was anxious to pick up as much know-how as possible, and so enjoyed the overtime that was involved on these occasions. His first close contact with express passenger locomotives impressed on him the roominess of their cabs and the large size of their injectors, while the various boiler fittings used to dwarf the ones on their own 0-6-0s that were tucked out of the way of the important strangers.

It is interesting to compare the services provided on Grand

National Day in 1913 with those in 1964. When Bill was firing, 34 trains used the race platform, while 57 called at Sefton Arms, including 45 electrics from the L.O.R. and the L. & Y. Over on the Great Central, 77 trains were dealt with, including the first-class special from Marylebone which provided excursionists with lunch, tea and dinner for their fare of 38s. 6d. Euston also ran a first-class-only excursion, as well as a sleeping-car special, and the Great Northern at times operated a Pullman car train via Retford and the G.C. line via Woodhead.

By 1964 the amount of traffic had shrunk considerably, and in this year for the first time, only Sefton Arms was used, Aintree Central having been closed completely, after having been kept open solely as a terminal point for the race traffic for 3 occasions after the ordinary passenger trains were withdrawn in November 1960. Pullman car excursions were still in evidence among the twelve long-distance specials running from places as far apart as London and Glasgow 1 an 8-car Blue Pullman set being used for the first time on a train from Swansea. The peculiarities of resetting the communication cords on this stock caused a lot of delay after the race, when some over-exuberant Welshmen pulled the chain. These were not the only Pullman cars to work into Aintree, as the Cleethorpes special arrived, as usual, with a 2nd class Pullman kitchen car in the formation, followed by the former Devon Belle observation car, now used in the summer between Inverness and the Kyle of Lochalsh. These two cars formed the guaranteed private excursion from Retford, organised by Alan Pegler, the Chairman of the Festiniog Railway.

The closing of Aintree Central posed difficulties for routing trains coming from the Manchester direction. In the past they had taken the Cheshire Lines route, diverging at Halewood to run via West Derby direct to Aintree across the north side of the Walton triangle. The altered arrangements necessitated them leaving Manchester on the former

L.N.W.R. route via Earlestown to Olive Mount Junction, where they crossed over on to the Bootle branch, where Bill used to see the coal trains going to the docks to bunker the Cunarders. Joining the route used by the Southport electrics at Bank Hall, they swung eastwards again over the line formerly used by the L.O.R. race services, reaching Aintree from the west. In the half century since Bill had played a part in the working of the Grand National specials, two wars, Grouping, Nationalisation, and Dr. Beeching have all had their effect on the railways, but in spite of them, the excitement of the day itself still remains.

6

After the excitement of his second day's firing for the 1913 Grand National, Bill settled down to the routine of cleaning once more, but began to fret at the slowness of promotion on Merseyside. He and Harry Edwards made up their minds to transfer to Neasden, the most southerly motive-power outpost on the Great Central, knowing that it would give them better opportunities and a greater variety of workings when eventually they got on the footplate. London was well known to him, of course, from his Bullion Messenger days, and although it meant leaving home, there was the excitement of life in the capital to compensate. Thus in 1913, Bill moved to London, which was to become his home for the next 46 years.

CHAPTER THREE

Neasden

When Bill moved to Neasden in May 1913, the Great Central's London Extension had been open for 14 years, and had settled down to a fairly steady pattern of operation. The story of the "Last Main Line" is an epic of the cut-throat competition that existed in the field of transport during late Victorian times. Under the chairmanship of Sir Edward Watkin, the Manchester, Sheffield & Lincolnshire Railway had launched out from its comparatively minor east-west axis in the North of England to rival several of the long-established trunk routes connecting these parts with London. Never wildly profitable, the old nickname "Money, Sunk & Lost" was promptly changed, when the name of the company altered, to "Gone Completely". Nevertheless it was not really until after Nationalisation, 50 years later, that the declining and altered traffic flows started to leave the Last Main Line without the will to struggle on. Shorn of its once-frequent express services, the final demise of the route cannot now be much longer delayed, but the highly competitive atmosphere in which the line operated during Bill's days as a fireman must have done much to inspire him with the love of fast running that he was able to exploit in his later years.

George Dow has ably chronicled the history of the London Extension, and in this biography we must confine ourselves to history only as far as it affected the lives of those working on the line. The "backbone" of the Great Central was the 92 miles of new line that were built in the years 1894 to 1898 between Annesley Junction and Quainton Road. Here the Metropolitan Railway was reached, whose metals afforded hospitality as far as Harrow-on-the-Hill. From this point the G.C. took itself to itself again, and after running parallel with the rapidly multiplying Metropolitan tracks as far as Finchley Road, dived into a series of tunnels, passing under Lord's Cricket Ground to terminate at Marylebone station. Not content with one joint route into London, the Great Central next allied itself with the G.W.R. which was early this century seeking to live down its nickname of the Great Way Round. In April 1906 the G.C. started its passenger services between Grendon Underwood and High Wycombe, four years before the G.W.R.'s direct Birmingham route was opened, which shared the same tracks between Northolt and the flyover at Ashendon.

On long distance services to cities like Leicester, Nottingham, and Sheffield, the Great Central was first and foremost rivalling the supremacy of Derby's Midland empire. The boardrooms at Euston and King's Cross, however, no doubt also heard numerous anxious comments about the newcomer, as the L.N.W.R. would have had some of its Rugby and Manchester traffic tapped off, while the Great Northern also ran services to Nottingham and Sheffield. Even when it was actually sharing metals with the Met. or the G.W.R., the Great Central still did not avoid the need to compete with its trackmates for the growing suburban traffic from the Chilterns. The motto of the company, "Forward", that appeared below its coat of arms, was thus no idle boast. Even in this matter of heraldic bearings, the Great Central did the job properly, being one of the few railways to get the College of Heralds to approve their coat of arms. Surmounted by a crest consisting of the front view of a locomotive between two raised symbolic wings, it was used on the tender or tank sides of their engines between the words "Great Central".

The G.C. footplate crews were thus well aware of the need for competition. While the fine dining cars which were provided must have helped attract passengers, competition first and foremost meant speed, to equal or better the rival's times over slightly shorter routes. By means of extensive engineering work, the ruling gradient was kept down to 1 in 176, or 30 feet per mile and it was only when arrears of maintenance sapped the condition of the track and its embankments during World War II, that full advantage could no longer be taken of the superb track layout to charge downhill with speeds rising into the eighties. The sparsely- populated countryside through which the line ran helped to achieve this freedom from restrictions, but in the end the resulting lack of intermediate traffic told against the viability of the route.

To get their first services off to a flying start, about ten drivers, who were to form the nucleus of the forthcoming shed at Neasden, were sent out to learn the road between London and Leicester before it was opened. They did this by walking the entire 103 miles. S. W. A. Newton's photographs, some of which have been published in book form by the Leicester Museum and Art Gallery, graphically record the conditions under which the Irish and Italian navvies worked. Living among them, these drivers shared their entertainments, the chief of which were the bare-fist fights that were arranged in fields alongside the line. With virtually no rules, the fights would last up to two hours unless the contestants became exhausted earlier. There was considerable betting on the outcome, and the drivers joined in, thoroughly enjoying the fisticuffs. In later years, Bill fired to many of the original drivers, and found it very interesting listening to their experiences. Like him and the other Neasden men, they were all part of an early "drift to the south", coming from the Midlands or Manchester.

From the enginemen's point of view too, the London Extension presented them with a pattern of motive power depots that was not to become general until the diesel age. Between Neasden and Woodford, 64 miles to the north, there was no intermediate source of engines in case of trouble, unless the train was travelling via the Met, in which case there were a few locomotives at Aylesbury. On most of the turns, the Neasden men only worked as far as Woodfood, but beyond this shed there was another 34-mile gap before Leicester was reached.

Although he had fired on two Grand National Days before he moved to London, Bill's seniority did not entitle him to any promotion, and he continued as a cleaner after his move to Neasden. There were changes, however, as the lads there worked in gangs on the small engines, booking on at 6 a.m.

or 6 p.m. and were paid piece rates. It was still a 12-hour day with two breaks of an hour each for meals, but just before the outbreak of war in 1914, there was a reduction in the working day to 10 hours as a result of the new agreement negotiated by Jack Bromley.

After a few months at Neasden, Bill was allocated as the regular cleaner on one of the large engines. There were no piece rates for this, and he worked on the opposite shift to the driver and fireman, booking on 11½ hours before they did. When the crew turned up 45 minutes before the locomotive went off shed, Bill was expected to have completed the cleaning, and had to make himself available to do any jobs the driver wanted carrying out while he was preparing the locomotive. On this system, the cleaner's turn finished when the engine went out for its train. When he first moved to London, Bill lodged in one of the railway cottages at Neasden, but these arrangements were not satisfactory. One of the other cleaners was Tom Ratley, whose father was a driver on the L.N.W.R., at Willesden, and Bill went to lodge with them at Brownlow Road. The family consisted of another boy besides Tom, and two girls, the younger of whom, Dolly, was then only 14. As a snooty young man of 19, Bill did not take much notice of Tom's "kid sister", but the lapse of 5 years was to see his opinion change very much indeed.

2

In June 1914, Archduke Ferdinand was assassinated in Sarajevo, and during the five weeks that followed, the resulting diplomatic and military threats escalated into World War I. The Oxford historian, A.J. P. Taylor, in his book "The First World War", suggests that it was the rigidity of the special railway workings which were required to bring about the mobilisation of the armies in Europe that caused the miscalculations of the statesmen to turn into widespread fighting. Following Britain's declaration of war in defence of Belgium, there was a general upsurge in patriotism, and amongst the half million who joined the colours in the first month were Bill, and a friend from Neasden, Bill Davenport, who volunteered for the Army at Willesden early in September 1914. Bill Hoole had spent two years as a Territorial private in the 10th Liverpool Scottish Infantry Regiment before he left Merseyside.

After they had signed on, the recruiting sergeant selected Bill and put him in charge of a draft of 40 who were being sent by the midnight train from King's Cross to Maryhill Barracks in Glasgow. Never keen on imposing discipline, Bill told the rest that they were free until midnight, and that as he had the warrant, it was up to them to report back at the station in time to catch the train. When they arrived in Scotland, they were treated to their first army breakfast. Lining up in the barrack square, they drew their rations from two soldiers who were working with their sleeves rolled up. One of them fished pieces of boiled bacon out of a tea chest and gave it to the men, while the other supplied them with half a loaf and some butter on a piece of paper. The British Government had only expected some 100,000 men to volunteer in the first six months, and were consequently overwhelmed by those who actually joined up. Supplies were, in consequence, strained to the utmost, and at Maryhill, cutlery was non-existent, as were beds and uniform. The men had to supplement their official rations with food they bought themselves, and they soon got tired of sending home for more money to supplement their shilling a day, although the 10/- allowance they received for using their own clothes instead of uniform helped a little. It was a fine autumn that year, and many of them slept in the open without any bedding, but when the weather changed this idea was smartly abandoned. A supply of bedding arrived at last, however, and they were surprised to find themselves issued with a pair of the finest white fleecy Witney blankets.

Bill had been drafted into the Royal Field Artillery, but they only saw one gun, and that was sent away after a week when the defect that had kept it at Maryhill had been put right. Their gun drill thereafter was carried out on a chart drawn in the sand, but Bill succeeded in "going through the motions" sufficiently well to pass out on his basic training. After this they asked for specialists, and Bill became a signaller, for which he had to learn morse. Having already had to cope without uniform, cutlery, beds, and guns, it is not surprising that the next thing they had to do without was a dummy key for practising morse. They improvised with a button stick wedged under a knife stuck into a crack in the barrack room table. The first dummy key he handled was when he took his passing-out test, although the Navy came along with Aldis lamps to enable them to try their hands at signalling at night. Their training completed, a parade was held, and the Sergeant-major split them into two lots, the dividing line falling between Bill and Davenport. Bill's half of the trainees went to Woolwich and from there to Flanders, whereas the others were drafted to Athlone and only reached France after the collapse of the Gallipoli campaign.

The stalemate on the Western Front that lasted for much of the war was again very largely due to the influence of the railways, which could bring up men and supplies quickly to the scene of action. Once the soldiers had left the train, however, their mobility was so reduced, especially in the face of even a few machine guns, that any gap battered into the lines of trenches would quickly be reinforced by more troops rushed up by rail. There, was, in consequence, an extensive army railway system, superimposed on the French Railways, and Bill tried to transfer to this Railway Operating Department, as he knew his seniority would get him a job as a driver. However, he was not allowed to leave the artillery, and became corporal in charge of the signals in "A" Battery, 123 Brigade, 37th Division R.F.A. In action his job was to go forward, often into no-man's land, to clear the barbed wire and establish communications between the guns and the forward observation post. When the observation officer came forward to take over, Bill would then put the guns in contact with back H.Q. where the horses were, and then connect them with the batteries on either side. Opportunities for sleep were not very frequent, and many times he curled up in a horse blanket in the open between the animals and their filth. He did once, however, have the opportunity of riding one of the officer's arab thoroughbreds, which he enjoyed very much indeed.

Bill still kept his eye open for railways, however, and was particularly interested to see the Baldwin narrow-gauge 2-6-0 tanks taking the supplies to the third-line trenches behind Ypres. Some idea of the scale of the railway operations in France can be gauged by the fact that there were over 2,000 of that company's 2-8-0s at work on the standard-gauge main lines. Railways were actually able to penetrate even nearer the front line in places where the communication trenches were wider. Light Decauville track was laid at night, and during the day would be folded up against the side. Heavily-armoured Simplex locomotives were used on the trains, the noise of their exhaust being drowned by the nightly barrage from the guns, Bill was to catch up with one of these locomotives at Portmadoc over 40 years later, and found the weight of its armour plating made it an excellent battering ram to clear the trees that grew up through the track during the "lost years" on the Festiniog. Their Simplex has now spent over 40 years in North Wales, but more recently the line has acquired four bogie coal wagons that once worked in the French trenches, which had been bought, together with several others, from a dump at Arras in the 1920s for use on the Smith's Potato Estates Light Railway in Lincolnshire. It was less than 10 years ago, while this unique farming railway was being slowly closed down, that the author drew their existence to the attention of the Festiniog, who subsequently bought four of them. Conditions in Flanders during the wet weather were very bad indeed, and in 1916 Bill was in action in front of Gommecourt Wood, in the Pas de Calais area where the trenches were very poorly supported, as there was not enough wood or netting. Both sides were more concerned with fighting the mud than fighting each other. At about this time Bill remembers a visit by Captain

Winston Churchill, who later wrote of two armies in the rear being required to keep one in action at the front.

Later in 1917, Bill was posted back to a hush-hush course at Luton Hoo, the large country house in the valley of the River Lea along which the Midland Main Line makes its way southward out of Luton en route for St. Pancras. The course was a mixed one of officers and N.C.O.s, and included several Australians and New Zealanders, whose other ranks were very free and easy with their discipline, calling their officers by Christian names. It was winter time and during the lectures one morning, it started to snow. The Anzacs became very restless and eventually left the hut to take a better look at the first snow they had seen. At the end of the lecture, the officers were the first to leave and were consequently the first to be hit by the volley of snowballs. After that the classes were called off for the rest of the day, while full advantage was taken of this opportunity for sport.

The course was on the first two-valve wireless sets being produced by Siemens of Woolwich, which were very hush-hush. They were told that the valves were extremely difficult to make, and that between 40 and 50 were discarded for every one that was used, a failure rate that would not be tolerated in the present days, even if it were the other way round. Their training over, the signallers returned to France by an unusual route and took up their duties for the Big Push on the Hindenberg Line. The sets were very susceptible to vibration, and they had to operate at least 30 feet down to avoid the concussion of the guns affecting the valves. With 100-foot aerials in each direction, their job was to give out false information to the Germans, and monitor the German signals they could pick up. The important messages were sent back by carrier pigeon, and Bill's small writing came in useful, enabling him to get the maximum amount of information on the lightweight message sheet. They only had two pigeons a day and the other, less important, messages were sent back by runner. On the day of the advance, they went forward right behind the infantry, and in a German dugout discovered a virtually identical set made by Siemens of Berlin. Bill still wonders how much time he and his opposite number spent sending messages to each other, and how the two sides came to be using similar sets.

During the war, Bill had several narrow escapes, and was wounded as well as getting a dose of mustard gas, which left him chesty. After he was wounded, he went back to base, but never returned to a battery, being attached to an ammunition column instead. Towards the end of the war, they relieved the Belgians on the coast, and Bill had the job of collecting all the British ammunition and putting it into barges. A German "pip squeak" landed nearby and he collected a bit of shrapnel in his left forefinger. At the casualty clearing station, a French officer removed it for him after freezing the finger-the first time Bill had seen a local anaesthetic administered. After he had rested, the officer asked him if he would mind doing a few simple exercises, like touching his toes. Bill tried to do so, and promptly grabbed his side in pain, where two other pieces of shrapnel had hit him. At the time he had not realised he had been wounded there too, and the doctor's simple test enabled him to discover whether the finger represented the full extent of Bill's wounds. After the Armistice was signed, symbolically in a railway coach, on 11th November 1918, the guns grumbled into silence, so ending the "War to end Wars" and leaving the world to set about licking its wounds. It was not until late in 1919, however, that 22889 Corporal Signal Instructor Hoole, W., was demobbed and returned to civvy street to help play a part in building a country "fit for heroes to live in".

3

While Bill was still in the army, two events took place which were to have far-reaching effects on his future career, as well as affecting those of everyone else employed on the railways. First of all, it was during the General Election in December 1918 that final negotiations were pushed through by Jack Bromley, the General Secretary of the A.S.L.E.F., with Sir Albert

Stanley, the President of the Board of Trade, to fix the starting date for the 8-hour day that the Government had promised in the middle of the war. This came into effect on February 1st 1919. At this time the 125 railway companies were still being controlled by the Railway Executive Committee on behalf of the Government, and they were involved in the negotiations on a national scale, as had been the case throughout the war. By 1917 all railwaymen were getting the war increases in wages of 15/- per week for adults, and a further agreement of the same sort resulted from the long negotiations that were carried out between the two railway unions and the R.E.C. from February to August 1919, the outcome of which was the first national agreement, standardising conditions of employment for enginemen throughout the country. The N.U.R. was not so quick in reaching agreement with the Railway Executive Committee, and called a strike from 26th September, which was supported by the A.S.L.E.F. Nine days later the strike was called off on the N.U.R.'s terms, and great unanimity reigned between the two railway unions, but only for a short time, as in January 1924, the N.U.R. did not support the 9-day A.S.L.E.F. strike that was then called, an incident that led to great subsequent bitterness.

As far as the locomotive men were concerned, they had achieved the following position as a result of their negotiations:

(1) They had a guaranteed working week of 48 hours.
(2) Overtime was to be paid at time and a quarter, each day standing by itself.
(3) Sunday duty was to be paid at time and a half.
(4) Night duty (10 p.m. to 4 a.m.) was to be paid at time and a quarter, with overtime during the same period at time and a half.
(5) There would be oneweek's holiday with pay for those with 12 months' service.
(6) Twelve hours rest would be allowed between each booked turn of duty from a man's home depot, but in

cases of necessity this might be reduced to a minimum of 9 hours.

As far as the actual wages were concerned, they ranged from 4 shillings a day for a 16-year-old cleaner up to 15 shillings a day for a driver of 8 or more years seniority. As a fireman of more than 5 years standing, under this agreement Bill could expect a wage of 7 shillings a day as a cleaner when he was demobbed and could return to the Great Central, with the prospects of 9/6d. a day when promoted fireman.

Bill lost no time in rejoining the Great Central, which throughout the war, unlike most other lines, had scarcely abandoned its 1914 standards of express train running. The average times between London and the principal G.C. destinations only increased by 8 per cent. during the four years, whereas on the L.N.W.R. the corresponding figure was 26 per cent. and on the South Eastern & Chatham, no less than 36 per cent. The day after reporting back, he was sent to Marylebone for a medical examination, which generally followed the routine he had gone through at Gorton. They used a dark room for the card reading, which was better, although the assistant still covered up alternate eyes with a piece of cardboard which could make them water if he was clumsy, and consequently sometimes caused an argument. They had improved the colour vision test too, using red, green, orange, and clear electric light bulbs instead of bits of wool.

Bill's seniority now entitled him to a firing job, and next day Inspector Harry Bailey rode with him on one of the 9F 0-6-2 tanks (later to become L.N.E.R. class N5) with a load of 30 loaded wagons from Neasden sidings to Marylebone Goods. It was as much an instruction course as a test, the Inspector watching Bill's antics with the shovel and advising him to keep his right hand on the end of the shovel up, and the same time not gripping it too hard with the other one at the front. Although the fire was incandescent, the needle would not rise to the 160lb. mark, and, at Dollis Hill Met. station, halfway up the 2 mile bank, which is as steep as 1 in 90 in places, Inspector Bailey pulled out a red glass to inspect the fire. He immediately spotted the weak spot, halfway up the right-hand side, and a couple of shovelfuls quickly repaired the hole, stopping the inrush of cold air which was cutting down steam production. The pressure gauge quickly rose to the blowing-off mark, and the rear Ramsbottom safety valve, which was always set slightly lighter than the front one, was soon sizzling satisfactorily. Bill's performance was considered adequate in view of his lack of practice, and from then on he became a "booked" fireman, so that his cleaning days were at last over. His first experience of proper firing, however, taught him one very important lesson. In his eagerness to put up a good show, he had gripped the hot shovel handle too tight, and his left hand blistered badly in consequence.

After this promotion Bill started to increase his railway experience, and in the next 7 years he worked rapidly up through the firing links, graduating from local turns to the longest regular workings on the Great Central, which took him over the 206 miles to Manchester. As early as 1904, it must be remembered, the G.C. had done nearly twice this distance with some excursions between Manchester and Plymouth, the 374-mile working being the longest then achieved in this country. The number of different locomotive classes on which he worked increased too, and, now that he was actually responsible for the way they performed on the road, he began to note their characteristics and peculiarities that he had not appreciated while he was only cleaning them.

Robinson had been in charge of the Great Central locomotives since 1900, and had provided that railway with an excellent stud of large modern engines. His 2- and 3-cylinder Atlantics, dating from 1903 and 1906, are still thought of by some as representing the nearest approach to aesthetic perfection that has been achieved in locomotive design. They certainly looked extremely impressive at the head of a train, with coats of arms on both splashers, the brass beading setting off the rust-red and Brunswick-green livery. His 4-6-0s were not, in retrospect, thought of so highly as the Atlantics, but most of them were popular with the men, although the last 4-cylinder class were known as "Black Pigs" because of their heavy coal consumption. As this title also indicated, the freight locomotives were painted black, but even they shone. The division between liveries was often not exactly clear-cut, as three of the six engines in the "Sam Fay" class were black, while the others were in passenger green livery, but with the claret-coloured frames which were first applied to No. 423 Sir Sam Fay when it was intended to send it to Amsterdam for exhibition. The painting specifications called for were very exacting, even requiring two days to elapse between each of the last three coats of varnish. Rather surprisingly it was the "Director" 4-4-0s that were most liked by their crews, even for the long distance turns between London and Manchester. Solid, robust, and masters of the work required of them, the 21 Great Central ones were supplemented after grouping by 24 more that Gresley built for work in Scotland, where they too became popular with crews who had a native suspicion of Sassenach designs. Their most serious defect from the drivers' point of view was the outside admission piston valves, the glands on which were, in consequence, difficult to keep tight. The footplate men did all their own gland packing in those days, and prided themselves on how many rolls of asbestos they could get in. Constant lubrication was required to keep the packing tight, but they would often make it last 2-3 months. When a crew were assigned a regular engine, it was standard practice for them to be given a shed day occasionally for squaring up the packing and trimmings. Since the advent of metallic packing, the job has become one for the fitters, but very much longer lives of up to nine months are now achieved.

On the freight side, the three principal classes were the 0-6-0 "Pom poms", the 0-8-0s (known to their crews as "Tinys" because of their small wheels), and the 2-8-0s, the last of which was to become the standard army freight engine in World War I.

Robinson had produced the 9J class, as the "Pom-poms" were officially known, in 1901, by putting a larger boiler on Pollitt's design of wheels, motion and framing, and the class finally reached a total of 174. They had deep fireboxes, and, as Bill said, "You could fill up the back corners to give them something to chew at". The larger eight-wheeled design, classified 8A, came out the following year, and all told, 89 of them were built. It was not until 1911, however, by which time Robinson had designed his own pattern of superheater, that the first of the Class 8K 2-8-0s appeared. 126 were built prior to 1914, those from the North British Locomotive Company costing £4,512 apiece. Between 1917 and 1920, no less than 521 similar locomotives were built for the Railway Operating Department, and after they had been sold off, survivors found themselves at work as far away as Australia even as late as 1963. Even the G.W.R., that arch-exponent of standardisation, considered some worth buying, and successfully operated them for the next 30 years. That company was not likely to have had its hard commercial head turned by sentiment for the Robinson family, either, although three of them served it in senior positions on the locomotive side, including J. G. himself until he migrated to Ireland in 1884. Gorton only built 6 of the R.O.D. series, and ultimately bought the last three back again when they were put up for sale. It is perhaps a fitting commentary on the rise in prices that took place during World War I, that they had to pay no less than £6,064 each for them.

In 1902, the local services from Manchester and London began to get too much for the existing tank engines, and Robinson produced 52 very neat 4-4-2 tanks of classes 9K and 9L, which always carried a pair of jacks on the framing in the London area, but fortunately Bill never had occasion to use them. They used to work these engines hard on the suburban turns, occasionally getting a "fire at both ends", or "snouting" them as it was referred to, with consequent damage to the paint on the smokebox door, but by the end of the war, their size was handicapping them in the ceaseless competition against the electrified Metropolitan Railway next door. Robinson's first class to be superheated from the start comprised the 9N 4-6-2Ts, better known perhaps by their L.N.E.R. designation, A5. First introduced in 1911, 21 had been built by the time Bill started firing, and 10 more were ordered in 1922 for the forthcoming Wembley exhibition traffic. The third of this batch was No. 7, which came out early in 1923, and was always a favourite of Bill's. It is an interesting coincidence that when he finally reached the Top Link at King's Cross, his finest feats of running were nearly always associated with what he considered was the best A4 of all, Sir Nigel Gresley, which also once carried the number 7.

Two of these locomotives figured in incidents on the Joint Line during Bill's firing days. Leaving Gerrards Cross on an up train on one occasion, travelling bunker first as was the usual custom, the locomotive slipped badly and buckled one of the side rods. While they were inspecting the trouble, one of the passengers came up and asked one or two questions. Bill's driver, known as "Razor" Smith because of his sharp way of speaking, told him to mind his own business and get back into the train. It was not until the next day that they discovered that the person concerned was one of the G.C. directors, and Driver Smith duly found himself on the carpet! This was a relatively minor incident, however, compared with the other, which took place while they were waiting in a siding at High Wycombe before an up working. Having run round the coaches, and coupled up again, the driver got down to feel the middle big end. Instead of climbing on top of the foot framing, he leant on the side rod and put his arm through the spokes of the driving wheel and the slot in the frame. Unfortunately, just at this moment the brake leaked off sufficiently for the compressed buffer springs to move the locomotive a few inches, catching the driver's arm in three places. He yelled and then collapsed with the pain. A G.W.R. porter and permanent way man came up and supported him, while Bill had the ticklish job of setting back just sufficiently far to free the arm again. They wanted to get him out as soon as possible in case he was badly injured, and there were no pinch bars available. Needless to say, if the locomotive had slipped, the results would have been disastrous, and when the job was over, Bill admitted having butterflies in his tummy!

The fine appearance of the Robinson engines owed much to the handsome boiler mountings with which he adorned them, and in this respect he was helped by the generous Great Central loading gauge. This permitted a maximum height of just over 13' 3½" but in the London area the clearances proved a bit tight at times. The dome covers on the 4-6-2 tanks were normally secured with a central nut having a lock-nut on top of it. On the Neasden engines, however, they were only able to fit one nut, and half the normal thickness at that. On two occasions Bill's locomotive finished its turn on a windy night minus the dome cover, which had been blown off, unknown to them, somewhere en route. The nut, unrestrained by a lock-nut, had either worked loose or, with some rather stiff new springs on the locomotive, it had been sheared off on an overbridge or tunnel. They also had the wooden sliding section of the cab roof blown out once by the wind.

Robinson also carried out a considerable amount of experimentation on alternative methods of firing locomotives. Various 2-8-0s were tried burning pulverised coal or colloidal fuel, the latter being a fluid mixture of coal with fuel oil, creosote, or pitch. The most successful of these con versions was on No. 699, one of the locomotives that was fitted in 1921 with a special 6' diameter boiler. This was provided with a massive, unbraked, double-bogie tender which had two small high-speed auxiliary engines mounted in cupboards on the tender front. One of these drove a fan through a train of gears and the other the feed screws. If one of them broke down, a system of dog clutches enabled the other to carry out both duties, and provision was made to supply steam to them from outside sources when lighting up. The arrangement was designed to deliver a ribbon of pulverised fuel into the firebox, surrounded by an annulus of air which gave intense turbulence to try and ensure that the firebox did not fill up with unburnt fuel as had occurred during some of the earlier experiments. Bill fired this locomotive on a couple of trips and found it easy to work, but the finely pulverised coal had one serious defect. The slightest amount of water getting in anywhere caused it to clog right back, and the only way of freeing the system was by separating the engine from the tender, a task that required several hours' work. Nothing ever came of these colloidal or pulverised fuel experiments, but with the troubled times that were being experienced in the coal mines during the early 1920s, Robinson modified a considerable number of locomotives to operate on oil fuel, including several of the 4-6-2 tanks. The quality of the oil provided was very variable too, a tankful on a "Director" at times being only sufficient to get them as far as Sheffield, while on other occasions it would be more than enough to reach Manchester.

Bill witnessed an unusual accident with an oil-fired 4-6-2 tank at Neasden one day, when he was standing outside the old coach body which served as the "Relief Bunk" at the outlet to the Shed. A crew had been preparing the locomotive for a turn and after getting the boiler pressure well up, the fireman turned the burner off until the arrival of the second crew who were booked to take the locomotive down to Marylebone. The standard way of lighting the burner was to turn the oil supply on, and immediately light an oily rag and throw it through the firehole door. Unfortunately, on this occasion, the oil supply had not stopped completely during the half hour or so during which the fire was out, and a consider able quantity had accumulated in the ashpan, while the whole firebox, tubes, and smokebox were full of an explosive mixture of gas. When the relieving crew arrived and were climbing up on to the engine, one each side of the cab, the first fireman carried out the standard re-lighting procedure, which, in this instance, had very spectacular results. The noise of the explosion made Bill look round, and from where he was, some 200 yards away, he saw a great cloud of dense smoke shoot out of the chimney, while a tongue of flame from the ashpan licked through the pit under the locomotive, reaching forward some six feet in front of the buffer beam. The crew on the footplate were injured by the blast and the force of the explosion also blew the other two who were relieving them into the pits in the adjoining roads. With four casualties the first job was to get them to hospital, and Bill was told to go as fireman for the driver who was to take the locomotive and the other four down to Marylebone, where the station staff were warned to expect them. The two more seriously shocked and injured men were given seats on the tool boxes in the cab, and they got them down to the terminus and off to hospital as quickly as possible. Once on their way, it soon became apparent that the blast had displaced the oil burner in the firebox, which always had to be adjusted fairly accurately or the locomotive went "off the boil". By the time they reached Marylebone, the boiler pressure was down to 60 pounds per square inch, but it was not until the locomotive was examined later, back at the shed, that they discovered the longitudinal seam along the top of the smokebox was split open and the chimney was hanging on by a thread of metal on one bolt, the others all having been sheared by the force of the explosion. Oil firing could thus produce its own particular difficulties and hazards.

While the Robinson designs were of a calibre that befitted the duties demanded of the motive power on the "Last Main Line", there were numerous earlier designs which Bill still had to work, either shedded in Neasden or working in on through turns from the north. There were still some of the early Sacre 2-4-0s about, and Bill and his mate would occasionally relieve a crew on one at Woodford, bringing it up to Mary lebone. He recalls that they were a handy engine on one of the light Sheffield trains. The gap between engine and tender was very wide, however, and the crew had to take care not to fall through. Bill had several trips on the two types of Sacre 4-4-0 that came through to Neasden from time to time, and well remembers watching the action of the side rods from the cab. These old timers were game engines, and Bill recalls one trip he had with Chris Peacock, who originally hailed from Barnsley. They were at Woodford awaiting their train from Nottingham, when the foreman informed them that, as there was no other locomotive available, the Sacre would have to go through with its load of 35 mixed goods wagons. Once out of earshot of the foreman, Chris turned to Bill and said, "Reet lad, na first thing we want is a Jimmy". They found a stout piece of wire that was just right for the job, and after the locomotive had come on to the shed for more coal and reconditioning, inserted the wire across the top of the blastpipe, centring it with one end wedged into a tube, and the other bent and inserted under the blower ring. This time honoured way of "improving" the effect of the blast pipe on a shy steamer has always been frowned on by officialdom because of the inevitable rise in coal consumption and the risk of lineside fires, but the rockets out of the chimney were a pleasure to watch when this form of "treatment" was used at night. When they set off with their train, Chris was delighted with the results, the needle keeping right on the mark. The harder he worked her, the better she responded, Bill having followed the yelled advice "Stick to it, lad, keep it thick and even over t'box". On his previous trip with one of these locomotives, Chris's fireman had let two large holes develop in the fire, giving them a difficult trip, but on this run Bill was able to keep them sealed, and only let the minimum amount of cold air into the box through the firehole door. As they left the locomotive at Neasden, tired out, but triumphant, Chris commented, "Mutual Improvement can't gie thee that kind a skill tha knows, Bill, thar's got to pick it up on t'road".

After 1902, when Robinson became Chief Mechanical Engineer instead of simply Locomotive Superintendent, he produced a number of interesting developments in the carriage and wagon stock. One that used to interest Bill was the anti-collision device that was fixed to the solebars of some of the suburban and long-distance coaches outside the buffers.

Each consisted of a stout steel plate bent into a series of horizontal corru gations. The idea was that if there was a collision, the corrugations on adjacent coaches would interlock and prevent one of the underframes riding over the other with subsequent danger of telescoping. They did not interfere with coupling up, but no one fortunately had occasion to try out their effectiveness in a bad accident.

Another safety device fitted on the suburban locomotives operating from Marylebone was the "Reliostop", a form of cab signalling introduced by Bound and Rowland. As the locomotive approached every distant signal, the apparatus sounded a siren in the cab and made a partial application of the brake, which the driver would cancel. If the signal was showing a caution aspect, a second similar warning would be given half- way to the home, but if they over-ran the home signal at danger, an arm beside the track broke a small wooden peg on the locomotive. As with ATC or AWS, it was possible to cancel the partial brake application associated with the caution siren, but once the peg was broken, a valve in the vacuum brake system sprang open and the train was rapidly brought to a stand with a full brake application. On each turn, the drivers drew three of these wooden pegs from the timekeeper. They were numbered, the one on the locomotive being marked "0", and the other spare ones, "1 ", "2", and "3". If a peg got broken, to get the brake off again it had to be replaced by the next one in the series, and questions would be asked about the incident on the driver's return to the sheds. Several drivers had their own blank peg made which they fitted at the start of each shift, keeping the one officially numbered "0" in their toolbox. This habit did not impair the safety of the device, of course, but merely made it less easy to detect that someone had run by a signal. Another trick was to put a bit of coal dust into the siren to quieten it down if its note was too raucous.

Bill worked with many different mates during his firing days, one of them being Sam Arrand, who had also come south to Neasden. He was very much a character, and smoked a small clay pipe "docker's style", while if there was anything he preferred to a pint of beer, it was two. He always carried a bottle in his tail-coat pocket (the G.C. crews still were not provided with uniforms) and would comment to Bill "Arr, this is what you want, something with some blood in it, something that'll pull you out, something that you can stand to." He was by no means a drunkard, but was up to all the tricks, always advising Bill to find a "father" for any incident about which he might be called to task. They worked on the 2-8-0s a lot, taking 40-60 coal empties down to Woodford. In those days they were all private owners' wagons, and had grease boxes, which were very sluggish, especially in cold weather. The maximum loading via High Wycombe was 60 empties, and during the winter they would have to work really hard for the first few miles until the grease got warm. It would then be comparatively easy to maintain a speed of 30 m.p.h. until the next stop for an examination, when the boxes promptly stiffened up again during the brief halt.

Sam was by way of being something of a sporting gent, and on certain turns used to take advantage of the sparseness of the traffic after 11 p.m. between London and Woodford, the point where the transfer freight for the G.W.R. from the north was siphoned off to make its way down to Banbury. The G.W.R. did not operate many trains during the night over the Joint Line via High Wycombe either, and many of the intermediate signal boxes would be switched out. The Neasden men had two overnight coal empty workings to Woodford, and in the early hours of the morning it was not difficult to get some time in hand between High Wycombe and Princes Risborough, or further on, depending on what Sam felt like. When the chosen section was reached, Bill would be given the regulator and told to look after the driving, as well as still doing the firing. Sam would then disappear around the cab side, and make his way up to the front of the locomotive, where he would proceed to lie down full length on the front buffer beam. This was not to have a rest, I must hasten to add, but to enable him to take better aim with his shot gun at any wild life on the cutting sides or in the fields adjoining the track. Bill's job, leaning round the right-hand cab side sheet, was to keep the train moving slowly along. If Sam succeeded in shooting anything, Bill would wake the guard by buffering up, and then sound the whistle to indicate to him where their prey was, so that he could jump down and retrieve it. If they were fortunate, the three of them would later divide the night's bag of rabbits and pheasants, but I am not sure who had the job of drawing the game. On the occasion when Sam shot a fox they did not bother to collect it, but one hopes that 40 years ago such an action never came to the ears of any of the G.C. directors who might have hunted with the Quorn or any of the other famous packs that abounded in the area through which the line ran. If they were late reaching the next signal box, Sam would have an excuse handy that something had gone wrong with the engine, so that even if his sporting exploits were known to others, no word of it ever reached the ears of Authority. They always had to be on the look-out for packs of hounds in the hunting shires, and on one occasion Bill's mate stopped his train when he saw one on the line ahead. This invariably resulted in a ten shilling tip from the master for each member of the crew.

4

When he returned to Neasden at the end of the war, Bill went back to lodging with the Ratleys, but found many changes in the household, as the Spanish "flu" epidemic in 1918 had claimed Mrs. Ratley and her elder daughter amongst its millions of victims throughout the world. Tom, a number of years younger than Bill and who had served in the Grenadier Guards during the war, also returned to Neasden but still as a cleaner. Bill was now 25, and suddenly realised that Tom's "little sister" had, in the intervening years, grown into a very attractive young lady. He duly proposed, and they eventually married, setting up home in Willesden, where their two daughters, Irene and Marian, were both born. Later, when the post-war housing shortage was not quite so intense, they moved to Ashmore Road, Paddington, where they stayed until after Bill's move to King's Cross.

As a family man, Bill always took full advantage of every free pass he could obtain, and often got permission to extend his one week's leave, before a fortnight's holiday became general. They went to stay at seaside resorts as far afield as Wales, the Isle of Man, and Scotland. It was their first holiday in Northern Ireland in 1922 that produced the most surprises, however. They had travelled overnight via Heysham on the boat to Belfast, where they were to stay with Bill's brother, Jim, who had not yet emigrated down-under. Going up Belfast Loch it was announced that, as snipers had been firing into the city from Cave Hill, a curfew had been imposed. It was due to be lifted at 7.30 that morning but anyone with definite arrangements to meet people would be allowed off at 7 with an escort. Bill and Dolly were duly provided with their own military chaperones, and after meeting Jim en route, got safely to his home. Bill's daughter was only a baby in arms, so when they arrived, Dolly put her to bed to catch up on the sleep she had lost on the boat. Bill and Jim decided to go out for a walk along the River Laggan, and on the way back paused to read the notices outside one of the Police Stations, announcing the restrictions being imposed. Before leaving London on the Friday night, Bill had been shopping, and had fixed himself up with an Italian velour hat, which was all the vogue at that time. They were nearing home again when two young men who had been walking along behind them suddenly closed in, covering them with revolvers. They immediately began firing questions at Bill, and before he could answer, one of them pulled his prize new hat off. He flung it on the ground, and then started to go through all his pockets. Apparently the I.R.A. had all adopted hats of this type with green feathers in them, and Bill had come under suspicion of trying to over throw the Northern Ireland government by force. They were able to prove who they were to the disgruntled members of the citizens' army, who, in spite of a repeated search, had fortunately been unable to find any feather stuck in the offending hat. Bill was told he was lucky to have got off so lightly and was warned not to wear the hat in question again. The fighting got worse during their stay, and as Bill's sister Ethel was now married and living some 30 miles away near Newcastle, they moved out of Belfast to stay with her instead. On the following Saturday they went in to Banbridge to enable the ladies to do some shopping, and while this was in progress, Bill sauntered up the road. Trying to kill time, he stopped outside a bank, and was promptly closed in on again by a couple of armed civilians, who thought he was intending to raid the premises for funds for the Southern Irish irregulars. It would appear that the Northern Irish were more than somewhat touchy at this time, as unless Bill as a young man was a more violent-looking character than he became later, one would hardly associate him with the possibilities of armed uprisings.

Bill's second family visit to Ireland was more peaceful, however. Ethel and her husband had found the job of househunting even harder in Ireland than Bill had in London, and finally had to settle on an old roofless smithy with walls nearly 4 feet thick. Ethel's husband was a handyman and soon had a roof on, a floor laid, and running water brought into the house. They were unable to manage a proper stove, however, and the cooking was done over an open fire, a crane with a plate hanging from it serving as an oven. Bill had taken up the wireless craze, and had brought with him a crystal set he had made, so they could tune in to 2LO. One day they had just succeeded in getting the cats whisker working properly on the bit of "silver" when the baker called. He was asked if he would like to hear the wireless, and was soon sitting down at the table with the earphones clamped to his head, enthralled at what was coming over the ether from 2LO. The programme was about to change, and a military band suddenly came on the air, whereupon the baker shot to his feet to dash outside and prevent his horses being frightened by the music. It took them all a long time to explain to him that the horses were unable to hear the programme too. Bill's visits to Ireland seem generally to have been more than usually exciting as on another trip from Heysham to Belfast on the steamer Londonderry, Bill went down into the saloon to be greeted by a group of Chinese sailors smoking opium. The fumes so put him off that he spent the rest of the voyage on deck in the fresh air.

5

At about this time Bill began to take up local politics, as well as being prominent in union circles at Neasden, where he held the posts of Assistant Secretary of the A.S.L.E.F. branch, and of the Local Departmental Committee. In the political field, he was a great admirer of George Lansbury and his Christian Socialist Party, and had been very impressed with what had been done by him during the 1911 strike. When the military had been called out, Lansbury went along to the railway pickets with some footballs, advising them to pick a team and challenge the soldiers to a match as soon as they appeared on the scene. As a result, tempers never became strained, and there were no incidents for subsequent regret on either side. Bill became Secretary of his Labour Ward Committee in Paddington, and got as far as standing for the Borough Council and the Board of Guardians, but without success. As Secretary he had to arrange a number of speakers, many of whom afterwards came back to his flat where they were entertained and discussed matters with the family. He once wrote to George Bernard Shaw, asking him to come, but received a snooty reply from his secretary, saying he was not available for local speaking. The Ward Committee also met Marie Stopes at a time when her early work with the Eugenic Society made her unaccept able in many quarters. Bill's biggest political blow, however, was just before one election when he had addressed nearly 2,500 envelopes at home, ready to be sent out to every house in the Ward. One of his daughters got measles, and they had to burn the lot to conform with the then-accepted standards of quarantine. When he moved to King's Cross in 1927 Bill gave up his various political activities as they were interfering too much with his social life, although I have a feeling that he also found that he did not care for the rough mud-slinging of local politics in those days. This background, however, was to provide a bond of common interest in his Top Link days, when he shared a locomotive with Charlie Simmons, thrice Mayor of Finsbury, a member of the Metropolitan Water Board, and Governor of St. Bartholomew's Hospital.

There was one interest of this sort, however, which Bill never gave up, and this was the Manor House Hospital at Golders Green, which had been started by volunteers during World War I, being then known as the Labour Hospital. They were short of funds in the early twenties, and one summer, Bill, with a railwayman from the Underground, toured the North of England seeking subscriptions from the local trades unions. Their expenses were met by their local A.S.L.E.F. branch for the fortnight, which was taken as their holiday that year. They visited Middlesbrough, the Hartlepools, and Carr's biscuit factory at Carlisle. The two of them found it a great deal harder to get into union meetings in the North than it was in London, where the branches conducted their business virtually in open session. Instead of just going in and taking a seat, they had to knock on a closed door, and were scrutinised by a pair of eyes through a peephole before they were allowed in. They then had to sign the visitors' book, and had their credentials examined before being taken and introduced to the Chairman. This northern caution was not reflected in the support that Bill and his friend were able to obtain, however. As a result of numerous voluntary efforts of this sort, the Hospital weathered the financial crisis that had brought them to the point where there were, in one week, no wages until a Grand Christmas Draw had been organised to bring in some funds.

The Manor House Hospital is run on democratic lines, with Ward Committees, and a House Committee that sits with the Medical officers. This last body was very informal, and Bill remembers that before one meeting a member once commented to a surgeon about a swelling on his arm. He was promptly taken into a corner and had the carbuncle causing it lanced while the rest of the committee was assembling. On Sundays, Bill would often volunteer to take visitors round the Hospital, part of which made use of the building where Pavlova had once lived.

One of the showpieces that used to intrigue him as well as the visitors was an infra-red heater that would cook the yolk of an egg without touching the white.

6

On January 1st, 1923, the London and North Eastern Railway began its operational existence as one of the four new groups into which the numerous small railway companies had been amalgamated by Act of Parliament. The process was somewhat more complicated than Nationalisation 25 years later, the second large-scale reorganisation that took place during Bill's working life. The boards of the old individual companies had, first of all, to reach agreement with the directors of their group before they could call an extraordinary meeting of share holders to ratify the arrangements and then vote themselves out of existence.

The L.N.E.R. was formed from seven "Constituent Companies", of which the Great Central was one, and a whole host of "Subsidiary Companies", including the Seaforth and Sefton Junction Railway-the nominally independent company that had previously owned the short section of line over which the Liverpool Overhead operated on Grand National Days. Their total route mileage was 7,000, and the nominal capital was £350 million. 223,000 staff of all grades, spread over the whole length of the country between London and Lossiemouth, were required to operate the new company, which boasted the most easterly as well as westerly metals in Great Britain. Many and impressive were the other statistics that were trotted out by the management in newspaper interviews, some of the claims being so tortuous as to tempt the reader to repeat Disraeli's well-known comment: "There are lies, damned lies, and statistics".

The total number of railway employees in the country at this time was approximately 677,000, so that, on this basis, the L.N.E.R. represented all but a third of the labour force. Of this grand total, there were nearly 36,000 drivers and motormen and approximately 15,000 cleaners, but the figures quoted never seemed to include the total of firemen, without whose backbreaking efforts the steam locomotives would never have left their sheds. Under the Grouping Act, however, two important sets of bodies were set up which enabled the railwaymen to discuss items of local or sectional interest with the management. These were the Local Departmental Committees, which covered small units such as a motive power depot or goods yard, while on the larger scale came the Sectional Committees, which ensured that the point of view of, say, all the enginemen in the company could be put to the management. It was this committee on the L.N.E.R. that got a new eyesight test accepted, as from the beginning of 1925, the colour vision part being based on the system laid down by Dr. Edridge Green.

As far as Bill was concerned, however, Grouping brought no immediate change in the conditions under which he worked, although in a few years' time he was to be very glad of the wider scope for transfer within the new company when redundancy reared its ugly head. As always with such an amalgamation, however, it was the ranks of management that were the first to find themselves engaged in jostling for the far fewer top jobs that were now available. Robinson, the most senior of the locomotive men in the constituent companies, was offered the post of C.M.E. of the L.N.E.R., but declined it in view of his age, making way for a younger man from Doncaster - Nigel Gresley, who returned the compliment by building a number of new locomotives to Robinson's design to meet his immediate requirements for additional motive power.

One of the first tasks that faced the L.N.E.R. was a decision on the livery of the locomotives, and, on February

22nd, nine engines were exhibited at Marylebone station to assist the directors in making their choice. Only passenger engines were involved, as most of the companies had adopted Henry Ford's policy with their goods engines. It was clear that the Great Northern colours were already highly favoured, as locomotives from the Great Central, Great Eastern, North British, and North Eastern all appeared in this livery, with the letters L. & N. E. R. transferred on to their tenders or tanks in 6" gold shaded letters above the number, which was in similarly-styled figures, 12" high. Another North British Atlantic, Dunedin, was there in its native dark brown livery, but carrying the new style lettering, and the North Eastern livery was similarly represented by one of their Class Z locomotives of the same wheel arrangement. A Great Central "Director", Somme, appeared in its Brunswick green livery, which was, in effect, a somewhat darker version of the Great Northern one that received the official blessing of the board. This cavalcade of strangers occupied two of the side roads at Neasden sheds for a week, and Bill took the opportunity of getting on all of them to see what they were like. He actually helped dispose of a North British Atlantic when it arrived, and was very taken with the novelty of the side-opening ash pan, the dampers on which were worked by a wheel on the frame by the firebox. It is an interesting commentary on the degree of which information on railway functions was not generally made public in those days, that no mention of this event appeared in the contemporary columns of the "Railway Magazine", although a rather similar collection of locomotives at York at the end of January was reported by an observant reader.

Also, following the Grouping, there was a change in the numbering of the Great Central engines. The new L.N.E.R. now possessed, in round figures, 7,600 steam locomotives, and some unified system of identification was obviously necessary. Each of the separate companies had originally adopted their own numbering system, and it was initially intended to retain these numbers. The now familiar small oval number plates were fixed to each locomotive, with the words "London and North Eastern Railway", and the name of the works which had previously been respon sible for it. The former G.C. "Director" Somme, for example, which had taken part in the Marylebone exhibition, sported the number 503 on its plate, together with "Gorton Works", while the number appeared in shaded gold transfers on the tender, as well as on the cast number plate on the cab side. The latest of the Robinson 4-6-2 tanks which were then being built for the Wembley traffic, appeared, however, without the large cast numberplate that had hitherto been customary on all Robinson engines. The number was applied in transfer form on the tanks, but their G.C. origin was indicated by that company's coat of arms on the sides of the bunker.

This interim system, however, did not last very long, as it had two defects. The most obvious one was that engines were virtually tied to the same tenders, and any temporary exchanges that were necessary to meet operational requirements made nonsense of the numbering system. The works plate idea, however, was also bound to lead to confusion, and after trying the use of a lettered suffix to the number, the L.N.E.R. in 1924 adopted the same sort of arrangement that was followed 25 years later after Nationalisation. Each of the constituent companies was allocated a group of numbers sufficient to contain all that company's engines. In deference to the large locomotive stock of the North Eastern Railway, their engines were allowed to retain the original numbers, but the G.C. stud had 5,000 added to theirs. None of their locomotives had been numbered higher than 1,800, and many of them had only carried three-digit numbers, so that Bill and his mates had to get used to the extra digit. The Great Northern, Great North of Scotland, Great Eastern, and North British numbers were similarly increased by 3,000, 6,800, 7,000 and 9,000 respectively. This was a reasonably neat arrangement, but for new construction the L.N.E.R., like the Great Central, went to pieces, and used any convenient blank numbers that were available at the lower end of the range, so that until Thompson sorted things out from 1946 onwards, any quick identification of a locomotive's class from its number was impossible. Consecutive numbers were not even used for a series of identical new locomotives, a group of ten K3s for example, being numbered 126, 127, 134, 135, 140, 141, 143, 153 and 156. It was the combination of this last locomotive, however, turned out from Darlington in February 1925, and the renumbering system, that once saved Bill and his mate from being hauled up in front of the Marylebone Bench and fined for excessive smoke emission.

The incident occurred when the railways were receiving quantities of German coal as reparations after World War I. Compared with our native British product, the stuff from the Ruhr was very poor indeed, earning the name of "Flea Powder" from the crews. No one liked it, either on the railways, in industry, or elsewhere, and Bill had four locomotives fail short of steam, with their firebars just a shapeless mass of iron, while working Marylebone-Manchester trains as a result of the slagging qualities of the ash. Being soft coal, too, it had a tendency to produce copious quantities of smoke, and even in those days the clean-air people were very active, obtaining numerous convictions for excessive smoke, since only one minute's grace was allowed for it to be cleared. A stoker that Bill knew on one of the Mersey ferries once told him that he had received three summonses from different authorities on the two sides of the river, which resulted in his having to attend three courts on the same day.

On one shift, after Bill and his mate had been having lunch, they climbed back on the footplate of A5 No. 5156, which was standing at the Marylebone coaling stage, just below Lord's cricket ground. The driver, who got on the footplate before Bill, was a bit over-anxious, and, without first opening the blower, got out the bent dart to lift the fire. As a result, thick black smoke oozed from the chimney, much to the delight of an L.C.C. smoke inspector who happened to be handy, with his camera at the ready. He duly obtained a suitably-incriminating shot of the locomotive, complete with the number on the tanks. Unfortunately for him, however, the end of the coal stage was obscuring the newly-added "5", and the summons was duly issued for the crew of locomotive No. 156. Either the inspector was not very observant, or was so used to three-digit numbers that he did not realise the mistake. In consequence, a rather surprised Geordie driver and his fireman were summonsed to appear before the magistrates at Marylebone. With the aid of the Company's lawyer, however, they had no difficulty in proving that their locomotive had been very busy in the Newcastle area on the day in question. The case consequently had to be dismissed, and as Bill put it, "We just grinned that one off". Compared with other crews, they were lucky to get off so easily, and did not have any fine to meet out of their own pockets.

7

The 1920s were noted for the pride which we, as a nation, took in the British Empire, those red-coloured countries and islands that spanned the map of the world, and on which the sun never set. As part of this national expression, it was decided to hold the British Empire Exhibition in 1924 and 1925, and a site was chosen for it at Wembley in the V between the two routes out of Marylebone. What part the Great Central directors had played in picking this site is not known, but although by the time it was opened their railway had become part of the L.N.E.R., the com paratively lightly-used terminus at Marylebone proved invaluable in handling the extra traffic that ensued during the two years, especially at week-ends. Together, with the exhibition itself, a vast new football stadium was built, and was first used for the F.A. Cup Final in 1923. Bill's first connection with the Exhibition traffic was long before it was opened, when they worked the trains carrying the constructional materials to Wembley. The Met. brought the wagons of cement and grit up from Brill to Harrow-on-the-Hill, where a Neasden 0-6-2T would collect them and take them into sidings serving the Exhibition area. The Great

Central also built a new single-track loop nearly a mile long, to serve the stadium and exhibition, and trains traversed this in a clockwise direction, reaching it via a new junction off the Northolt line, controlled by Neasden North Junction Box. It was constructed in four months, well over 30,000 cubic yards of clay having to be removed, mainly from the deep cutting that leads into the 600-feet long platform. From here into Marylebone, the signalling was improved, colour-lights being installed at a number of locations. Although the Great Central was thus very strategically positioned, there was competition from the L.M.S. services out of Broad Street and Euston to Wembley, as well as from the intensified Met. service from Baker Street to Wembley Park, where a new double-sided platform had been provided.

The scene was thus set for the events of Saturday, April 28th, 1923, when Bolton Wanderers met West Ham in the first Wembley Cup Final. For weeks the spaciousness of the new stadium had been referred to in every newspaper, while the railways concerned were all vying with each other to attract the maximum number of passengers. The Met. was offering special return fares of ls. to Wembley from Baker Street and some other stations, and by using all available stock, were able to book trains at l½ minute intervals into Wembley Park. The Great Central offered the same fare from Marylebone, and aimed to provide a two minute service, but this had to be worked over the one pair of tracks. The Stadium station, then in open country, was provided with eight double gates set along the length of the rear fence, with large raised notices marking their position. So effective were these arrangements that it was found possible to empty and dispose of an eight-coach train load of up to 1,000 people in a minute. This allowed ample time before the next arrival came slowly round the approach curve, passing at yellow the colour light at the south end of the platform while the one at the far end still showed red, protecting the empty stock as it picked up speed around the north side of the loop.

Back at Marylebone, platforms 3 and 4 were allocated exclusively for the use of the Wembley service, and each was therefore called on to dispatch a train every four minutes during the peak period between 1 and 2 p.m. As a train of empty stock ran in past the departing train on the next platform and stopped, the shunter standing by would un couple, so the driver could run forward to the water crane and put the bag into the A5's tank as quickly as possible. Another locomotive came on to the country end of the stock and after two minutes it would be away, the locomotive at the rear end providing banking assistance as far as the platform end. The points changed and the "Tommy Dod" (subsidiary signal) cleared, directing them into the siding, ready to set back on the rear of the next incoming train which was by then due to be running in alongside. They had tried operating this intensive service on an experimental basis during off-peak periods on the Thursday and Friday so that the various bugs could be overcome. One of the snags proved to be the difficulty of sighting some of the signals in the tunnels with so much steam about. Even so, on the Saturday everyone was really keyed up, and nerves got a bit frayed at times, especially as their water supply was continually dropping lower and lower, since less than two minutes at the column was not sufficient to make up for that used on a round trip with eight packed bogies. During one of their visits to Maryle bone, Bill was out of the cab making certain that they got the maximum amount of water when the guard's whistle blew, and jumping back in again, thought that the driver had already spun the handbrake off, which he was actually relying on Bill to do. By the time they had realised what had happened, the departing train was two coach-lengths away, and his driver shouted at him to get it off so they could catch it. Bill did not fancy chasing a train up the platform like that, so did not budge and his driver got a bit hot under the collar about it. Mr. W. G. P. Maclure, the Locomotive Running Superintendent, who was watching the special workings from the platform end with Mr. Matthew Robinson (the son of J. G.), came up, inquired what was the matter, and told them to carry on, so that the incident was smoothed over. At Neasden North Junction, too, the signalman on one occasion misrouted a train, failing to realise from its special headcode of a black diagonal cross on a white square, that it was destined for the loop. The driver saw from the lie of the points that something was wrong, but although he braked hard, the engine overran them by a few yards. He shouted to the signalman that he was setting back sufficiently to permit the points to be changed, and they were thus able to sort the matter out to their satisfaction. Unfor tunately, one of the passengers leaving Wembley station was heard by one of the inspectors to remark on the unusual shuttle service over the points, and he reported the incident on the Monday morning. So intense had been the service, however, that in spite of repeated enquiries from all concerned, they were never able to pin down the culprit, helped of course by the communal smokescreen put up by the locomotive crews!

The services that the railways had laid on were admirable, but the organisers of the sporting event had failed to realise that a Cup Final on a fine Saturday without tickets would attract far more than the 150,000 spectators which the new stadium would hold. The main line railways worked over 140 special trains into the London terminals alone, on the Saturday morning. Long before kick-off time, more than 200,000 were packed into the ground, spilling out on to the pitch itself, while thousands more strove to get in or, giving up hope, tried to return while others were still arriving. The position was saved, largely by the work of Police Constable Storey on his white horse and his colleagues, the incident being still well known as a classic example of crowd control, so that it was finally possible to start the match. Outside, however, the railways, expecting an hour and a half of peace in which to regroup for the homeward rush, were suddenly faced with the need to keep up a continuous supply of trains. As a consequence, two of the Neasden crews ran out of coal and had to be rescued by other locomotives, while at one time the services in and out of Marylebone all but came to a standstill. The lessons of April 1923 were very quickly learnt, however, and to this day, admission to Cup Finals is by ticket only, a prize much sought after in sporting circles. The train service from Marylebone still operates in the same way, although diesel multiple units have ousted steam.

The British Empire Exhibition itself opened the following year, and the railway exhibits from Britain, Ireland, South Africa and India formed a considerable attraction. The L.M.S. and Met. provided full sized coaches, and Beardmore's exhibited the 4-6-0 No. 5845 that they had built for the former company, fitting it with Prince of Wales nameplates for the occasion. A South African electric locomotive also appeared at the head of a three-coach train in a "station", and visitors could take meals in the restaurant car. The most interest, however, was aroused by "Flying Scotsman" and Caerphilly Castle, standing tender to tender on adjacent stands. Bill had seen the Pacific at Neasden sheds waiting to go to the exhibition, with the new L.N.E.R. coat of arms on its cab sides. This was a special exhibition livery, its tyres being burnished too, a task that has daunted her present owner from emulating. Alongside was the Stockton and Darlington Locomotion, just 99 years old, but the G.W.R. was not able to produce any broad gauge counterpart. Few of the thousands of spectators that filed through the rivals' cabs would have expected that these two modern locomotive classes were, as a result of the exhibition, to take part in direct comparative trials in the following year, and that, in them, the smaller 4-6-0 would beat her larger sister, thanks to the efficient valve gear that she had inherited from Churchward's pioneering.

Throughout 1924 and 1925, the L.N.E.R. were able to make full use of the former Great Central line to work their special trains into London, taking advantage of the relative peace and quiet of Marylebone to handle the crowds, ferrying those who wanted to go to the Exhibition on the shuttle service around the loop. By this time, the stadium station had taken on much of the appearance that it has now, with a brick rear wall from which the platform awning springs. It was well positioned for the Exhibition, being in the centre of the ground near the India Pavilion. On the other side of the line, with a fence separating the tracks, was part of the " Never Stop" railway, that ingenious internal mode of transport used in the exhibition. The vehicles on it were propelled by a lug which engaged with a continuous helical screw set between the rails, and by decreasing the pitch of the screw at the stations, it was possible to reduce forward motion sufficiently for passengers to get in and out without difficulty. The peak Exhibition service out of Marylebone settled down to eight trips an hour, which took twelve minutes for the journey, and the traffic handled was enormous. On Whit Monday, 1924, for instance, no less than 321,000 people visited the Exhibition, and from June onwards, the Met. decided to pay all their staff a fortnightly bonus of 10 per cent. of their basic weekly wage to mark their successful handling of so many additional passengers. Neasden men would usually relieve the crews of long- distance L.N.E.R. excursions at High Wycombe or Northolt, and Bill and his mate frequently had to take over strange locomotives that they had never even seen before. One of these was the Ivatt Atlantic

No. 1419, which Gresley had fitted with a booster. Large pipes ran along the foot-framing on each side to take the steam to and from the booster, and when he first saw them, Bill thought they were to provide central heating for the new, more commodious cab with its side windows. The booster, providing over 8,000 lb. of tractive effort, cut out as soon as the main valve gear was linked up to 25 per cent. It was an excellent device for getting heavy trains out of King's Cross, as Bill was to find in later years when he worked her to Cambridge on one occasion, but by then the cab had become loose, and was always wobbling, which he found very irritating.

8

Bill was by now firing on the longest Neasden workings, which would take him over Woodhead to Manchester with freight and passenger trains. Much the hardest work came at the end of the 206-mile northbound journey. After the racing stretches of the Last Main Line, there was the climb to Pilsley, but even in those days, six minutes recovery time was allowed for colliery subsidences over the 38 miles between Nottingham and Sheffield. This climb paled, however, almost to insignificance, beside the 18-mile slog out of Sheffield, with a third of the distance inclined at an unbroken 1 in 120. With a "Director" or a Robinson Atlantic on five bogies, the long climb was not so hard a job, however, as when they were toiling up the same gradients with a heavy freight. In either case, by this stage of the through working, the coal would be well back into the tender, with the consequent need to double-handle it into the firehole. In this direction, however, once they had charged into the smoky left-hand bore at Dunford Bridge, it was downhill all the way. In the up direction they had to contend with three miles of wet single-line tunnel inclined throughout at 1 in 200, which could tax the footplate crews considerably. Nowadays as we hum behind a 2,490 h.p. electric locomotive into the concrete vault of the new double-line tunnel, with its rows of lights arcing ahead on either side, it is rare for passengers to spare a thought about the conditions that used to face the drivers and firemen on a steam locomotive behind the now bricked-up gothic arches of the old tunnels. Even with a comparatively light passenger train, a lot of sand would be used on the way through, and at 30 or 40 m.p.h., the three mile journey through the backbone of England seemed to last an age, as the exhaust blasted off the dripping roof and swirled back overhead in the flickering light from the fire, while wraiths of steam curled into the cab, poking with red-tipped fingers at the open firehole door. On a heavy freight, even with two locomotives on the train, the crews might be anything up to 20 minutes " underground", and slipping would add even greater quantities of smoke and steam to the already saturated atmosphere. No distance at all inside the tunnel the daylight would be obscured, and, in spite of the diameter of one of the ventilation shafts being doubled in 1912-15, the atmosphere would thicken steadily until they could see nothing but a white sulphurous mist, with the open firehole just gleaming as a diffuse oval ahead. Bill remembers on one trip when a couple of oil burners had been through before them, he and his mate took it in turns to look after the regulator, while the other lay on the cab floor to get the best of the air available. Unlike some of the shorter tunnels such as those on the Worsborough Bank, where they could fire up before entering them and let the fire burn clear, a heavy eastbound train in Woodhead would require more or less continuous attention from the fireman, the inevitable smoke adding to the other conditions that would be rapidly approaching those of Turkish Baths, until they passed the enlarged No. 2 shaft, which provided some relief. From this intense heat, therefore, they would emerge into Yorkshire, their perspiration striking instantly chill in the cold air off the windswept Thirlstone Moors, where, as often as not, the weather was totally different from that they had left behind them in Lancashire. It must be remembered too, that there was no sick pay on the Great Central, although other companies had been more considerate, especially the Met., possibly because so much of their working was in tunnel.

By this time the footplate crews were being provided with caps and overalls to provide some degree of uniformity in their dress, which also saved them having to use their own clothes while at work. Bill found that the peaked cap provided good protection for the eyes from the particles of ash, and was no longer quite so envious of their opposite numbers on the Met. who had had them for several years. When the "opposition" had first appeared in them, the Neasden men had scornfully referred to them as "Letting (alighting) boards for pigeons", their own idea of a status symbol for footplate crews being a cloth cap and muffler. Some of the firemen were inclined to be rather scruffy before uniforms came in, and on one occasion, a driver, knowing he was going to work a special train next day, asked his mate to come suitably attired, or at least clean.

The fireman concerned, however, went to the other extreme, and turned up in his most disreputable outfit, thereafter always being known as "Lord Raglan". Although they were issued with blue overalls as uniform, individual preference came to the fore on the question of whether to "bleed" the dye out of them or not, but Bill's own choice was for as dark a uniform as possible, which he still adopts on the Festiniog.

9

With the prospect of having to take his driver's examination in the near future, Bill had been studying the rules and had attended Mutual Improvement Classes. The Great Central were not so generous as the Great Eastern, who had provided a lot of facilities for their footplate men at Stratford, but even so, they offered the M.I. classes the use of a room, although they did not lend them any models. Bill found the Science Museum at South Kensington handy, however, and would regularly make use of the working models of the different types of valve gear and so on that were on exhibition there. It was in about 1919 that Driver Bailey from Neasden, whose fast running had often been referred to by Cecil J. Allen, was appointed Inspector, a job which he held for nearly ten years, being a stickler for rules. On several occasions, when Bill was on a locomotive preparing to leave Marylebone, especially if he was splashing with the slacker pipe, his mate would remark "Remember Bill, there is one above who sees all". This is not an allusion to the recording angel, but to Harry Bailey in the old signal box he used as an office, who would in due course examine Bill on the rules and on the proper way to work a locomotive.

One day in 1926, therefore, Bill and five of his mates made their way at 9 a.m. into the old signal box, which was provided with a table, some chairs, and a blackboard, as well as some home-made models of valves and lubricators. The six of them took their seats, and Harry told them how he proposed to conduct the examination. He would ask one of them the various questions, and then when the replies had been given, would get each of the others to say whether their "spokesman's" answer had been right. In retrospect it does not seem to be too equitable a way of dealing with such an important examination, but with the various butterflies that there were in his tummy, Bill did not feel like arguing, especially when he found that he was the one who had to give the answers first. Once he had successfully dealt with the first question, however, he lost his nervousness, and thoroughly enjoyed the day. There were about a dozen questions all told, half on the locomotive and half on the rules. This was followed by a short written examination, and then they had to make trimmings with wire and worsted. One of the lads failed this part of the exam, and he was the only one out of the six who had not attended the Mutual Improvement Classes.

Next day came the practical part of the examination, when Harry rode with Bill on the footplate to Aylesbury and back. It was accepted that the drivers would occasionally let their firemen drive on the easier turns to gain experience, and this had been a principle that Bill had followed ever since, countless firemen having been given that feeling of trust that results from such a gesture. On his test run, Bill was able to stop at the right spot in each platform, and did this easily without dropping time, so that from then on he became a passed fireman, able to work a train as and when required.

While 1926 was a notable year in Bill's railway career, on a national scale it also marked the only General Strike that this country has ever known. The coal miners' strike, which in all lasted for nine months, led up to the sympathetic national stoppage of work on May 4th and although the majority of the nation then creaked back into action once more on the 12th, the railwaymen stayed on strike until the 14th. During the main part of the strike, volunteers from many walks of life took part in operating skeleton railway services, not without accident, but once the strike changed from being a national issue to one that only concerned the railways themselves, most or all of the volunteers ceased "playing at trains", as the railwaymen referred to it.

During the coal strike and other disputes involving the coal industry during the 1920s, supplies of locomotive coal became very scarce, and attempts were made to import suitable fuel from elsewhere, with comparatively little success, while oil firing was tried on a limited scale. There was less traffic for the railways to move too, and a lot of cleaners had to be dismissed in 1925 because of the lack of traffic on the railways. The Guaranteed Week agreement was suspended, and only came into opera tion again in April 1927, while immediately after the General Strike, the railways only took back their staff as they managed to get the services working once more, with consequent hardship to many railwaymen. At week-ends there were still many excursions to deal with, and Bill got in 13 driving turns during the next few months, mainly going out to Northolt to relieve an incoming crew, working the train forward into Marylebone. This was a good arrangement for a young driver, as the more experienced man he relieved was in a position to settle any queries he might have. As a result of this arrangement, however, he never handled a London-based locomotive in all the trips he worked as a driver from Neasden.

Early in 1927, there was a fall off in traffic on the Great Central, and Bill became redundant, being given the chance of moving elsewhere as a driver. Now that the move could be made to any depot in the Southern Promotional Area of the L.N.E.R. that was short of drivers, there was plenty of scope, and Bill was not surprised when he was given a form containing a large list of places on which he could put "yes" or "no" to indicate which he was prepared to accept. He duly bracketed the lot together, and wrote "yes" beside them, fully expecting to be moved north again. He was exceedingly surprised, therefore, when the official notification arrived at Neasden, to find that he was now transferred to King's Cross, less than six miles away. Not only did this not involve moving home, but King's Cross offered perhaps the greatest possibilities for an ambitious newly-promoted driver of any shed in the whole country.

CHAPTER FOUR

King's Cross

Bill moved to King's Cross in 1927 and although he was to be involved in very minor roles for many years, it is of interest to review the general position on the East Coast Route as it was at that time. Now that the L.N.E.R. had inherited the operation of the through Scottish expresses as a single company, they naturally boosted them, making full use of the slogan "King's Cross for Scotland". The agreement with the West Coast Route that had followed the races to the north was still, however, in force, and no day train was allowed to take less than 8¼ hours between London and Edinburgh, so that promotional efforts had to find some other form of expression than time-saving. One of the things tried was to hire ear phones to passengers at ls. a time, so they could listen to the wireless. Forty years later, the advance of technology was to see the introduction of the transistor radio on such a large scale that the railways had to ask passengers to refrain from using them if the noise caused annoyance to others. As early as 1923, Gresley, aided, of course, by Bulleid, had intro duced four new sets of stock, the Press run being made to York and back on 29th September that year. Fitted with Buckeye couplings and with all-electric kitchens, the interior finish was of a high standard for those days. The first-class dining cars were panelled with mahogany, while the seats were of green morocco leather surmounted by lace antimacassars, their pattern being designed around the initials of the company. Four of these 12-car sets were built, two for the "Flying Scotsman", and the others for the 1.15 p.m. down and the corresponding up train. Fine though these vehicles were, however, they were to be superseded on the "Scotsman" within 4 years, following the events of May 1928, when the world-beating regular non-stop schedule was introduced. Its first trip in the north-bound direction behind No. 4472 stirred everyone's imagination, and hundreds turned out at King's

Cross to see the inaugural train, complete with its cocktail bar, ladies' retiring room, and barber's shop, pull out at 10 o'clock. Although the "Scotch" expresses (as the nomenclature of the day still had it) attracted most of the publicity, the East Coast Route actually handled more trains for other destinations. This meant that the movements were increasingly more dense as one moved towards the south, with the Newcastle, the Hull and West Riding, and the Lincolnshire trains superimposed on those from Scotland.

The scheduling of long distance runs that culminated in the "Flying Scotsman's" 393-mile journey started in July 1927, when the relief train, leaving King's Cross at 9.50 a.m. four days a week, was booked non-stop to Newcastle. A schedule of no less than 5½ hours was allowed for the 268 miles, however, and the inaugural train consisted of only eight coaches, so the crew of Flying Fox would not have had a very exacting task. Nevertheless, their arrival at Newcastle was marked by telegrams from the Chief General Manager, and a reception by the Lord Mayor, who presented them with pipes and cigars. Easy though this trip was, within a month the August Bank Holiday crowds resulted in the train being lengthened to 15 bogies, a far tougher proposition. It was the regular introduction of trains of this sort that prompted the decision to lengthen Platform 10 at King's Cross by 45 feet, so providing the vantage point from which so many platform-enders were to observe Bill's departures in later years.

Special trains were also run for numerous different events. The half day excursion was very popular on the L.N.E.R., nearly 3,000 trains being run in the first nine months of 1927, and their booking from Leeds to London was advertised as the longest and fastest such excursion in the world, and for the Calcutta Cup match at Murrayfield that year, the return excursion fares by both the East and West Coast routes were only 24s. There was, however, one event in 1927 that produced no less than eight special workings out of King's Cross in the space of two hours on the evening of June 28th. This was the total eclipse of the sun visible early the following morning in North Yorkshire, and the trains, some conveying sleeping cars and with up to five restaurant cars apiece, were filled to capacity. Most of them packed themselves up the Richmond branch, while one went to Leyburn, one to West Hartlepool, and the last stopped on the main line at Croft Spa. The posters for these excursions referred to it being "Your only chance until 1999", and at approximately the halfway point in this 72-year gap, it makes an interesting speculation as to what form our railways will have taken by the turn of this century.

On the freight side, conditions were very different from what they are today, especially with the multiplicity of short-distance loads that the railways were handling as a matter of course. In the mid-1960s we would not contemplate sending half a ton of potatoes, say, from King's Cross to Potters Bar by train. Even with road conditions getting steadily more crowded year by year, it could nowadays scarcely take more than an hour and a half for the round trip from door to door by mini-van. When the only means of local delivery was the horse and cart, however, the trip to Potters Bar would represent a whole day's job for animal and carter. Thus the railway network of this country, which, during the Victorian era, stretched out to bring a pair of metals to within a day's striking distance of any appreciable-sized locality, was in 1927 still playing the dominant part in the structure of the nation's transport economy.

On the motive power side, the L.N.E.R. in 1927 boasted a stud of 52 Al Pacifics. These had taken over the principal trains from the large boilered Ivatt Atlantics, which were now showing the benefits of the superheating that Gresley had applied to them, as well as the piston valves with which he had equipped many of the class. Since the 1925 locomotive exchanges, when the performance of Pendennis Castle had beaten the

L.N.E.R. engines on their home ground, Gresley had been applying the lessons of the exchange to his original Pacifics.

The significant change was not, however, the increased boiler pressure that appeared on Enterprise in July 1927, but rather the modified valve gears that were fitted to the locomotives, following the experiments tried on Gay Crusader the previous year. Nevertheless it was the appearance of the first A3, Felstead, with its 220 psi boiler in 1928 that finally convinced railway enthusiasts that it is boiler pressure that really matters, a myth that is likely to see out the steam age nearly 40 years later. The Pacifics could cope single-handed with any train the L.N.E.R. operating authorities could provide, but the Atlantics would call for assistance as far as Potters Bar with heavy loads. On such occasions a Dl 4-4-0, one of the 0-6-2 tanks, or even an 0-6-0 would be attached as pilot, to help provide adhesion as much as tractive effort, during the climb through the Northern Heights. Since 1921, when the North British Locomotive Company had turned out 50 of the Gresley 0-6-2 tanks (later known as Class N2) to supplement the ten built at Doncaster, the King's Cross suburban and empty carriage stock workings had largely been in the hands of these powerful-looking locomotives. With the steam pipes of their condensing gear writhing in and out of their tanks like the curves of a sea-serpent, they became an invariable part of the scenery at King's Cross for almost the next 40 years, until the advent of the Birmingham Type 2 diesels swept them to the scrap heap in the early months of 1959. The leaner N1s, some of which were superheated by Gresley, either during the planning stages for his own N2s or subsequently, were also at work, while in the numerous yards where Bill was first to spend his time, Gresley J50s operated side-by-side with Ivatt and Stirling saddle tanks, some of them without backs to their cabs and sporting the old G.N. ball-type injectors. Long-distance freight traffic was in the hands of the O2s, which had been introduced from 1921 onwards, but these large locomotives were surpassed in size by the solitary pair of 2-8-2s (the Pls) that Gresley built as an experiment but never multiplied further. Taken all round, when Bill transferred to King's Cross in 1927, the L.N.E.R.

motive power was well on the way to attaining the supremacy it was to achieve a decade later.

The Stephenson Locomotive Society was already active in the locomotive preservation field in 1927, raising a fund for the restoration of the Stroudley 0-4-2 Gladstone to its original condition after it had been presented to them by the Southern Railway for ultimate display in the South Kensington Museum. As that institution could not house it at that time because of the rebuilding taking place, the locomotive was sent for temporary exhibition at the Railway Museum at York, where it can still be seen 40 years later. The SLS was founded in 1909 and after nearly 20 years was able to report that membership was well on its way to completing the second century. It now has well over 2,000 members, and in the 10 or so years since Bill joined, he can probably claim to have introduced as many new members as there were altogether in 1927. On his visit to address the Tees-side Centre in 1964, when the plans for this biography were laid, I had eight applications for membership on that evening alone. There was great public interest in railway matters, and the Great Western particularly was taking advantage of this at that time. Excursions from Paddington to see the new "King" class locomotives under construction at Swindon were sold out, in spite of the trains being duplicated, while the Press carried accounts of King George V's progress during its American tour on the Baltimore and Ohio Railroad, for which it was fitted with a Westinghouse pump on the side of the smokebox. The report that this "toy engine", by American standards, had been asked to slow down from a speed of 75 m.p.h. at one point at the request of the railway officials caused great delight amongst Swindon supporters.

2

Bill's first job was in Number 7 Link, which was responsible for the Shed Duties and Relief Work in the King's Cross area. The work was rather humdrum in nature, but vitally important in the area of a large and very busy terminus like this. Up at "Top Shed", he would have the job of preparing engines and disposing of them at the end of their turn of duty. These duties would also involve having to work light engines in both directions between the shed and the station, so that he had to learn the details of the new main-line signalling in this area that had been installed in 1923 and 1924, enabling up trains to be routed into the departure platforms. There was one particularly unusual feature about this signalling-a 3-position upper quadrant that was installed on the up main at the north end of Gasworks Tunnel.

At the other end of this tunnel lies the station locomotive yard, which had been carved out of the old retaining wall four years previously, so permitting the old yard to be replaced. This was situated between the suburban platforms and the "Drain", as the King's Cross men term the platform with its steeply-inclined track leading up from the Metropolitan "Widened Lines". In the place of the old yard they were able to build two new suburban platforms (Nos. 15 and 16). A 70-foot turntable, capable of taking the new Pacifics, was installed in the new yard, and was first used by No. 1475, then unnamed. As one of his duties, Bill would relieve main-line crews in the station platforms, and, after the N2 had removed the empty stock to Holloway or further afield, would take the locomotive over to this yard and recondition it for its returning working. Modest coaling facilities were provided, but things have changed considerably since the coming of the diesel age. Now, with the yard often accommodating anything up to a million pounds' worth of diesel-electric motive power during their very brief turn-round periods, tank wagons of diesel fuel and drums of lubricating oil have replaced the turntable and the "Black diamonds".

Between Gasworks Tunnel and Copenhagen Tunnel, almost under the high bridge carrying the North London line over the cutting, lies Belle Isle signal box, controlling the two single-line "creep-ups" that connect with the higher-level tracks on the west side. The average East Coast traveller will do no more than take in the name "Goods and Mineral Junction" on the lofty box set against the retaining wall, or perhaps note the long brick bridge carrying York Way over the tracks that begin to fan out at the higher level south of this box. Beyond the bridge, however, lies the 85-acre Goods Yard, with a capacity of no less than 3,000 wagons, in the middle of which used to stand the King's Cross motive power depot, or Top Shed. The main access to and from the yard is not via the "creep-up", but through the twin-track tunnel north of Goods and Mineral Junction, at a higher level but parallel to the other pair of bores that comprise Copenhagen Tunnel, at the north end of which there is a flyover that enables up trains to reach the yard without fouling the down lines.

The bridge carrying York Way forms a major obstacle to the operation of the yards, and its 20 arches each accommodate one or more tracks, many of them sharply curved because of the cramped layout. The five most southerly arches lead to the main section of the yard, where there is a building still known as the Midland Shed, from the days prior to 1867 when the Midland Railway reached London via Hitchin and G.N. metals. Outside the arches, and next to the main lines where they disappear into the Gasworks Tunnels, are Cemetery Sidings which are reputed to have been built on the site of one of the burial grounds from the Great Plague in 1664. Opposite them, on the other side of the six main-line tracks, set high up above the retaining wall of thecutting, is some of the plant now being used in the construction of the new Victoria Line of London Transport. This side, too, has a connection with death and burials, as it was here that the old Cemetery Station existed until less than 1O years ago, from which funeral trains were at one time operated to the cemetery behind the Standard Telephone factory at New Southgate, where the name of the nearby signal box still serves as a reminder of the old arrangements. Similar trains used also to run to Brookwood from Waterloo in L.S.W.R. and Southern Railway days.

Stretching around the east and south-east sides of King's

Cross Goods Yard is the old potato market, by 1965 almost completely disused, but 30 years ago all 40 of its "runs" would contain three or four wagons apiece, being unloaded by the various merchants, while up to 400 loaded wagons awaited their turn elsewhere in the yards. Each "run" consisted of a short line at right angles to the perimeter track, and wagons were placed on them with the aid of turntables and capstans to be unloaded on to the covered platforms. Bill and his fireman would sometimes be given half a sack of potatoes when they were working in this part of the yard. They would promptly open the smokebox door and put them inside, so that by the time the meal break had come, they were nicely cooked and ready to share with the others! With a spot of butter, pepper and salt, they made a very welcome addition to the meal, especially on a cold day. West of the potato market are the despatch roads, where wagons can be put under cover to be loaded by traders. One of the roads leads down a steep incline underground and is used for the vulnerable traffic, while another pair of tracks cross the Regent Canal to Carnley Street Coal yard, where over 200 coal wagons can be positioned by the electric transporter for unloading. Capstan working is again common in this area, the power to turn them being provided hydraulically. In one of the buildings to the south-west of the fine granary, there are two hydraulic accumulators weighing 100 tons each, together with their associated pumps. Some of the capstans rotate clockwise, and some anti-clockwise, and it is of interest that appropriately twisted ropes must be used with each type, or the rotation will cause the strands of the rope to separate. "Dummy" capstans are also provided in places, to take the sideways pull of a rope in a curve. North of Carnley Street yard, the slow waters of the Regent Canal pass below the approach tracks into St. Pancras, and from here as far as the North London line, Eastern and London Midland region property adjoins all along the western side of the yard. The present-day servicing facilities outside St. Pancras that suffice for the Midland's diesels are alongside the site of the former King's Cross shed offices, being only separated by the width of the ring road that surrounds the yard. Between the former Shed roads and the warehouses away to the south-east are a number of sidings, laid out in pairs, where heavy mobile cranes can position themselves to transfer loads from rail to road and vice versa.

Between the flattened expanse of ground where Bill once prepared so many locomotives for their journeys down the G.N. main line and the elevated North London line, are more goods sidings, all of them reached by sharply curved connections from Goods and Mineral Junction. Under cover are the Sundries sidings, while bricks are dealt with in the open, and there is even a "manure road". As the name implies, this was where they used to load stable manure from the railway's own carriage horses as well as from elsewhere in London, to take it out into the country for use on the land. This traffic has ceased with the coming of the internal combustion engine, but the siding was still in being in 1965, and is used to load some 40 wagons a day of rubbish from Chapel and Hoxton Markets which is taken out for disposal to Holwell Sidings on the Hatfield to Luton line. As already mentioned, the yard is terminated by the elevated North London line crossing the northern boundary, and there is a connection from Goods and Mineral Junction up to St. Pancras Junction on this electrified east-west route. This steeply-inclined line is single and worked by a train staff, while a siding leads off it into the cramped Eastern Region Civil Engineer's yard. Behind Goods and Mineral Junction is another steeply-graded line, running parallel with the Main Line to a dead end above Copenhagen Tunnels, where there is a trailing connection that crosses the tunnel to reach the Caledonian Road goods yard. Wagons for here are propelled up the inclines, and even the 350 h.p. diesel-electric shunters are limited to a maximum load of 12 vehicles, to allow room for running round the load when the reversal takes place.

King's Cross Goods Yard is still a comparatively busy

place, employing over 1,000 men altogether, but 30 years ago was even busier. The activities on the rail and road sides reach their peaks at different times, but traditionally it is during the night shift that the yards are busiest. Thirty years ago, 16 trains were despatched between 7.35 p.m. and 4.35 a.m., most of them at half-hourly intervals. The "Arcade Gang" would assemble the rear half with their capstans inside the sheds, while one of the pilots made up the front half and joined the two sections together, under the eye of the Train Starter, George Foster. His job was to check on the wagons making up each train, and ascertain the cause of any delays, passing all the necessary information on to Control in due course. In 1965, George, after 49 years on the railway, had risen to the post of Chief Inspector, being in charge of all outside movements in the yard: he recalled Bill's days in the yard, and told me that he had a reputation of being a "cracking pilot driver", never moaning, and always ready to work fast if the shunter wanted him to do so. Once the pilot had made up the train, the guard would check it over, and pass on the details to the main line driver after the locomotive had set back on the wagons. Then the signals that were normally kept off to allow free shunting move ments at Goods and Mineral Junction would be put back, the gongs on some of them sounding to draw people's attention to the fact, and off would come the signals for the road up the bank to Holloway. The signalman who shared Five Arch Cabin with the train Starter would lean out to sound his large bell fixed on the outside wall, and the K3, cylinder cocks hissing, would gently pick up the couplings and wheel its load up the bank with steadily sharpening exhaust as the fireman looked back to exchange signals with the guard. In his Top Link days, Bill regularly used to work the Scots Goods out from here at 3.15 p.m. behind his own A4, beating the "Talisman" (due out of King's Cross passenger three quarters of an hour later) to York on occasions.

Top Shed, Bill's working home for 30 years, was reached by two connections off the goods line at Goods and Mineral

Junction. Each passed under its own arch in the York Way bridge, the more southerly of which was used for locomotives going in shed, and the other for those coming "off". This layout relative to the Main Line produced the rather unusual practice that locomotives always left and arrived at the shed smokebox first, an uncommon arrangement for a shed serving a terminus. The incoming locomotives would stop briefly outside the number-takers' hut, and then continue to the turntable. Beyond this on the south side was the coaling stage, and then came the ash disposal pits. The covered shed roads were at the back of the yard, with the offices behind them, and the workshops with their 30-ton overhead crane lay immediately to the north. These had formed the original King's Cross shed, which accounted for the large number of very short roads they contained. The men's mess rooms, oil stores, and toilets were in a block stretching alongside the north side of the shed roads, which were spanned by a gantry carrying the water cranes. In the south-west corner of the shed yard is the only part of it that remains standing, the water-softening plant, and even the tender that does duty as sludge carrier for the spent line now stands on an isolated section of track, its weathered paint still showing the traces of its former livery, and the initials L.N.E.R.

When they were on a relieving turn to bring locomotives up to Top Shed, Bill and his mate used to deal with four engines per shift. After booking on, they would walk down to the terminus, and take a locomotive over from its main-line crew. This gave Bill the opportunity of handling every different class that came through, and he soon developed the habit of discussing the trip with the men they were relieving. Their accounts inspired his ambition for Top Link work, and he stored all the knowledge he acquired for future use. He would also note the condition of the fire and the locomotive generally, looking it over to see if anything else was wrong. When the empty stock had been removed, and they got the road, they would be away up the bank through Gasworks Tunnel to the Belle Isle "creep up", stopping under the North London line, just clear of the signal that permitted them to set back through the Goods Yard to the Sheds. Here they would go straight on to the turntable, and with one of the heavier engines, they sometimes had trouble turning it, especially if the low levels of coal and water in the tender prevented them balancing it properly. All they could do then would be to position it as best they could, and call for assistance with the pinch bars. After the engine was turned, they would take it over and replenish the coal sup plies, before positioning it over the ash pit for someone else to drop the fire. They would then walk down to King's Cross again and repeat the process.

Another of their duties was preparing engines, and a driver and fire man on such a turn would have to deal with up to seven locomotives per shift, building up the fire for the forthcoming journey, and checking over the motion to see that the lubrication was in order. Bill always used to like dealing with five out of the seven locomotives before knocking off for his meal break. On most turns, the main line crew would take the engine down on to its train, and it was accordingly rare for men on a preparation turn to go down on to King's Cross passenger station. When Bill got into the Top Link, it was only when a crew were working the infrequent summer turn to York and back in the day that they would take over the locomotive at the terminus. This was in contrast to the turns already mentioned where a crew from the north would be relieved in the station while their locomotive was turned and reconditioned for the down journey later the same day.

In addition to the duties already referred to, Bill used to have turns relieving the drivers on the various pilots in the East Goods and King's Cross Goods Yards, as well as at King's Cross "Passenger". East Goods is on the up side just south of Finsbury Park, and handled interchange traffic for the Southern, as well as wagons to and from the docks. The system then was that the men on each yard or station pilot were relieved for a 20-minute meal break every shift, and Bill and a fireman would therefore go round from engine to engine to provide the necessary relief crew. These arrangements did not work out in practice for a number of different reasons. Some men did not like being relieved, while on other occasions, when Bill and his mate had succeeded in tracking down the locomotive, they found that the crew had already taken advantage of a slack period earlier in the shift to have their food. The pilots were some times sent out on trip workings to other nearby yards, too, and if this had occurred, the relief crew would be unable to find the engine for which they were looking, and the relieving system thus fell into disuse.

Relieving in the middle of a shift could, on occasions, produce other difficulties too, as Bill found out one day at King's Cross Goods Yard. As he came up to relieve Dick Nutting on one of the yard pilots, he found that the locomotive had stalled with a load of wagons. The shunters had got him to empty one of the roads, and he had gone back under the line leading to Caledonian Road without using sand, slipping to a stand still when he came forward again due to the combination of the sharp curvature and the gradient. Dick explained the position to Bill, who then told the shunter that he would go back again, out of sight, laying sand and then propel the load forward smartly once more. This was not correct, of course, as he should only have made the forward move ment under the shunter's direct instructions, after he had specifically been given the "all clear". As Bill came round the curve under the bridge, he suddenly saw that about a dozen of his wagons, all of them containing fresh peas, were off the road ahead of him. A pair of points were not closing properly, and the person whose duty it was to hold them shut when any movements were in progress, was not prepared for Bill's return, and the vans had consequently split the points. Not only did their load never manage to make Covent Garden, but when the wagons came off, they cut 13 signal wires and point rods, stopping the yard and only leaving one road operating in and out of Top Shed. It was some time before they had sorted the mess out, and normal working was resumed. As soon as the derailment occurred, the Yardmaster turned up and asked Bill whose fault it was, and was rather surprised to be met with the immediate reply “Mine”. In the subsequent inquiries, he remembered Bill’s honesty and the way in which he had avoided trying to pass the blame on to anyone else, and in consequence Bill was let off with a “cau tion”-the minimum punishment. In those days, three “Reprimands” (the next more serious punishment) were followed by two days’ suspension, and any further similar incident would bring about the driver’s dismissal.

As one of his later superiors commented, Bill’s very genuine penitence and frank apologies whenever he was hauled up before authority for some offence he had committed was to stand him in good stead on a number of occasions many years later.

Another time when he was working in King’s Cross Goods Yard, Bill remembers seeing the trials being conducted by an autogyro for the Post Office. These flights were to see whether mail could be transferred between the G.P.O. at Mount Pleasant and the main line termini at King’s Cross, Liverpool Street, and Paddington. The experiments were not a success, and nothing further came of the idea. On one of the days of trials, however, a large airship happened to come over too. Bill was fascinated by the sight of these large silver monsters, having once previously seen one of them at Benfleet flying up the Thames to London.

As a newcomer, Bill was faced with the problem of learning this new area, and his task was complicated by the fact that his arrival at King’s Cross was not, by any means, greeted with the universal approval of all his new colleagues. This was not due to his own personality, but to the fact that the changes that had followed the formation of the L.N.E.R. caused deep divisions between the old Great Northern men, and those from the Great Central who transferred across. Before Grouping, the

G.N. crews were in the unusual position of being able to retire at 60, and then draw a pension. As a result, promotion for all crews was rapid. If one assumes that, even when retiring at

65, a driver does no more than 10 years on the crack workings, the G.N. system would have halved this time, thereby doubling the rate of promotion into these links, a process which inevitably continued all the way downwards through the footplate grades. After the formation of the L.N.E.R., this eminently satisfactory system, as the King's Cross men viewed it, quickly came to an end, but not before the other former lines in the Southern Promotional Area had begun to transfer men across to fill many of the vacancies that occurred. Many of the former G.N. crews, resenting this change very much indeed, made all outsiders extremely unwelcome. So much was this so, that at times a G.N. man would not speak to his mate on the footplate if he happened to have come from the G.C., while if a stranger was supposed to be learning the road from a G.N. man, only the bare details would be communicated. Such strained relationships would make an 8-hour shift seem like 16, and the two men concerned would never get the best out of one another or out of the machine, so in later years, whenever he had the opportunity, Bill always endeavoured to encourage a good relationship with his mate, as many of his former firemen will testify.

3

After spending four years on the duties already described, which had confined him to the first mile or so out of King's Cross, Bill was promoted to Number 6 Link. This covered yard shunting anywhere in the first half-dozen miles out of the terminus, as well as occasional trip working somewhat further afield. There must be few such complex areas as this, and Bill had to learn the details of all the numerous yards so that he was available to work in any of them.

North of Copenhagen Tunnel, the steep initial climb out of King's Cross finishes, and, with the line no longer below ground level, the retaining walls on either side give way to the first of the additional yards that now concerned Bill. On the down side are Holloway Carriage sidings, and opposite them the cattle dock, used as such in 1927, whereas now, in the role of terminus of the Anglo-Scottish Car-Carrier service, it plays a vital part in one of the railway's more successful enterprises involving the private car, exemplifying the old adage "if you can't beat them, join them". From Finsbury Park, there are connections running south-eastwards from both sides of the main line to join the North London at Canonbury, the lines from the down side passing under the East Coast metals. The considerable interchange traffic, which has always existed between the two lines, produced a plethora of yards in this area, some of which also meet purely local requirements: Highbury Vale and Ashburton Grove, reached off the connecting line, are reminders of the unspoilt countryside that once existed hereabouts. One of the jobs carried out by Bill in the latter yard was weighing wagons of refuse. Disposing of this product of our urban domesticity has always been a problem in London, and the railways still play a large part in handling this traffic, working it in sheeted wagons to Blackbridge sidings on the Welwyn-Luton branch. Elsewhere, too, in places like Middlesbrough, wagon-loads of "night soil" would be taken by the railways to nearby country stations, where the farmers came to collect it for spreading on the land. The job of shunting wagons could be a smelly one, and in summer time, the refuse would act as a breeding ground for blow-flies.

The next two yards that Bill had to work in were East Goods, already familiar to him, and Clarence yard, which sit astride the main line before the suburban carriage sidings are reached, shortly before Finsbury Park. Gresley's "Quad-Artie" sets used to be kept here, on the down side of the line, their fussily-panelled exteriors belying the spartan facilities provided inside. As long ago as 1924, when this stock was being built, it was officially being stated that the carriages were capable of being converted to electric working, a change that was never to come in their lifetime.

North of Finsbury Park, the Edgware and High Barnet lines swing away westwards, and the East Coast route then crosses the

Tottenham and Hampstead Joint, which Bill used to traverse on his way to Mint Street with the bullion. After Harringay comes the Ferme Park flyover, recently modernised, but now only carrying a single track on the steel bridge sections that connect the numerous brick arches, many of which were to be converted to air-raid shelters in World War II. On the up side, at the south end of the flyover, are some more carriage sidings, while the Ferme Park goods yard-the terminal point of many main-line freight workings opens out to the west beyond the arches at the country end of the flyover. On the opposite side are the Hornsey sidings, and behind them the motive power depot, which used to be the home of the two booster fitted Pl Mikados, in addition to numerous other freight and suburban locomotives.

At Wood Green come the most extensive carriage and wagon sidings of the lot, where the sleeping cars are prepared for their next trip, and general servicing and repairs are carried out on other types of passenger stock and freight wagons. North of this station there is the flyover that takes the down connection with the "New Line" via Cuffley and Hertford North eastwards over the main line. Freight trains had regularly been running through to Langley Junction by this route since early 1921, but the first use of the line for passengers actually took place as early as February 1920, when the single line that was then in existence was used after an accident had blocked Welwyn North Tunnel. Regular through passenger services were not, however, introduced until 3½ years after freight traffic commenced. Passenger trains north of Hertford had a short life, however, but the development of this part of Hertfordshire in the 1960s has seen their revival. As part of their 1924 Bill before Parliament, the L.N.E.R. obtained permission to connect the G.E. Palace Gates branch with the Enfield Line at Alexandra Park, which would have provided a new link between the two former rival systems, but the line was not actually built for nearly 20 years. This point, just over five miles from King's Cross, represented the northern limit of the area over which Bill had to acquire his route knowledge.

It took Bill between two and three months to master all the yards that he was now expected to know. Throughout this time, he would be booked out with a regular driver each day and spent the shift with him on the footplate. Not only were there something like 1,000 signals to learn, but he had to pick up the various operating practices, as well as the positions of the "jack catches" (as the G.N. vernacular referred to trap points), protecting the running lines, that marked the yard limits. Although the standard L.N.E.R. upper-quadrant type of signal was beginning to make its appearance, most of them were still G.N. somersaults, and Bill liked the clear gap they gave from the post in the "off" position. It was not, however, until he actually started working the yards himself that he was able to get the feel of the haulage capacities of the various locomotives over the numerous sharp curves and gradients that abounded. Bill always reckoned that the job of a driver in one of the junior links was an excellent training ground. Numerous interesting incidents would occur, all of which would provide additional experience and greater confidence for the next time something similar cropped up.

No. 6 Link also involved trip working from Highbury Vale to High Barnet, Edgware and Alexandra Palace. At this time, of course, the L.N.E.R. was operating the passenger service over these three branches that fanned out to the north-west of Finsbury Park, and the N2s battled with the steep gradients en route to High Barnet and Mill Hill that are now served by the Northern Line Tube trains. It was a real slog all the way up from Finsbury Park to Highgate Wood, with a ruling gradient of 1 in 59, which was steep enough to prove difficult with the maximum load of 25 full wagons. From Clarence Yard, the Nl or N2 on the trip workings would be assisted by the Highbury Vale yard pilot, usually a six-coupled saddle tank. Bill enjoyed the experience of working the loco motive hard, as besides wagons of coal, there were numerous loads of bricks to be worked out over the branches to meet the demands of the speculative builders. The housing estates that sprang up alongside the line were subsequently to justify the first (and so far the last) electrification of any former G.N. line. The Alexandra Palace branch was due to be electrified too, and conductor rails were even laid, but World War II intervened, so that when passenger trains over this line finally ceased operating in 1954, it was still steam-worked.

There are twin-bore tunnels either side of Highgate Station, and if the trip engine was in trouble, this stretch could be pretty sticky for the banker, especially in the second tunnel, before they emerged on to the level beyond Park Junction. The Alexandra Palace branch swings away to the right here, past the carriage sidings in the V now occupied by Tube stock, but which then used to house the L.N.E.R. Royal Train. The banker would drop off clear of the junction and after the signalmen had made the seven lever movements required, the small semaphore between the splitting homes would come off, allowing the locomotive into the yards to await its return path. The former Great Northern lines out of King's Cross were provided with more than their fair share of tunnels, nearly all of them on appreciable gradients. Not only did the King's Cross suburban stock always seem to have its own particular smell flavour might even be a more appropriate word-but the conditions the footplatemen had to put up with considerably taxed their vitality. Any one who suffered at all from chestiness could be badly knocked back by tunnel work. When working locomotives fitted with condensing gear (such as the Nls and N2s, as well as some of the 0-6-0 tanks), it was possible, of course, to cut down the production of steam in the tunnels, but the sulphurous fumes from the coal still pervaded everything. The use of the condensing gear cut out the draught-producing action of the blastpipe too, and steaming consequently fell off, so it was not indulged in, except when demanded by the authorities on such sections as the Widened Lines round to Moorgate. Too much condensing would also raise the temperature of the water in the tanks, and lead to difficulties with the injectors, whose operation depends on the coldness of the water condensing the flow of steam through the cones. Like the G.W.R. pannier tanks of the 97XX series fitted with condensing gear, the G.N. locomotives were also originally provided with a mechanical feed-water pump to supplement the usual injectors, but they had nearly all been removed by the time Bill got into the Met Link. There was consequently nothing to fall back on if the water in the tanks got too hot.

To cope with any sudden emergencies at a shed like King's Cross, it was customary between the wars to roster three or four locomotives as spares on each shift. As well as the drivers and firemen on these, there would prob ably be several more crews who were available to cope with any changes that might be forced on the operating authorities by, say, a train running late, or the last-minute need to run an extra train to cater for a sudden influx of passengers. Bill did his share of these turns too, spending the shift, if they were exceptionally lucky, in the mess room. This would provide the opportunity of yarning with the other crews about their experiences on the road, the deficiencies of the Government, or the failure of the Arsenal centre-forward to put the ball into the open net the previous Saturday afternoon. One of the other duties that would come the way of these spare crews was going out with the breakdown train. This train came under the charge of the Foreman Fitter, and one of the junior fitters, being only 22 years of age, was keen to take every opportunity of riding on engines. Whenever, therefore, it was called out with its 35-ton crane, he would ride on the footplate to the scene of the derailment. Such a trip might well take him anywhere between King's Cross and Peterborough, or even, in exceptional circumstances, north of the latter point, since, if there had been a major accident, the joint efforts of the London, Peterborough and other cranes would be required to clear the wreckage ready for the permanent way gangs to replace the damaged track. On occasions such as this, the breakdown gang could spend upwards of 48 hours continuously on the job, the mess van providing welcome food and shelter in wet or cold weather when accidents have a perverse habit of occurring.

When the breakdown train was called out, if Bill happened to be on the locomotive, he would let the fitter, with whom he was very friendly, do the driving. In typical Bill fashion, he made him do it properly, including watching for the relevant signals ahead. This caused the temporary driver, who was not used to being out on the road anyway, some concern, particularly in view of the complicated junctions that abound in the first dozen miles out of London. The Great Northern somersault signals were still in the majority and many remained on the slow lines and elsewhere more than 20 years later, well after nationalisation. The G.N.'s habit of stringing anything up to half a dozen stop signals on the same post, one above the other, can hardly have made things particularly easy for a strange driver. The train was fairly light too, in those days, so express speeds were usually attained and they carried the Express Passenger headcode of two lamps, one at each end of the buffer beam. Anything from a J52 to a Pacific would be used on it, depending on where the accident had occurred, and the motive power available. If the fitter got anxious enough to ask Bill whether certain signals were theirs or not, Bill would either completely ignore him or just turn away in a very nonchalant manner, leaving the driver very perturbed, whilst Bill was hugely delighted at the whole matter. When the pupil is left to "get on with it" in such circumstances, confidence is much more quickly developed from experience, rather than having someone fussing in his ear all the time. The fitter concerned remarked to me, too, that if the signals did happen to be theirs and were at danger, no one would have moved quicker than Bill to take the necessary action.

4

Bill's stay in No. 6 Link also occupied approximately four years, so it was in the mid-thirties that his second promotion took place, putting him in the Odd Metropolitan Link. For the first time his duties now involved working the occasional local passenger train, but many of the other turns also took him to King's Cross, either to shunt, or work empty stock to and from the various carriage sidings serving the terminus. The eight years that had elapsed since he moved to King's Cross had already brought many changes, but by now the dramatic events that were to characterise the East Coast route in the latter half of the decade were beginning to cast their shadows before them, even before the chime whistle of Silver Link first pierced the swirling steam and smoke that wreathed the tunnels outside King's Cross. In May 1934, Gresley had turned out the first P2, Cock o' the North, from Doncaster, and her great size and unorthodox appearance caused a great deal of interest throughout the country. Bill took as much notice of all the excitement as he could, especially when, in the November of that year, "Flying Scotsman" made her celebrated test run to Leeds and back. On this trip, for the first time on our railways, a locomotive achieved an undisputed 3-figure maximum speed on that wonderful racing ground south of Stoke that was to become one of Bill's favourite stretches of line 20 years later. Flying Scotsman's run immediately made the headlines, and Cecil J. Allen broadcast a hurriedly-prepared account of the trip in the B.B.C. news at 9 o'clock that evening. On the down journey, the Pacific (still in its Al form) had cleared Stoke Summit at a minimum of 81 m.p.h., a performance that seemed completely unbelievable to the recorders on the train at the time. Flying Scotsman's load was a very light one of only four bogies, weighing 147 tons, but even so the performance far surpassed anything that had previously been considered possible. Although the trip stirred Bill's imagination, he little thought that 25 years later at the regulator of Sir Nigel Gresley, he would have the opportunity to better this climb of Stoke Bank on the Golden Jubilee Special with twice the load, and a higher minimum speed over the summit.

The ranks of the Gresley Pacifics had now been swelled by the addition of the 27 A3s, and it was Papyrus, one of these Super-Pacifics, as they were known, that took part in the next high-speed runs four months later, this time to Newcastle and back. September 1935 saw the arrival of a new shape and livery at King's Cross, when the silver-grey form of Silver Link, the first of the A4s, appeared on running in turns. Few loco motives and trains can have had such an outstanding introduction as was achieved with the "Silver Jubilee". The almost unbelievable schedule advertised for it was beaten hands down on the press run of the 27th, and the locomotive's feat of maintaining a speed of over 100 m. p.h. for no less than 25 miles on end, twice touching 112 in the process, was one that even Bill was never able to emulate. Pamphlets were issued about the new streamliners, and Bill still has some of the special circular luggage labels that were printed in distinctive colours, with an A4 surmounting the name of the destination station which was blazoned across the centre. Those who were able to take part in these special runs were considered very lucky, and even after nearly 30 years, Bill still recalls the day when he went down to King's Cross to relieve Driver Haygreen on a Leeds turn, and found that he was taking over the regulator of an A4, the first of them he had seen. It is of interest, in passing, to comment that in steam days a driver would frequently be called on to take over a completely strange type of locomotive that he had never previously handled, or, on occasions, had never seen before, whereas in the diesel era everyone goes through several days' instruction on each different class.

Although the excitement of the streamliners caught everyone's imagination, there were still allthe old routine jobs to be done, and the Odd Met link with their Nls and N2s had their share of these to perform, even if they were at times called on to shunt the articulated stock of the "Silver Jubilee", "Coronation" or "West Riding Limited". It is one of the fundamental precepts of terminal working that if the empty stock is got away promptly, the loaded trains will more or less look after themselves. At King's Cross, the bottleneck represented by two tunnels and only six tracks on a rising gradient of 1 in 107, made conditions especially difficult in steam days, particularly when the war-time trains appeared. Their great length on occasions would leave the last coach of up trains still in the tunnel, while down trains would have the locomotive standing in the tunnel mouth before leaving. The sleeping cars were a special job for the Odd Met Link, and as the overnight expresses arrived, they would gently cut out the sleepers, making them up carefully into complete rakes in the platforms and providing a supply of steam for heating purposes until about 8 a.m. when the last of the sleepy-eyed passengers had emerged in search of the bathrooms, barber or breakfast. Then they would take the heavy train up the bank out of the terminus, propel it slowly through the carriage washing plant and put the vehicles in the appropriate sidings where they would be prepared for their northward journey the following night. The crew that got away on the first train of stock was able to get the job over smartly, and would be back at King's Cross "Loco" well before the full eight hours were up. The last man would have a very different story to tell, however, as there was only spacefor one train at a time in the washer and doing the shunting. The later trains would inevitably be kept waiting, therefore, and it might well be as late as 1 o'clock before the last of the pilots had finished its job for the day.

Working these heavy trains without delaying the following traffic was a challenge for Bill, and he enjoyed getting them up the gradient through the tunnels. Another awkward spot was at Wood Green, where to reach the carriage sidings, they were routed over the fly-over and then set back on the up side of the main line. Not only is the fly-over on a sharp curve, but the gradient is 1 in 53, and many trains have stalled there in their time. They were unable to set back and have another go until they had arranged with the Station Master for someone to hold the catch points closed. It is of course very easy, especially in tunnels, to start moving backwards with a heavy train on a steep gradient, and the old trick of feeling for the tunnel walls was sometimes necessary before the driver could be certain which way he was moving. In Gasworks Tunnel, of course, they had the advantage of the gas lamps at 25-yard intervals, their distances from the tunnel mouth painted on the glass, glowing with yellowish light through the swirling smoke.

In the late 1920s the now-familiar electric signalling was installed at King's Cross, and the searchlight beams from the colour-lights greatly improved signal sighting in the area, especially when the weather pro duced a London "Special". They did, however, have some difficulties with the installation in the early days, and on one occasion when Bill was on the night shift, there had been a failure at Belle Isle on the signal controlling the movement from the down main to the "creep-up". The signal fitter had repaired it, and normal working had been resumed by the time Bill backed on to a rake of empty coaches for Hornsey at about 11 p.m. Going up through Gasworks Tunnel, he sighted the signal off for the main line, but the smoke stopped him seeing the lie of the points in the dark. He suddenly felt the locomotive take the turn-out to the left, cross over the down slow, and continue up the "creep-up". The signals were off for the down slow too, so he kept going as hard as he could, and told his fireman, "Ginger" Lunnis, to get the detonators, jump down, and protect the slow line. He carried on until the train was clear of the latter, and then shouted up to the surprised signalman at Goods and Mineral Junction. "Ginger" succeeded in stopping the train on the down slow, and nothing serious resulted, but there was a company inquiry about the incident, at which Bill had to give evidence. He was later informed that the signal fitter had made a wrong connection, leaving the points working in the opposite sense to the signals, and had been "dealt with suitably".

The men in the Odd Met Link had a very wide route knowledge, as they had to carry out numerous interchange trips with fish and freight to destinations south of the Thames like Clapham Junction on the Southern Railway. In those days too, the live theatre in the suburbs and provinces had not succumbed to the twin onslaughts of the cinema and television, and at week-ends the railways ran numerous theatrical specials, conveying the scenery and "props" from one theatre to another, ready for the new opening on Monday night. With only horses and carts for local delivery work, they tried to get a special to a station as close as possible to the new theatre, and Bill worked many of these trains from the G.N. Line to Charing Cross, Victoria or Waterloo.

The route across the Thames, which Bill and the other King's Cross men used to work, took them straight through the City, via the Widened Lines, and the Snow Hill incline that lifts the railway from the level of the Inner Circle at Farringdon to the level of Blackfriars Bridge. A banker had to be provided here, in the smoky depths, ready to provide rear-end assistance up the 1 in 39 gradient, and they would exchange whistles with it before blasting their way up to Ludgate Hill. They were not expected to know all these routes for the theatrical specials, of course, and used to be provided with a pilotman over the strange parts of the journey. The trips into Victoria were particularly unusual, as they had to call on the services of two separate pilotmen, one from Clapham to the L.B.S.C. side, and another for the S.E. & C.

5

The four years from 1935 to 1939, during which Bill was in the Odd Met Link, saw the L.N.E.R. reach the summit of its pre-war achievements. The first of the streamliners, the "Silver Jubilee", had entered service in 1935. Its booking of 3 hours 18 minutes in each direction between King's Cross and Darlington has, in 1965, still to be equalled or bettered by the fastest "Deltic"-hauled schedules, although, to be fair, the diesels are hauling much heavier trains and are subject to more intermediate speed restrictions. The A4s showed themselves so much the masters of this working that, in July 1937, the "Coronation" was introduced with a slightly heavier train, and an even tighter average of 71.9 m.p.h. to York, the fastest schedule that had at the time appeared in a British timetable. The locomotives worked through between London and Edinburgh, and coal supplies often ran short towards the end of the 393-mile trip, providing an additional worry for the fireman who was already faced with the task of going further and further into the tender to bring the coal forward. In the early days, the A4s were provided with a streamlined fairing from the cab roof along the top of the tender, and this fitting caused a fatal accident one day when the up and down expresses passed on Wiske Moor troughs. The rush of water from the down express broke the cab window on the London-bound engine, and a piece of glass hit Inspector Charlie Skinner who was riding on the footplate of the southbound A4. He was a former G.C. man, and was the driver of Earl of Kerry at the time when Bill worked on it as a cleaner at Neasden. High speeds were thus not entirely free of risk for those on the footplate, and it is of interest to recall that, nearly 30 years later, close to the same spot, a part from the bogie of a "Deltic" came off and killed someone in the cab of a similar locomotive, travelling in the opposite direction.

It was in July 1938, after the last of the streamliners, the "West Riding Limited", had entered service the previous October, that Gresley staged the series of test runs that were to earn Mallard its entry in the annals of steam locomotive history and, one hopes, its ultimate resting place at Clapham Transport Museum. Gresley had been knighted in 1935, and George Dow has described how Sir Nigel discussed the plans for the record-breaking attempt with his assistant, Norman Newsome, who was in charge of some high-speed braking tests being carried out at the time. The object of the run was to beat the record of 114 m. p.h that Coronation had set up for the L.M.S. in June 1937 as she tore down the bank from Whitmore into Crewe, her final approach into the station being marked by taking the first turn-out at nearer 60 m.p.h. than 50! Gresley had to obtain approval from the Civil Engineers'

Department for his attempt, and, according to the story Bill recounts, he was only given permission to go to 120 m.p.h., Sir Nigel's reply was "anything more will be mine, then". There was thus no attempt by Driver Duddington to curb the locomotive's running until the speed began to fall off as the gradient eased, when one of the high-speed braking tests was then carried out. Thirty-one years later, the decision to adhere to the Chief Engineer's limit of 1 10 m.p.h. robbed Bill of his opportunity of trying to beat Mallard's record with Sir Nigel Gresley at the head of the Stephenson Locomotive Society's Jubilee Special.

Other motive-power developments took place on the L.N.E.R. during this period, and the large-engine policy that was being followed by Sir Nigel was to stand the L.N.E.R. in great stead during the dark years that lay ahead. Four new P2s were built in 1936, their front ends being streamlined in A4 style, and in the same year Green Arrow, the first V2, appeared. These latter locomotives, finally totalling 184, shouldered the brunt of the heavier L.N.E.R. mixed traffic duties, and provided their crews with machines that had almost the same capabilities as the Pacifics. During the war, as well as in their later years, the often run-down condition of this class was marked by the extreme syncopation of their exhaust beat, but in pre-war days, they were regularly rostered to work such trains as the "Yorkshire Pullman". At this time No. 3 Link had nine of the class, including Green Arrow, booked to regular drivers, and their green livery was kept spotless. Their advent thus displaced the Atlantics - the big engines of Ivatt's days- from some of their top-link workings.

No. 10000, the largest of Gresley's locomotives, which had been built at Darlington in 1929, was rebuilt at this time as a 3-cylinder simple. In its new guise, it appeared more reliably on East Coast workings now that an orthodox boiler had replaced the 450 psi design which tended to produce ash and slag deposits in the most embarrassing places.

Unhappily, the period 1935-39 was not one in which the

L.N.E.R. was free from serious accidents. In the early summer of 1935, just north of Welwyn Garden City, K3 No. 4009 at the head of the 10.58 p.m. express for Leeds, running at 70 m.p.h., piled into the back of the previous down train, bound for Newcastle behind Atlantic No. 4441, which was recovering from a signal check. Thirteen passengers were killed as a result of the error by the signalman at Welwyn South, and to avoid accidents arising from similar mistakes in future, the block instrument controls were interlocked with a track circuit which has to be occupied and cleared each time before "Line Clear" is given to the box in rear. This arrangement, a now familiar installation on most of our main lines, is referred to as "Welwyn Control", still recalling the events that led to its introduction that June night 30 years ago. The death toll was nearly three times as great in the L.N.E.R.'s next major accident, 2½ years later, when in the snowy darkness of a December evening, an A3, Grand Parade, over-ran the Castlecary signals between Edinburgh and Glasgow, and hit the rear of a Dundee express, carrying on for 1 00 yards beyond the point of collision before it came to rest embedded in the side of the cutting. In the official report on this disaster, in which 35 people were killed, the M.O.T. inspecting officer, Colonel Mount, put forward a plea for the installation of some form of Automatic Train Control, which was not to be installed on the East Coast Route until the concluding years of Bill's main-line service.

While these events were taking place on the L.N.E.R., on the national and international scenes thc position was very different. The rejoicings for George V's Silver Jubilee in 1935 had seen our towns and cities disappear under festoons of red, white and blue, while commemorative tea parties for the children were held in the streets. Within twelve months, however, the body of our dead monarch was to be brought into King's Cross station behind Bl 7 Helmingham Hall, en route from Sandringham to its final resting place at Windsor. Then came the crisis of Edward VIII's abdication, and the Coronation of his brother, which produced another wave of national rejoicing, so that Coronation mugs joined the Jubilee ones on the shelves of Dolly's kitchen at their flat in Tufnell Park. On the international scene, the actions of a former Austrian house-painter had produced the Munich crisis, and were now building up to the final series of events that plunged Europe into the Second World War in September 1939. The wail of the air raid sirens that so quickly followed the official declaration of hostilities turned out to be a false alarm, but in the 5½ years that were to elapse before VE Day, the London that Bill knew was to be altered almost beyond recognition by the attention of Goring's Luftwaffe. These events were also to result in the standard of pre-war East Coast running disappearing for more than a decade, as arrears of track and locomotive maintenance forced even the A4s to comply with the war-time all-line limit of 60 m.p.h. that was to descend on the L.N.E.R.

6

Bill was promoted from the Odd Met to the Regular Met Link in 1939, and spent the next three years on these duties, which took him as far afield as Welwyn Garden City and Hertford. There were over 60 different turns in this link, and since crews spent a week at a time on each of them it consequently took them over a year to work through all the turns. The Regular Met Link was also the "highest" link that did not involve the more exacting duties of fast running on the main line, and consequently those drivers who did not want to go forward to main line work could opt to stay in it. At times so many drivers did not want to go forward, that even this large link could not accommodate them all, and men were faced with the alternative of going forward or being relegated to shed duties, which involved nothing more exciting than preparing and disposing of locomotives. Some of the main line links involved lodging, and this was always a snag from the men's point of view, especially in the early days when the crews had to take pot luck at finding somewhere to stay in one of the poor districts of the town. Bill knew of men who would kip in a locomotive or passenger coach in some siding rather than put up with the sometimes unsavoury conditions in the local "digs". With the coming of wartime conditions, however, it was agreed between the unions and the railways that as many lodging turns as possible would be abolished, and joint committees were set up to discuss how this should best be brought about. The reduction was probably greatest on the L.N.E.R., with a cut of over 90 per cent. in the rostered number of these turns. With the wartime requirements for train services (long-distance passenger traffic on the G.N. main line rose to 200-300 per cent. of its 1939 figure), and the public exhortation "Is your journey really necessary?", the attraction of long non-stop passenger runs was no longer a selling point, but when peace time condi tions returned once more, there were unofficial Sunday strikes over the reintroduction of lodging turns. New lodging allowances came into operation in 1940, the footplatemen being paid 2d. per hour on rostered turns, from the time they booked on at their home depot, to the time they booked off again, subject to a minimum payment of 4s. 6d. If the lodging turn was not a rostered one, they got 2½d. per hour, with a slightly higher minimum payment. Wartime emergencies also led to crews being transferred to other depots either temporarily or on promotion, and for this they received 4s. 6d. per day for the first fortnight, after which the daily payment dropped to 3s. 6d., although on the L.N.E.R. this was later modified so that the rate remained at 24s. 6d. per week until such time as the man concerned could move his home.

The summer of 1939 had seen the threat of a railway stoppage, which was called for August 26th, but because of the national emergency, the strike notices were withdrawn. The A.S.L.E.F. was asking for an increase of a shilling a day in pay, 12 days holiday a year, and the abolition of extended rosters, with certain alterations to Sunday pay, and, after the resumption of negotiations, the minimum rate of pay for drivers was increased from 12s. to 13s. per day. From June

1940, however, there was a general increase in railwaymen's pay, the most junior drivers getting 14s. 2d. per day, while those with six years or more standing received 16s. 2d. Right at the bottom of the locomotivemen's ladder, a young cleaner of 16 would get 4s. 7d. per day, which represented an appreciable increase since Bill first went to Walton Shed. During the war, the cost of living increased sharply, and railwaymen received special War Allowances; 4s. per week from the beginning of 1941, with an additional ls. a week from June 1942. Less than 12 months later, there was another all-round adjustment, with the top drivers' rate becoming 18s. 5d. per day. Ultimately the War Allowances reached 28s. per week, and after the end of hostilities this payment was incorporated into their basic wages.

As already mentioned, it took a full year to work through all the turns in the Met Link, and as Bill's three years covered the early years of the war when everything was being altered almost daily to cope with the emergencies of the Blitz, he probably never worked exactly the same turn twice in the whole of this time. The imposition of the black-out brought far more stringent conditions in which the footplate men had to operate. They had tarpaulins to stretch between the cab and tender so that the glare from the firehole door did not reveal their whereabouts to hostile aircraft during "Alerts". The atmosphere inside this improvised tent rapidly became hot and stuffy, while outside, all the lighted land marks disappeared into the all-enveloping darkness with only the flash of exploding bombs to set off the dim glow of the signal lights. In the coaches, lights were dimmed and wide black strips around the edge of the compartment windows ensured that when the rexine blinds were pulled down, only the minimum of light escaped. Corridors were dimly lit by blue lamps, and the lighting on stations was cut to the absolute minimum. Wide lines of white paint were laid along the platform edges to assist passengers to board and alight, but in spite of these precautions there were numerous accidents as people stepped out into the inky blackness thinking that their train had halted in a station.

To help the drivers position their trains, a small white light was provided near each platform end, opposite which they were supposed to stop.

It was the anti-glare tarpaulin that landed Bill in trouble one trip with a 2-8-0 on a 60-wagon coal train for Ferme Park. Leaving Hitchin they got the warning of an "Alert" and having seen that the signal ahead was "off", Bill set about putting up the tarpaulin. Unfortunately, Control rang through to the signal box asking them to stop the train so that the guard could be relieved, and the signal was put back to danger. Bill did not look out for it again, and was stopped at Stevenage to be told he had run by the board. As a result of this he was suspended for two days. The oil lamps on ordinary signals were not altered during the war, but arrangements were made for the electric searchlight ones to be dimmed when enemy aircraft were about, after one of them had used the colour lights north of York to position itself for bombing one of the nearby R.A.F. airfields. This section of line seems to have had more than its usual share of incidents involving lights and aircraft, as only a few years ago the railway staff at Northallerton hurriedly extinguished the station lamps one night when a training aircraft had mistaken them for the local runway lights, and was preparing to land on top of them.

At the beginning of the war, Bill left his footplate duties for a few months, taking over the duties of A.R.P. Warden for Top Shed. This was a full-time job, as it involved instructing other people on the precautions they had to take in various circumstances, as well as liaising with the neighbouring Civil Defence Units in the district. Bill got fed up with the job after a while, and asked to go back on the footplate, and Bert Dixon, now Headquarters Locomotive Inspector at King's Cross, took over the job from him.

From the railwaymen's point of view, one of the most gruelling turns was to act as "Bomber Pilot". When an air raid had occurred over London, and bombs had fallen near the railway, it was important to find out at the first opportunity whether the lines were clear. Control would have received reports of places where there had been any attacks and with normal communications probably interrupted, the N2 on "Bomber Pilot" duty would be sent out after the "All Clear" had sounded to investigate the extent of the damage to the railway. Such a turn might take them to Hitchin by either of the two routes, the locomotive probably making a circular tour. More often than not these trips took place in the dark, and they had to creep along, aided perhaps by the light of fires left burning by a stick of incendiaries, hoping they would not fall into an unseen bomb crater. Bill fortunately escaped this experience, although others were not so lucky. It was entirely up to them to carry on at their own speed, and the only thing to do was to keep going and hope for the best.

King's Cross itself was badly hit one night in May 1941, when two bombs landed on the offices behind No. 10 platform, where the temporary replacement building and the corrugated sheeting on the station wall to this day still show the site of the main damage. The N2 on the back of a newspaper train in the platform was covered by debris from the roof, but this train and all the other scheduled trains left King's Cross that day in spite of the resulting difficulties. Further out, in another raid a bomb hit the retaining wall separating the goods and passenger lines at Goods and Mineral Junction, but the signalmen and the booking lad in the box escaped injury, thanks to their small steel shelters. Fire raids also caused widespread railway damage, and in one attack at Holloway sidings the staff were reduced to trying to extinguish incendiaries with carriage watering hoses. Bill's old line, the Great Central, was more unlucky in the Blitz. Marylebone Goods Depot was almost completely destroyed, and the shallow tunnels in the Lord's area were repeatedly blocked, while the breakdown crane was once called upon to remove an unexploded bomb from one of them.

Bill's duties in the Blitz also involved him away from the railway, as an Air Raid Warden, lending a hand to man the local reporting post where details of all "incidents" came in.

IV

The Civil Defence arrange ments that were perfected under Anderson and Morrison as successive Home Secretaries played a major part in maintaining morale during the Blitz, proving to the world that “London Can Take It”. Many of the children from the capital had been evacuated at the beginning of the war, including Bill’s younger daughter, Marian, who was sent to Bedfordshire where she could finish her exams unaffected by the nightly bombing. The job of transporting the evacuees fell on the railways, and King’s Cross was thronged with thousands of youngsters .clutching their gas masks among their belongings, and identified by ·luggage labels tied through the button-holes of their coats. The pressure on housing eased in spite of all the damage by bombing, and Bill and Dolly were able to move into a top flat in Boscastle Road. They had always wanted to live at the top of such a house, and it was only when the war temporarily rendered such a position somewhat less desirable, that they were able to achieve this ambition. For someone working on shifts, the absence of any overhead disturbances considerably helped sleeping during the day.

The railways were being continually pressed to move more traffic than ever before, and at the same time, damage to locomotives, permanent way, and rolling stock made the job even more difficult. Maintenance of locomotives became haphazard, and even such elementary jobs as boiler wash-outs would get overlooked when the locomotive rosters went haywire. An engine might be used by half a dozen different depots before it reached its home shed again, perhaps only after the lapse of several weeks. One day, Bill got a K3 on a down freight turn, and when they set off, he found there was no water in the gauge glasses, just a thick white scum, which rapidly built up into a solid emulsion. By the time they had reached Hatfield, where they were turned slow line, they had no idea where they were with the water level. Bill stopped at Welwyn Garden City and went forward to tell the signalmen they were going to throw the fire out, but by the time he got back he found his mate had already done this, although his efforts were too late to prevent one of the fusible plugs going. They got another engine, and the K3 was taken forward to Hitchin and examined. The corner of one of the firebox seams was blowing, and when, later on, the records had been examined, it was found that the boiler had not been washed out for three months, during which time the locomotive had covered a huge mileage.

Throughout the war, and especially during the period of the Blitz in London, many of the footplate crews were called on to work long shifts, at times up to 18 hours on end if something had gone wrong with their relief arrangement. Occasions such as this made them draw on their stamina, especially as they would often have to go without food for much of the turn if they were unable to cadge anything locally. Canteens were, however, introduced for railwaymen, and platform refreshment kiosks were built to replace the restaurant cars that were withdrawn from 1943 onwards. The run-down condition of the locomotives and shed installations did not help either, and Bill suffered a double hernia from the strain of turning locomotives at King's Cross during the winter when the cold made the grease on the badly-worn bearing especially stiff. The effort of linking up the lever reverse on the Atlantics did not help either, and in the summer of 1943 Bill finally had to have an operation in the Manor House Hospital. The medical attention he received there amply repaid him for his earlier efforts on the Hospital's behalf. Over 20 years later he has had no recurrence of the trouble, and his spryness at 71 would do credit to many younger men. The severe winter of 1941 played havoc with the East Coast Line, and in the February of that year all the lines into Newcastle were blocked, with three down expresses completely lost "somewhere near Durham". Conditions like these inevitably made their effect felt further south, and added to the long hours and improvisation required to keep the services running.

The war also brought about some new railway construction

in the London area, as on other important lines throughout the country. A north-to-west connection was built at Harringay, linking the G.N. main line with the Tottenham and Hampstead Joint. In conjunction with a similar connection at Gospel Oak, which was built in this case by the L.M.S., it permitted through running on to the North London line, with its connections at Willesden for the L.M.S., G.W.R., and S.R. Out at Wood Green, the few hundred yards of line authorised as long ago as 1924, were built to connect the Cuffley Loop south of Bowes Park with the former Great Eastern Palace Gates branch. This proved invaluable during the later years of the war, when trains for D-Day could be worked direct down to the London Docks, the Hornsey men learning the road right the way through. Although they did not come into this working area as yet, there were new wartime works at Sandy connecting with the Cambridge-Bedford line where it crossed the East Coast route, and north of York, during the latter half of 1942, quadrupling of the line as far as Northallerton was completed, apart from the up slow from Pilmoor to Alne that had to wait nearly another 20 years before it was con structed. This post-war construction resulted in the abandonment of the Alne and Easingwold Railway, which had remained in private hands after the Grouping and which handled very large quantities of the war material that was dispersed round the countryside to support the air bomber offensive, and later the invasion of Europe. The vast amount of extra traffic being handled made the East Coast line busier than ever, and the difficulties of shunting the slower trains into refuge sidings resulted in many of these being converted into full running loops, with the points at the far end from the signal box operated electrically. New siding capacity was put in in numerous places, one site that involved Bill being at Welwyn Garden City. The four East Coast lines north from Hatfield were originally flanked by the two single-track branches leading to Luton and Hertford, and the latter was converted to an additional goods line after a new connection had been constructed at Welwyn.

All these changes meant that the crews constantly had to keep refreshing their route knowledge of the area over which they operated.

7

Bill's promotion from the Regular Met Link took place approximately half way through the war, and he now found himself in the Odd Main Link for the next three years. This took him further afield, to Peterborough and Cambridge, on mineral and freight trains mostly, although the occasional passenger train came within his duties. Far more route knowledge was now required of him, with just over 100 miles of double or quadruple track involved. On some of these longer turns too, Bill was now paid for the mileage he covered and for the benefit of those not conversant with this method of payment, I had better explain the system, as it was to involve him more and more as the years went on.

Under the 1919 National Agreement already referred to, enginemen worked an 8-hour day, with "Time and a Quarter" for any day overtime, and "Time and a Half" for night overtime and Sunday duty. The roster could be split, however, so that it occupied up to nine hours, but once they had worked for more than eight of them, they were entitled to overtime. On "Mileage", however, the system was different, and the first 140 miles they covered in the day was considered as their basic day's work, for which they were allowed eight hours' pay. Thereafter, for every 15 additional miles, they got an extra hour's pay. A trip of 170 miles, therefore, brought the crew 10 (8 + 2) hours' pay. Overtime payments went on the hours worked, but only if they exceeded the normal eight hours a day. On an express turn, it was quite frequent for the 170 miles to be booked to be covered in only three hours, but if something went wrong and they were detained beyond their normal rostered time, the crew could not receive any additional payment until more than eight hours had elapsed since they had signed on. On a mileage basis, the King's Cross-Peterborough round trip only just qualifies, with a distance of 152¾ miles, and the extra they received from the mileage was very little, often less than they got for overtime on the suburban services in the Met Link. The locomotive situation was still difficult because of the war, and many of the engines they handled were run down, which added to their already hard job of tackling maximum loads with indifferent quality coal.

Various different classes of locomotive came their way too, and Bill once handled one of the Pl Mikados on a tank special. Changes were taking place on the motive power side too, since Gresley had died in 1941, being succeeded by Thompson, who introduced a number of fundamental changes in the new designs for which he was responsible. His Bls of 1942 were excellent engines, and set the pattern that he was to follow during his 5-year reign at Doncaster. Two cylinders only were provided, while many other Gresley engines were similarly converted, and it was only the Pacifics that retained the 3-cylinder layout, but even then they had three separate sets of valve gear in place of the Gresley conjugated arrangement, while the six P2 2-8-2s were radically rebuilt as Pacifics in 1943. Strangers, in the form of Riddles' "Austerity" 2-8-0s, had also made their appearance, and after many of them had returned from service on the mainland of Europe, the L.N.E.R. took over 200 of them, giving them the classification O7. Bill was badly burnt on one of these engines on one occasion, when the valve that isolated the steam supply from the lubricator failed to seat properly. When he loosened the plug to drain out the accumulated water, the steam pressure blew it out, together with the scalding mixture of water, oil and steam which hit his hand. Fortunately no permanent damage was done, and his hand healed completely after some days' discomfort.

From the L.N.E.R.'s point of view, the latter half of the war saw them supporting the vast air offensive that this island was mounting against Hitler's "Fortress Europe". Dozens of airfields sprang up in the eastern half of the country, and nearly all the materials for their construction had to be transported by rail. Three hundred wagons a day of rubble were at one time leaving London to be used in the foundations of the runways, which in some places were built across the railway lines. Once operational, the loads for the airfields changed from bricks and cement to bombs and petrol, a far less companionable type of traffic, which was not so tolerant of the carelessly-discharged cinder from a locomotive's chimney. The southern end of the G.N. main line, however, did not see all that much of this special traffic, which was mainly of a cross country nature, but there were plenty of other loads for them to wheel southwards during the nights and days that preceded VE day.

In 1944, after the Allied Armies had re-established their bridgehead on the mainland of Europe, Hitler unleashed his V weapons against southern England. As luck would have it, the first of the "Doodlebugs" to arrive hit one of the bridges out of Liverpool Street, and in the weeks that followed every ear in London became attuned for the sudden cut-out of the "Flying Bomb's" motor that was the prelude for its dive to earth where the warhead exploded. Special "Imminent Warning" systems were improvised, and at King's Cross the warning was given by the flying of a red flag by day on the western tower of the station. One night alone, they had 54 such alarms in just over seven hours. Large numbers of people voluntarily evacuated themselves from the capital, and in spite of down expresses leaving with "18 on", several hundred would-be passengers were left on the platforms after each had departed. On one day in July the booking office sold no less than £20,000 worth of tickets. Bill had his own special "Doodlebugs", a pair that appeared to be after his train one night. He was working the 2.10 a.m. down staff train via the New Line, and as they left Wood Green to go over the fly-over a couple of these Vls appeared behind them, one on either side of the track. Bill saw them from the footplate of his Atlantic, and tried to decide whether it was best to stop or carry on. Meanwhile the men in the train were leaning out of the windows offering conflicting advice as to what he should do. Fortunately the two Flying

Bombs carried on with their pulsating flames flickering out of their propulsion tubes, and all was well. After the Vls came the V2 rockets, which were much less appreciated than Gresley's 2-6-2s that carried the same designation. Again the L.N.E.R. caught the full force of this limited onslaught, one severing the New Line just north of Palmer's Green, while another landed on the 8-track section just south of Wood Green. Fortunately it only put six of the lines out of action, and down trains were able to get through by using the "Khyber Pass", the sharply-curved line around the back of the flyover, which has now been lifted. So practised were they with track repairs by this time, that within 12½ hours of the rocket exploding, six out of the eight lines were back in action. Bill also had to put up with attacks from enemy aircraft during this period, especially on his trips to Cambridge when lone bombers would infiltrate amongst our own return ing aircraft and attack the railway installations. The clearing of the enemy forces from the Channel Coast, and the final collapse of the Third Reich thus brought considerable relief all round to the London railwaymen, and Dolly could spend her time in the ration queues without worrying about what was happening to Bill on his rostered turn that morning.

Bill's three years in the Odd Main Link took him to 1945, so that in 18 years he had worked through all the junior driving grades at King's Cross, and was due to be promoted to express passenger working. He would now be in a position to enjoy sustained fast running again, and with the war over, everyone hoped that performance standards would soon return to those that had characterised the L.N.E.R. in the days before 1939.

CHAPTER FIVE

Express Passenger

When Bill was promoted out of the Odd Main Link in 1945, he was 51 years old and thus had another 14 years to go before he retired. He was now in the Express Goods Link, but in spite of its name, they also handled express passenger trains, and even when Bill got into the Top or No. 1 Link, they still had a regular express goods working, the 3.15 p.m. down from King's Cross to Newcastle. Between the Express Goods and Top Links was the Doncaster Link, consisting of 12 sets of men. Unlike those in the Top Link, the Doncaster and the Express Goods men did not regularly lodge, and those drivers who did not want to sleep away from home would elect to stay in the Doncaster Link, although their seniority entitled them to promotion to the Top Link. Most summers the No. 1 Link was enlarged from 12 to 14 sets of men to provide crews for the non-stop Edinburgh working, and although Bill was still only in the Express Goods Link, he was promoted for the duration of the 1950 summer services into the Top Link, as no one else with sufficient seniority was prepared to lodge. A similar arrangement should have applied for the next summer, but because of the general difficulties that the Railways faced in 1951, Bill did not actually work to Edinburgh again until 1952. The Top Link was enlarged to 18 sets of men in 1 953, and after this Bill remained permanently on these "Lodge" turns for his last six years on British Railways. His promotion into the Doncaster Link took place in the Autumn of 1952, and he therefore spent less than a year in it before his final move.

With the coming of peace in 1 945, which coincided with Bill's promotion to the Express Goods Link, the L.N.E.R. lost no time in trying to shake off the lethargy of wartime, but they were still hampered by the arrears of track and locomotive maintenance. It was possible to raise the general speed limit from 60 to 70 m.p.h. north of Hatfield, but difficulties with locomotives and adequate suitable supplies of coal resulted in a public announcement in 1952 of the policy of changing locomotives on nearly every train at Grantham or Peterborough in the interests of punctuality. In the summer of 1946, I travelled between King's Cross and Welwyn Garden City fairly frequently over a period of a couple of months, and even on the outer suburban trains, latenesses of 20 minutes were common, while on one occasion an Atlantic failed half-way to London.

From October 1945, however, the "Flying Scotsman", now with its restaurant cars once more, had 50 minutes knocked off its wartime 8 hour 55 minute schedule, and, later on, the number of stops made by it was reduced, producing an unusual non-stop run from Grantham to Newcastle. As well as the restaurant cars, other pre-war facilities returned, and by late 1946 the "Yorkshire Pullman" had been re-introduced, to be followed a year later by a new all-Pullman express, the "Tees-Tyne Pullman". In later years it was on this train, which took the place of the pre-war "Silver Jubilee", that Bill achieved some of his finest runs. With the summer service of 1949, non-stop running commenced between London and Edinburgh, but the train concerned was no longer the "Flying Scotsman", but the "Capitals Limited", a relief to the main train that left King's Cross at 9.30.

With the coming of peace time, the funereal black of the L.N.E.R. locomotives was discarded, and green adopted as standard livery, apart from the A4s which returned to their pre-war garter blue, with red wheels, now more clearly visible because of the absence of the streamlined shrouding below the curved foot-framing. Men working on the engines found these deep valances a considerable nuisance, as they hampered them getting at the motion, and during the war they were discarded, to everyone's relief. From an aesthetic point of view, too, I must admit that I always preferred the locomotives without this awkwardly-shaped covering, and find Mallard in the museum of British Transport has a very definitely "dated" appearance. The first A4 to be repainted blue was

No. 8, which was renamed Dwight D. Eisenhower, in honour of the Supreme Allied Military Commander in Europe. The L.N.E.R. had provided him with his own special train during the war, and perpetuated the connection by renaming Golden Shuttle after him. Several of the other A4s were also renamed after directors and officials of the L.N.E.R. Now, with most A4s displaced from active service by the diesels, Dwight D. Eisenhower reposes in the National Railway Museum at Green Bay, Wisconsin, alongside numerous other preserved steam locomotives, including a Union Pacific "Big Boy". The A4, in British Railways' green livery, arrived without any headlamps, and when Brian Hollingsworth visited it in the summer of 1964, he was immediately asked why the locomotive did not have headlamps, and admitted that it looked slightly wrong without them. We hazarded a guess, however, that the Americans would have been somewhat puzzled if a pair of small, white-painted oil lamps had arrived, in place of the single powerful electric one they were envisaging.

New coaching stock was also introduced by the L.N.E.R. after the war, and represented an appreciable departure from their previous designs, which had inherited many Great Northern features. The long-familiar bow-ends to the roofs disappeared, and cross corridors were provided, which did away with exterior doors in the compartments. The flush panelled exteriors were still painted in simulated varnished mahogany, and on the special stock for the "Capitals Limited", which was also pressure-ventilated, the panelling was carried down and round the sole bars. This new design represented a considerable step forward in comfort and amenities for the passengers, and 20 years later the vehicles are still at times used on main line services. Some of these new vehicles, however, achieved a measure of notoriety a few years after their introduction, as the lacquer used in the interior was highly inflammable, and there was a bad fire in one train as it entered Penmanshiel Tunnel. In the tests that followed, it was found that a lighted match thrown against the corridor side rapidly involved the whole corridor in flames, and different types of paint had to be applied in place of that originally used.

During 1947, Bill was involved in two mishaps on the main line. In the first, he was approaching Huntingdon with a V2 on an up passenger train. From Abbots Ripton up to Stukeley the locomotive had been pri ming and after coasting down the bank, he opened the regulator again by the South signal box. They had been running freely down the 1 in 200, and had reached about 65 when he applied steam again, but as he opened the regulator, the small end of the connecting rod on his side fractured. Freed from any support at its front end, the heavy rod dropped down, hit the sleepers, and dug into the ballast, the resultant thrust rolling the locomotive fiercely to the right. Bill made an emergency brake application, but the rod continued to flail around until they stopped. Several sleepers were broken, but the locomotive fortunately was not derailed and did not overturn on to the down fast line, either of which could have produced a very nasty result.

The other incident was rather more serious, and occurred in the early hours of the morning, when Bill was on one of the last of the original Als, standing two to three engine-lengths behind "99 Up" (the 7.50 p.m. from Edinburgh) in Grantham station. The guard of the sleeping car train had shown a green light to his engine and the train had just started to move forward, when Bill's fireman suddenly shouted "Get Set", as he had seen a WD 2-8-0, running light, coming off the "Branch" (the line from Nottingham), past the signals at danger. The "Austerity", still with its regulator open, hit the back of their tender and the impact drove their Al forward into the back of the express, whose driver felt the jerk and applied his brake. Bill and his mate got off their locomotive, and immediately saw that the front of the 2-8-0 was very badly damaged, with various of the parts thrown on to the platform by the force of the collision. Its crew were in a bad way, as they had been unprepared for the shock, and Bill told his fireman to look after them while he went forward to see whether anyone was hurt in the train ahead. The last vehicle was a restaurant car, which worked down on an evening train as far as Doncaster, where it was transferred, with its crew, to the rear of "99 Up" for the balancing working, although in this direction it was closed to passengers. Bill put his head through the window and asked if anyone was hurt. The crew, thinking Bill had been the cause of the mishap, gave him a saucy answer, and then showed him the condition of their kitchen, which was plastered with butter, jam, flour, and numerous other stores. They reckoned that instead of their usual snooze on the way to London, they would have to spend the whole journey cleaning up, and even then the job would not be finished until well after they had arrived in King's Cross. This was the only damage to the passenger train, however, except for the broken tail lamp. Once everything had been checked, and a new lamp found, the express left, leaving them to sort out things in the platform. The injured crew off the WD had been treated by first aiders from the depot, where they had heard the noise of the crash, and later another locomotive was sent over. It came up behind the culprit, coupled up, and then pulled it back on to the branch again, before propelling it into the locomotive yard where it could be dealt with at leisure. The force of the collision had buckled the Al's tender frame, and on the fireman's side the rear axlebox had been forced nearly off the journal. The tank had been punctured underneath, and all the water lost, but they were able to crawl their way along the platform and were then put "inside", where they could throw the fire out and wait for a replacement locomotive.

2

Exactly 25 years after the Grouping took place, the railways of this country were Nationalised, so that on 1st January 1948 the whole of the 648,740 staff employed on British railways were again plunged into the turmoil of reorganisation. Although nearly 20 years have now elapsed since this reorganisation took place, most readers will be familiar with the major changes that were involved then, or which have occurred since. As far as Bill was concerned, there were few changes that affected him very much, although the former L.N.E.R. locomotives now grew an additional 6 (and perhaps some noughts as well) in front of their existing numbers. The figures painted on the front buffer beams migrated to become the familiar smokebox number-plate that we now know, while the initials L.N.E.R. on the tenders were replaced by a lion seesawing on the name "British Railways". The use of this emblem followed a short period when only the words themselves appeared in large letters that occupied nearly the full length of the side panels. The locomotive colours changed too, and after some experiments the Al, A3, and A4 Pacifies, like other express passenger classes throughout the country, appeared in dark blue livery. Later on, the task of keeping this livery clean was found to be too difficult, and the blue gave way to the G.W.R. Brunswick Green that had been adopted for other passenger engines. The varnished mahogany coach livery that the L.N.E.R. inherited from the Great Northern was far from appropriate for modern steel-panelled stock, but the garish crimson lake and cream that replaced it after Nationalisation was not a happy choice. Bill now sported a dark blue totem-shaped cap badge; but there were generally few changes following nationalisation that involved him very deeply for the next five years.

Amongst those who were appointed to the Railway Executive, which now ran the railways, was W.P. Allen, the General Secretary of A.S.L.E.F. who had started his railway career on the Great Northern as a cleaner at Hornsey. It gave the enginemen considerable pleasure that a member of their union was now on the management, but although Allen's job was specifically concerned with the manpower side of the railways, there were not the immediate improvements that many thought would inevitably follow hard on the heels of Nationalisation. As in 1923, it was amongst the higher ranks of management that the initial changes were first felt, and the sheer problem of welding an industry that employed over 600,000 people into a single organisation occupied most of the Railway Executive's efforts for the first few years, especially since the wartime arrears of track and motive power maintenance were still far from being wiped out.

Just after Bill had retired in 1959, the interviewer in a B.B.C. programme slipped in the inevitable political question on what he thought of Nation alisation, failing to realise that from the point of view of the man on the job, it was the contribution that the local management made to raising morale and interest which would affect him most. Without getting involved in political matters, the comment might nevertheless now be made that Nationalisation of itself does not solve the problems of an industry that is facing fierce outside competition. It was only when the railways started to move forward again technologically, following the Modernisation Plan of 1955, that they were able to sharpen the competition they offered to the onslaught of the private car and C-licence lorry. Unified control resulting from Nationalisation then enabled full advantage to be taken of these new developments.

As a matter of deliberate post-war policy, the Government allowed little new investment in our national transport systems, concentrating instead on the construction of new homes. The post-war plans for improvements published by the L.N.E.R. in their booklet "Forward" made impressive reading, but it was a good number of years after Nationalisation before many of them were carried out. To this day, however, the severe restric tion remains at Peterborough North, reducing the speed of every non stop express in both directions from at least 60 down to 20 m.p.h. through the platforms, and yet the rebuilding of the station was actually started as long ago as 1939.

In the Spring of 1948, the Railway Executive announced that they were going to conduct a series of Locomotive Exchange Trials, the whole programme, which involved mixed-traffic and freight designs as well as express passenger classes, lasting from mid-April to early September. The geographical range too, covered nearly the whole of the British Isles, stretching from Plymouth as far north as Inverness. For the express passenger classes, around which most interest centred, the East Coast route between King's Cross and Leeds was one of those chosen, and turned out to be the only "foreign" line over which clearances permitted a G.W.R. "King", King Henry VI, to take part. It was joined by a South ern "Merchant Navy", Belgian Marine, and two L.M.S. designs, a Pacific, City of Bradford, and rebuilt "Scot", Queen's Westminster Rifleman. The locomotive class chosen to uphold the honour of the L.N.E.R. was the A4, and for the test runs over the East Coast main line, Lord Faringdon was used, which together with Mallard and Seagull, represented the Eastern Region, as it now was, in the "away" matches. Of all the classes to take part in the trials, the A4s fared worst mechanically, registering three failures which necessitated a change of engine, all caused by the over heating of the middle big end. It was events like these which helped found the popular impression in the post-war years that the A4s were "done". The results of all the Trials were made public, but although the very bulky report giving all the official figures was available for loan, it was never printed and put on sale, like the subsequent test bulletins. Many long and possibly acrimonious discussions have since ensued in railway enthusiast circles about the rival merits of the different designs and their performance, but the quoting of the coal consumption figures to the second place of decimals has misled many into believing that this represented the true accuracy of the results, whereas lack of consistency in the tests themselves produced much larger day-to-day variations which consequently made overall comparisons less sure than the average figures indicate. I would very much like to see a full statistical analysis of variance done sometime for these tests, so that it would at last be possible to pinpoint those differences which are truly significant and which are not due to random variations in handling and operating. The Railway Executive was not misled by the results, and drew only two conclusions, both of the broadest nature. The first was that because of the ability shown by the different classes to operate satisfactorily on "foreign" routes, there was no need to limit the proposals for producing their new range of standard designs then under consideration. The second conclusion arose out of the first, and was to standardise where possible on certain items such as large boilers and features leading to good riding that had shown up as superior qualities during the Trials.

During the Exchanges, the locomotives were worked by crews from their "home" Region, who had two round trips during which they could pick up the route before the test runs proper, with the dynamometer car, the following week, which also comprised a pair of round trips. Bill was not personally involved in any of the workings, but his brother-in-law Tom Ratley, by then also a driver at King's Cross, was selected to take the Bl down to work over the Western Region line between Bristol and Plymouth, where he achieved the fastest of all the recorded climbs of Hemerdon Bank during the Exchanges, even beating the A4 Seagull, although with a lighter load. Great interest was shown by railway en thusiasts in the Trials, and R. S. McNaught was able to get up to Peter borough from Spalding on Tuesday 27th April to see the "Rebuilt Scot" on its first down test run. When the stranger ran in to the station on the 1.10 p.m. from King's Cross, A3 No. 106 Flying Fox was standing in the other platform road, with Bill and his fireman, F. Ruffell, leaning out of the cab to watch what was happening. Amongst the railwaymen the trials produced a considerable amount of partisanship, and when Bill saw the Eastern Region pilot driver struggling to fasten the side door on the footplate, he proffered the advice, "That's right, fasten her up or you'll be shaken off". This exchange was clearly audible across the platform, in spite of the fact that safety valves on the "Scot" were now lifting as she got ready to lift her train up Stoke. Bill also took exception to a character in sports coat and flannels who was spreading sand on the line in front of the 4-6-0, as well as the train previous to it, which might have caused a delay, remarking to McNaught that they never got anything like that themselves, and it was distinctly unfair to accord this treatment to the stranger. Ten years later, McNaught referred to the incident in the "Railway World", without realising it was Bill who was involved, and was very surprised to receive a letter from him filling in the gaps in the story, demonstrating not only his interest, but his remarkable memory for detail.

3

With the beginning of 1948, we have moved into the period for which Bill's diaries are still in existence, recording in his tiny clear handwriting the details of every day's work that he carried out, including the number of the locomotive, and any other items of special interest. For those not familiar with Bill's writing, I must point out that it is very small indeed, especially so for someone who has spent a lifetime engaged in manual activities of various kinds. Although I have never seen the results, he is reputed to be able to write the Lord's Prayer on the space occupied by a sixpence, and I can certainly well believe that it is possible. His small signature used to cause the time-keepers at the various sheds some difficulty, so much so that at Leeds on one occasion, one official thought he was having a joke with him, and words ensued. At King's Cross, where they were used to it, it caused endless difficulties, as the following driver would often fail to notice it, and sign his name on top, with consequent confusion. One of the time-keepers decided to stop this, and provided a pen with a specially broad nib, which he thought would force Bill to adopt a larger signature. Instead, Bill used one corner of the nib only, and deliberately made the signature smaller than ever, so that the time-keeper had to admit defeat. It was the coming of the ball-point pen, I think, that really provided Bill with his ideal writing implement, and none of the numerous letters I have received during the course of writing this book have lacked the ornamental capital letters and signature that are included in the example that has been reproduced opposite.

In the early months of 1948, Bill was engaged mainly

on freight workings and some of the turns would take him no further than Hitchin, with the return trip being made "on the cushions", as a passenger. On such occasions, like all drivers, Bill would sit in one of the end compartments of the train, in the most strategic position for booking-off at the end of the journey. He would prefer to travel with his back to the engine if possible, as travelling in that direction he did not subconsciously find him self watching the road ahead. Little incidents cropped up from time to time, such as that on February 4th, when they stuck at Wood Green with K3 No. 1853, while on the last day of March they ran hot with A2/3 Chamossaire on a Peterborough turn. The differences that occurred from day to day on a nominally identical turn were surprising too, especially when freight trains were involved. From Monday 4th April to the follow ing Saturday, Bill signed on at 3.10 a.m. to work "1068 Down" as far as Peterborough, returning "passenger". For some reason on the Tuesday, he got no further than Hitchin with Fireman H. Ellis on Isinglass, but they then transferred to No. 3063, one of the WDs that had been taken over and renumbered by the L.N.E.R. as Class O7, to work "1035 Up". In spite of this short trip, his time worked that day amounted to 9 hours 40 minutes. Ellis fired for Bill on three other nights that week right through to Peterborough, with K3 No. 1862 on Wednesday, another WD, No. 78522, on the Thursday, and an A4, No. 28 Walter K. Whigham, on Saturday. On the two remaining days he had another two firemen, and two additional classes of locomotive; V2 No. 814 on the Monday, and A2/1 Highland Chieftain on the Friday. The "hours" worked, which of course would include mileage, were as follows on successive days, starting with the Monday: 10 hours 30 minutes, 9 hours 40 minutes (the Hitchin trip), 10 hours 30 minutes, 8 hours, 8 hours 20 minutes, and 10 hours 30 minutes. Amongst the locomotives that he handled during April were a "Claud" (driven to Cambridge as a light engine), and the unique W1 4-6-4, then still numbered 10000.

Occasionally in his diaries, there is reference to Bill's

regular turns being altered while they were out on the road. Control would stop them, say, at Tempsford on the down trip, and arrange for them to change over with the crew of an up train in order to cover the workings with the men that were available. These changes mainly concerned freight trains, although passenger ones were occasionally involved, but only if they were running sufficiently out of course to prevent them to be covered by the booked diagrams. With special and parcels traffic, however, it used to be very different, as a hold-up in a yard miles away could throw the whole service out of step and disrupt all the carefully balanced crews' workings. For the footplatemen these unexpected changes could be rather hard in certain circumstances. They might have been booked to Grantham, say, and "Home Passenger", only to find themselves being made to change over a few miles short of their destination, and work a train straight back, instead of lording it on the cushions for the return journey. If traffic was badly out of course, too, it might be several hours later than their normal booking-off time when they got back to London, after a much harder turn than they had expected. As a result, they would sometimes try and refuse these change-overs on the grounds of disturbance from diagrammed working, and Bill recorded a number of these incidents in his diary. There was a spell, shortly after Nationalisa tion, when he considered that undue advantage was being taken of the footplate crews in this respect, and he consequently disobeyed instructions on a number of occasions to mark his objections. Over a period of 4½ years he got into a considerable amount of trouble in consequence, collecting a number of Severe Personal Reprimands. It was, of course, absolutely vital for the railway management, as exemplified by the Locomotive Department, and Control, to be able to make last-minute alterations of this sort to cope with unexpected difficulties that cropped up. If any unfairness resulted, the Local Departmental Committee could always make representations on behalf of its members, but when a driver takes the law into his own hands, there is no excuse if it leads to a train being delayed, as occurred on several occasions as a result of Bill's actions. It was perhaps as well that standards of discipline were somewhat easier 15 years ago than they are now, or the incidents to which I have referred might have brought Bill's footplate career to a close.

4

One of the overnight turns they had at this time involved working down to Grantham on the 11.15 p.m. train and after a break, returning on "99 Up", the 7.50 p.m. from Edinburgh that Bill had rammed when the WD hit his Al. On Thursday 15th July 1948, he and Albert Young had No. 60508 Duke of Rothesay, another of the V2s that Thompson had turned out as Pacifics of Class A2/1, on this turn, the trip passing off uneventfully. The following night they had the same turn to work, and coupled on to their load of 11 coaches at Grantham, setting off in the early morning light of Saturday 17th July for the 105½ mile return trip. Duke of Rothesay was steaming well, and with the comparatively light load of 362 tons tare, Bill had no difficulty in picking up time, in spite of the isolated patches of mist about. They had left Peterborough 20 minutes late, and by Hatfield had regained half of the arrears. A good climb was made to Potters Bar, which was passed at 5.55 a.m. Over the summit, Bill continued steaming until after Hadley Wood, by which time their speed had reached 60 m.p.h., the overall limit that still prevailed south of Hatfield, where the arrears of maintenance and drainage work in the London clay formation still made it unsafe to raise the limit to the figure of 70 that applied elsewhere. No. 60508 was not fitted with a speedometer, and on the long 1 in 200 falling gradient, speed crept up to about 70 m.p.h. as they entered the centre bore of the three parallel Barnet Tunnels. With the hard work now over, Albert Young had swept up the loose coal on the footplate and hosed down the dust before finally washing his hands in the bucket. This job over, he put the soap away, and moved into his seat on the right hand side of the cab as they plunged into the darkness of the tunnel. Half-way through they both heard a rattling noise, apparently from the front right-hand side of the locomotive, and Bill immediately put the brake handle fully down. Among the steadily increasing noise, he shouted to Albert to try and see what was happening. As they emerged into the daylight once more, Albert looked out of the side window of the cab but could see nothing, so he got up and moved back to the gap between engine and tender, where he would be able to lean out further. Unknown to them, the trailing axle on the bogie had been derailed to the right just after a rail joint that had been left ¾ inch high following some permanent way work the previous Sunday. The derailed wheels badly damaged the chairs of the track, and flying debris hit a down parcels train on the slow line whose driver saw the express emerge from the tunnel with sparks coming from the bogie.

This far, the derailment was not particularly serious, but 300 yards further on there was a facing connection to the up slow, and as they passed over the V crossing, the whole of the bogie was derailed, which promptly started to tear the track to pieces. As Bill put it, "the debris did not really begin to fly until we got through the points", which is probably something of an understatement, as just over 200 yards of track were completely destroyed. Unfortunately one of the dislodged rails caught Albert Young, snatching him off the footplate, where he was crushed by the overturning first coach and killed. The noise was by now indescribable, and Bill grabbed hold of the two injectors on the back of the boiler, clinging on like grim death. Coal crashed forward from the tender as a result of the rapid braking effect, and one of the lumps caught him a nasty bump on the back of the head. Then the screw coupling parted between the tender and the leading coach, and the locomotive went forward on its own, slowly turning over on to its right-hand side. This caused some of the fire to be flung out of the firehole door on to Bill's legs, but fortunately one of the displaced rails had penetrated the right-hand side of the tender, and the resulting cascade of water put out the fire that was threatening to burn him seriously. Ahead were a signal gantry and the four arches of Bridge No. 37, which carried a road across the six tracks, and Bill saw them looming up as his motion suddenly became smoother since the overturned locomotive had started to slide on its side along the now-intact section of the Up fast line. They caught the gantry and demolished it, but the locomotive slid through the arch of the bridge without hitting anything, and came to rest 50 yards further on.

As the locomotive stopped, Bill shook himself free from the coal that came almost up to his waist and climbed out, noticing as he walked round the front of the engine that the leading bogie wheels were still gently rotating. He was badly shaken up and was not really able to walk properly, so that when the guard came up, he asked him to go forward and protect the train. But the accident had been seen by the signalman in Cemetery box, who sent "Obstruction Danger" for all four running lines, and phoned Control. Bill was upset by the disappearance of Albert, and after trying to get his belongings out of the tender, set off back along the track to try and find him. A group of sailors from the train were· working like Trojans getting the passengers out (none of whom were seriously injured), helping them up the embankment on to the road, and a driver and fireman who had been riding back "on the cushions" helped too. Bill could see nothing of Albert, and then got worried about the fire left in the box. He made his way slowly back to the locomotive again, but all the tools had gone, so he could do nothing about the small amount of fire that remained, and it eventually went out of its own accord. After a bit, someone came up to Bill and told him he was in a bad way and ought to get some attention. He was offered a cigarette, which enabled him to have a smoke at last, as his own had been soaked by the water that poured over him, and he was then persuaded to go into the ambulance centre of the adjoining factory that belonged to the Standard Telephone and Cable Company, where the first-aid staff took care of him. He had only been there a short while when two police officers turned up and started to question him closely about the whole incident. After putting up with their questions for a few minutes, Bill asked if they had seen the aftermath of the accident, and if so, did they think he was in a fit state to answer questions. He told them it was more important for someone to go and see about his mate's four youngsters, who were now orphans. The nurse was also rather short with them and they went away. Bill feels that their visit was prompted, as much as anything, by a desire to find out whether he had been drinking, but is nevertheless still rather bitter about this particular facet of the accident.

After the first aid people had patched Bill up, he was sent off to hospital, where the cut on the back of his head was dressed and bandaged. By now he was getting anxious about Dolly, who was out queuing for rations. He wondered who would be the first to tell her of the accident, and whether the story would be the correct one, with no exaggerations about the extent of his injuries or even survival. The hospital people wanted to keep him in for observation, but by following the doctor out of the ward, he finally persuaded them to send him home in an ambulance, with somebody to see him in to the flat. By the time Dolly had arrived back from the shops, Bill was nicely settled down and had a cup of tea all ready for her. As she had come in, she had heard from neighbours of the ambulance's arrival and the fact that Bill, with a bandage round his head, had been helped into the building, but on entering her kitchen, was greeted by Bill's usual puckish figure without any bandage on, since he had carefully taken it off himself so it would not frighten her. The reporters soon got word of who had been the driver in the accident, and arrived to interview him. Bill bargained with the first that he would give him a bit of a story in exchange for a lift to the Sheds, where he could make out a proper accident report. He therefore had a drink of tea, with something to eat, and then got "squared up", giving the press only the bare facts on his way down to King's

Cross to make his official report. There were more reporters waiting when he got back, and as he was tired of parrying their questions, he suggested to Dolly that they should go to the pictures, which they did.

The usual round of inquiries that follow a fatal accident started the following Monday, with the Joint Inquiry, held by W. E. Green, the District Superintendent, in his office at King's Cross. On the Wednesday, the coroner opened the inquest on Albert Young, but this was then post poned until 5th August, after the usual evidence of identification had been given. Bill was naturally particularly concerned about Albert's family, and was pleased when the local branch of their union raised a fund under the control of the Branch officials which helped very consider ably with the children's education in later years. The Ministry of Trans port Inquiry by Lt. Col. G. R. S. Wilson took place on Friday 23rd July, and the whole accident was investigated very thoroughly to deter mine its cause. Col. Wilson, in his usual kindly but penetrating way, questioned Bill about the details he could recall, and expressed surprise that he had been able to remember so much of what had happened in such a short time. Bill had been able to describe the various parts he had seen flying, including the bogie from the leading coach, and the right-hand cylinder cock, which was thrown right over the locomotive, finishing up on the left-hand side of the line. It became clear that the high joint in the tunnel had led to the initial derailment, but as it had been like this for nearly a week, it was surprising that no-one else had complained about it. Duke of Rothesay was subsequently found to have one slightly weakened spring on the bogie, but it was finally concluded that it was probably chance that the derailment had not occurred previously, al though the higher than usual speed at which Bill was running may have accentuated the trouble. From various items of evidence, the Inspecting Officer concluded that the speed had been 70 m.p.h., although he did not blame Bill for this, and pointed out that the locomotive was not equipped with a speedometer. In any case, no engineer fixing a restriction would allow a safety factor of less than lO m.p.h. at a speed of a mile a minute. There was one interesting sequel to the incident, which has not, as far as I know, been mentioned previously. During Col. Wilson's Inquiry, he showed Bill some photographs of No. 60508 after she had been got back on to the rails, and the two of them used the illustrations to point out where the various parts of the motion were missing. A few days later, Bill was asked into the Shedmaster's office at King's Cross. He was shown one of the photographs of the right-hand side of the locomotive that had been used at the Inquiry, and asked whether he noticed anything unusual about it. He could find nothing particular to comment on until his attention was drawn to the number on the cab side, which clearly showed 60507. Either there had been an exchange of cabs sometime between Duke of Rothesay and Highland Chieftain, or when the former was being repainted, the wrong transfers had been applied and subsequently covered up with a fresh coat of paint. The rubbing action as the locomotive slid along on its side exposed the lower incorrect number, and it is of interest that the original Ian Allan "Renumbering ABC", published in 1949 and recently reprinted, showed the number of Duke of Rothesay as 507. The various formalities concerned with this derailment, and his nervous shock, kept Bill off normal working until Monday 26th July, when he spent the day on shed duties before taking up his rostered turns on the Tuesday, just 10 days after the accident. On his first up run that day he did not feel so good as he came over the fatal stretch, but everything was all right, of course, and from then onwards it became just another bit of road for him. When Frank Mayes was firing for him in 1953, he once asked Bill whether the accident had had any real effect on him. Bill's reply was typical, to the effect that he had a cold shudder while he was standing at Hitchin the first time out after the accident. In spite of this nonchalance, however, I think the derailment had more effect on him at the time than he thought (or will admit) as the daily records in his diary ceased for six weeks, which included his fortnight's annual leave. It was not until the beginning of September that things apparently returned to normal, and the usual entries were resumed. Bill did not handle Duke of Rothesay again until March 27th the following year, and he once more had occasion to find something wrong with it, but this time it was nothing worse than a faulty injector. Bill thus survived the one really serious accident of his career with nothing worse than a bad personal shaking and a cut on the back of his head. I can never make out how large a part luck played in his escape, or whether it was his foresight and quickness in knowing what to do in such an emergency that saved his life. It is quite certain, however, that it was entirely Bill's spirit and character that enabled him to come through the accident with his love of railways and fast running still intact.

5

The human brain has a wonderful ability to suppress unpleasant mem ories, and forget things that it wishes not to remember. This process has been demonstrated not only in the way Bill's recollections of the New Southgate incident have faded as far as his own pain and fear are concerned, but also in the way in which numerous railway enthusiasts fail to recall the chaotic conditions that ensued in some railway motive power circles in the late 1940s and early 1950s. Many people have been very ready to point the finger of scorn at the difficulties that British Railways have experienced with their change-over to diesel and electric traction, but few now realise the sort of conditions Bill had to put up with in his early days on express passenger workings.

The devotees of the Great Northern main line have always been especially good at collecting locomotive information and chronicling it for posterity. R. A. H. Weight probably formed the original nucleus from his house overlooking the line at Wood Green, and in later years Eric Neve, christened "The Foreman Spotter" by the railway people, presided over the "Grape Vine", gathering and farming out the information at the country end of No. 10 platform. Each edition of the "Railway Observer," whose editors print locomotive numbers even more assiduously than the average provincial weekly newspaper records names, includes a paragraph on the G.N. Section, and faithfully records the major happenings month by month. As late as 1950, the reports of the Christmas traffic into King's Cross referred to such confusion and congestion as had never previously been experienced on the East Coast Route, with a line of as many as 24 engines waiting at Holloway South to gain entry into King's Cross shed. Winter weather conditions were not responsible for these happenings either, as on one Saturday during the following summer the up "Capitals Limited" took no less than 1 hour 15 minutes to cover the last 8½ miles from Oakleigh Park, arriving in the terminus virtually empty as most passengers had alighted at Finsbury Park and taken to the Underground, a regular practice amongst the knowledgeable on such occasions. It must be remembered, of course, that petrol rationing was still in force throughout the 1940s, and new cars could, by and large, only be obtained by people like doctors, but the conditions that resulted at these times of peak traffic made many passengers decide to switch to road as soon as they possibly could, and they are now, in consequence, among those who overheat their idling engines in the queues on Exeter bypass on summer Saturdays instead.

To get some idea of the conditions under which the East Coast Route was operating its express trains during these years, it is first necessary to review the post-war motive power developments. Prior to 1939, Gresley had provided the L.N.E.R. with the largest stud of Pacifics of any of our railways, and these were backed up by the ever-capable V2s which frequently deputised even for the A4s when circumstances made it neces sary. After Gresley's death in 1941, Thompson had continued building the V2s, but turned out the last four of them in the form of A2/1 Pacifics, which were later given Scottish names to continue the series from the rebuilt

Mikados. Neither of these classes was an unqualified success, and after the New Southgate incident, Bill never had a good word for the A2/ls. All these locomotives had three separate sets of valve gear, doing away with the Gresley conjugated arrangement, but were nothing like so free running as the older designs. In 1945 Thompson rebuilt the first Gresley Pacific Great Northern along generally similar lines, but the result also was not an outstanding success, and certainly lacked the aesthetic appearance of the original. It was officially intended to carry on with these rebuilds, and subsequent locomotives were to have been streamlined, although whether Thompson would have perpetuated the A4 outline is not known. As it turned out, it was Peppercorn, his successor, who set about the construction of 6 ft. 8 in. Pacifics again, and Thompson's only other Pacifics were the 15 A2/3s, introduced in 1947 with the 6 ft. 2 in. wheels like the previous A2s.

During his 5-year tenure of office, Thompson rebuilt one or more locomotives of nearly every Gresley class of smaller engines with two cylinders in place of the original three, following the example he had set with his Bls, which were ultimately to total over 400 and prove the most successful locomotive he designed, if one goes on numbers built. The rebuilding process was also applied to some fifty of the Robin son 2-8-0s which received new boilers, cylinders with outside valve gear below raised foot-framing, and side-window cabs, which were now classified O1. To supplement the tank engine classes, he built the Lls from 1945 onwards. They were a businesslike-looking class, but were not so generally popular with the crews as were the older Gresley Vls and V3s, because of the roughness that developed relatively quickly from the wear on the axleboxes and hornframes. Introduced three years after the Bls, they all disappeared to the scrap heap several years ago, which would also indicate they were heavier on maintenance. In passing, it should also be recalled that the Thompson era was also noted for producing some semblance of order in the numbering of the L.N.E.R. locomotives. It was the advent of

The Cunarder *Campania* alongside the landing stage at Liverpool. Note the crowds on the landing stage, the paddle tugs, and the Mersey ferries moored at the southern end of the landing stage. *Cunard Steam Ship Co.*

The paddle steamer, *La Marguerite*, on which Bill, Jim and Christopher made a day trip to Llandudno in 1905. This picture, taken some three years later, shows the vessel, well laden with trippers, churning up the waters of the Mersey. *E. Jone*

The arrival of the first passenger train in Riverside Station, Liverpool, on 12th July, 1899. The L.N.W.R. were clearly not very lavish in their embellishments, but the effect of the repetitive detail is not unattractive. *Reproduced from the collection in the Brown, Picton and Hornby Libraries, Liverpool.*

Single- and double-deck trams pass Liverpool Central station at about the turn of the century. Bill's journeys with the bullion were made on a dray similar to the one behind the lamp on the left. Liverpool City Engineer's Dept.

Great Howard Street Goods Station in L. & Y. days. The main line into Exchange Station passed over the viaducts in the background. The warehouses behind the elevated signal box belonged to the Leeds & Liverpool Canal Co., whose terminal basins were situated beyond them. Note the numerous bales of cotton in the yards, some covered by tarpaulins. One of the capstans used for moving the wagons can be seen beyond the turntable in the foreground, and the van to the right of it is dual-braked, as well as being fitted with a steam-heating connection. *Liverpool City Engineer's Dept.*

The former L. & Y. pug No. 51229, complete with deflector plate on the chimney, trundles a solitary wagon under the remains of the Liverpool Overhead Railway near Wapping during dismantling operations in February, 1958. *Reproduced from the Collection of Liverpool Museums by permission of the Liverpool Libraries, Museums and NU Commission.*

Bill in his Midland Railway messenger's uniform. *Bill Hoole's collection.*

A Great Central outside-framed 4-4-0 wheels her light train of two six-wheelers and a bogie coach out of a station on the Cheshire Lines. Note the chaired fish plates. *H. Casserley's collection.*

No. 970, one of the Pollitt single-wheelers of the Great Central, on the Cheshire Lines. Bill acted as fireman on one of these on Grand National Day, 1912. *H. C. Casserley's collection.*

A Midland "Spinner", No. 623, heads a 40-minute Manchester-Liverpool express on the Cheshire Lines. *H. C. Casserley's collection.*

Robinson 's 2-8-0 No. 966, as built, and, below, as later fitted with a larger boiler, side-window cab, and bogie tender with pulverised fuel system. *H. C. Casserley's collection. Modern Transport.*

R.O.D. 2-8-0's stored at Neasden in July, 1922, after World War I service. Note jacks on the footframing, and the Westinghouse pump under the tarpaulin. *H. C. Casserley's collection.*

One of the Robinson 8B 2-cylinder Atlantic at Neasden in spotless condition, with Willesden old parish church in the background. *Locomotive Publishing Company.*

Two of the Neasden cleaners pose in front of "Director" No. 437 Prince George after producing the immaculate finish on the locomotive, ready for working a Manchester express. Note the space between the tracks and absence of any ashes. *H. C. Casserley's collection.*

"Director" No. 5434 *The Earl of Kerry* at Neasden after Grouping. Bill was one of her regular cleaners at Neasden in 1914, when Charlie Skinner was driving this locomotive. *H. C. Casserley's collection.*

A Robinson 4-6-2 tank at Neasden sheds in L.N.E.R. livery. Note the " gimp" on the side tank. Bill did his first mileage turns on these locomotives, with round trips from Marylebone to Brackley and South Harrow in the 7½ hours. *H. C. Casserley's collection.*

A shed scene at Neasden on 6th June, 1925, during the Wembley Exhibition. A fitter works on "Director" No. 5430 Purdon Viccars, while on the next road the driver prepares the former Great Eastern N7 No. 992E which was transferred to Neasden to help with the Exhibition traffic. In the foreground is N5 No. 5913. H. C. Casserley's collection.

Wembley Exhibition. The former Great Eastern N7 0-6-2T No, 997E approaches the Exhibition station on the loop line on 4th July, 1925. The minarets of the Indian Pavilion tower in the distance, and the covered footbridge across the tracks almost hides the colour-light signal protecting the platform. Beyond the fence on the right can be seen the "Never-Stop" Railway. *H. C. Casserley's collection.*

Wembley Exhibition. The Horwich "Baltic" No. 11114 dwarfs the other exhibits on the L.M.S. stand on 26th September, 1925. The notice on her smokebox reads "L.M.S. Horwich. This engine has been withdrawn direct from traffic after having run 21269 miles." *H. C. Casserley's collection.*

Wembley Exhibition. The reversing loop of the "Never-Stop" Railway on 4th July, 1925. Notice how the vehicles close up in the stations. The carriages were very popular as picnic places as well as a means of transport. *H. C. Casserley's collection.*

G.N. Atlantics. Left : No. 4410at King's Cross, in 1937, and below : No. 3295, Bill Carter's 5"-gauge model, standing in steam on the track at Beech Hurst in 1965. *C. C. B. Herbert & W. A. Carter.*

Former Great Northern 0-6-0 shunter No. 3140. Note the absence of a dome, the rudimentary cab, and the wooden buffer beams. In his early days at King's Cross, Bill drove locomotives of this type. *P. Ransome-Wallis.*

An NI at King's Cross Top Shed in early grouping days. The locomotive is still carrying its Great Northern livery and number although the L. & N .E.R. initials have replaced the G.N.R. on the side tanks. *W. J. Reynolds.*

Opposite At the beginning of World War II, Bill demonstrates what a driver would have to wear in the event of a gas attack. *Fox Photos.*

BILL HOOLE

An evening rush hour scene at King's Cross on 22nd March, 1948. A2/3 No. 517 *Ocean Swell* leaves Platform 10 with the 5.30 p.m. for Newcastle, while N2 No. 9541 comes out of "The Drain" with a Welwyn Garden City Train. The two drivers would be indulging in the usual race through Gas Works Tunnel, each trying to keep in front, so the other crew got the benefit of their exhaust. *C. C. B. Herbert.*

A2/2 Duke of Rothesay on its side after the New Southgate accident on 17th July, 1948. The badly battered tyres on the rear wheels of the bogie contrast with the almost pristine condition of the others, showing that it was these wheels that ran derailed for a considerable distance before the remainder came off the rails. *Associated Newspapers.*

] The first A2, built by A. H. Peppercorn, was turned out from Doncaster Works in the last few days before Nationalisation of the L.N.E.R. on 1st January, 1948. This model was made by the apprentices at Darlington to present to the last Chief Mechanical Engineer when he retired in 1949. Built to a gauge of 1/4 in. to the foot, the model is interesting in a number of respects. It carries a British Railways' number, but is otherwise in L.N.E.R. livery and is fitted with a double chimney, rather similar to those fitted to the first Als. Many of the A2s later had double chimneys fitted, but not of this pattern, and No. 60525 carried a single chimney until it was scrapped in the spring of 1963. The engraved works plate on the cab side reads "Built at Darlington 1949". *Author, by courtesy of Mr. & Mrs. w. Mather.*

Seagull awaits departure time at King's Cross with the "Elizabethan" on 1st September, 1955. Bill is in conversation with a youngster on the platform. R. I. Nelson rode with Bill on this occasion, and they cleared Stoke Summit at 70 m.p.h. *P. J. Coster.*

Bill doing his usual daily stint of firing on Quicksilver. *P. J. Coster.*

Bill leans out of the cab of Lord Faringdon at Retford, watching for the guard's "Right-Away". *Eric Treacy.*

Above left Bill at the controls of *Sir Nigel Gresley* doing 80 m.p.h. on the 1 p.m. from King's Cross on 22nd June, 1959. Note the Working Timetable on the seat. *Kenneth Leech*.

Above right Top-Link drivers from three Regions have a conversation at King's Cross before Bill leaves on No. 60156, *Great Central*. Sammy Gingell of Stewart's Lane (Southern Region) is in his working clothes, with Walter Harris of Old Oak Common (Western Region) behind him. *Kenneth Leech*.

A group in front of *Sir Nigel Gresley*, at King's Cross one evening before the departure of the "Yorkshire Pullman". Albert Leech stands behind Bill, with Allan Garraway on his left. *Rev. B. C. Bailey*.

Bill drives the late H. Philpot's 5"gauge 4-4-2 No. 5457 *Lady Lynne* on the occasion of the S.M.E.E.'s visit to Hayward's Heath in 1957. *The late H. Philpot*.

During a visit to Middlesbrough, Bill and the author visited Brian Hollingsworth's 3½" -gauge track at Croft Spa. Watched by Brian and his daughter, Bill stokes up No. 3051, *Stormy Petrel*, which was built by Dick Simmonds & Co.-"The original Backyard Foundry" -at Erith, Kent, in 1949.

Bill on the Tallyllyn Railway. This was his first acquaintance with the Welsh narrowgauge when he fired No. 4 *Edward Thomas* to Jeff Hayes on two round trips on 4th September, 1954. *A. G. W. Garraway*.

From the footplate of Sir Nigel Gresley. *Left*, crossing Welwyn Viaduct. *Right*, leaving King's Cross and passing under the bridge carrying the North London Line, with Copenhagen Tunnels ahead. One of the creep-ups leading to Top Shed can be seen immediately ahead of the smokebox, with the former Copenhagen Junction signal box on the right. *Kenneth Leech*.

The fireman 's view of Peterborough North as Bill brakes *Sir Nigel Gresley* down for the slow passage of the station. *Kenneth Leech*.

Bill slips the headlamp on the bracket of Lord Foringdon in Leeds Central Station. *Eric Treacy*.

V2 No. 60869 on the down "Flying Scotsman" passes Benningborough on 30th May, 1958, on the run described in Chapter VI. *C. Ord*.

Bill waves from the cab of Dominion of New Zealand on the down " Talisman" near Tollcrton. *C. Ord*.

Sir Nigel Gresley on the "Yorkshire Pullman" passing New Southgate. The tail of the 5.20 p.m. King's Cross-Hatfield can be seen under the bridge on the down slow line, and Bill would sometimes try and beat this train to New Southgate with the Pullman, managing it on at least one occasion. *P. J. Coster.*

Al Amadis near Benningborough on "266 Down", the King's Cross-Niddrie express goods. *C. Ord.*

Sir Nigel Gresley at the head of the King's Cross-Niddrie Goods passes the Midland Yard at Hitchin at 70 m.p.h. *P. J. Coster.*

Sir Nigel Gresley accelerates away from Peterborough Station with the up "Northumbrian" on 30th May, 1959, and out past Crescent Junction on the sharp climb up to the Nene Bridge. This was the journey with Jack Boston aboard that is described in Chapter VI. *R. F. Roberts*.

English Electric Type 4 No. D208 on the Up "Tees-Tyne Pullman" on 1st July, 1959, stands in the deserted No. 4 Platform at King's Cross at the end of the run. *R. F. Roberts*.

Bill in the cab of the prototype "Deltic" at Peterborough on 20th February, 1959. *A. Aylard*.

With the dynamometer car behind it, the prototype "Deltic" eases its train southwards out of York on one of the test runs from Newcastle in March, 1959, for which Bill drove. *C. Ord.*

Bill's last run. Merlin at the head of the up "Elizabethan " takes the curve at Chaloner Whin on 7th July, 1959, and with Alan Pegler and Alf Hancox visible in the cab, eases into King's Cross Station. *K. Len.*

With a double-yellow signal threatening in the distant, No. 990 and 251 leave Doncaster with the "Plant Centenarian" on 27th September, 1953. *W. G. Jackson.*

The "Westminster Bank Special". Bill with Inspector Sam Jenkins in the cab of *Flying Scotsman* at York on 3rd April, 1955. *Bill Hoole's Collection.*

On behalf of those aboard the train, Alan Pegler presents Bill with a clock at Doncaster after the down run of the S.L.S. "Golden Jubilee Special." *P. J. Coster.*

Bill autographs itineraries at Doncaster before the return trip of the S.L.S. "Golden Jubilee Special". Inspector Bert Dixon watches from the front of the tender. *P. J. Coster.*

Sir Nigel Gresley, in the lengthening evening shadows, storms up Stoke Bank at the head of the up S.L.S . "Golden Jubilee Special", before reaching 112 m.p.h. on the descent towards Peterborough. *P.H. Wells.*

With the speed in the 90s, *Union of South Africa* speeds the RCTS/SLS "Jubilee Requiem" northwards between Arlesey and Three Counties on 23rd October, 1964. *P. Riley.*

Jack Boston, President of the S.L.S., and Bill discuss a model of a Volga train ferry in the Museum of Science and Engineering at Newcastle on the occasion of the "Jubilee Requiem" on 23rd October, 1964.

Almost 30 years are covered by these three photographs of Sir Nigel Gresley. In pre-war days the locomotive, No. 4498, works the up "Flying Scotsman" through Naburn. *C. Ord.*

On 2nd June, 1962, she climbs Stoke Bank with a King's Cross-Leeds express. She spent another year at King's Cross, until Top Shed closed in June, 1963, and after 4 months at New England, migrated to Scotland. *P.H. Wells.*

In the summer of 1965, she leaves the Mound Tunnel at Edinburgh on the 10.30 Saturdays-only train for Aberdeen, which only operated for 10 weeks during the peak of the summer services. The leading vehicle is a former Great Western Railway coach. *P. Riley.*

Early days on the Festiniog. Bill prepares *Taliesin* at Boston Lodge for the 2.30 p.m. from the Harbour Station in September, 1956. Note the corrugated iron fencing, now removed. *J. Shores.*

The official opening of the 1957 Summer Service on the Festiniog. From left to right in this group, taken before the departure of the first train from Portmadoc Harbour Station, are Mr. W. B. Broadbent (a Director of the Festiniog Railway Company), Messrs. E. Roberts & I. C. Jones (Members of the Portmadoc Council), Alan Pegler, Major-General Ll. Wansbrough-Jones (Secretary General B.T.C.), Bill, and Allan Garraway. *Bill Hoole's Collection.*

Bill eases *Earl of Merioneth* over Lottie's Crossing with a down train in August, 1962, while Lottie herself waves to the fireman on the other side of the locomotive. *D. Mackintosh.*

Above left At Tan-y-Bwlch on 13th September, 1960, Bill stands with Bessie Jones, while his fireman. Alan Ramage, sits behind them at one of the tables outside the Jones' house. *R. F. Roberts.*

Above right The staffs of the various narrow-gauge railways throughout the country get together from time to time. In 1965 a party from the Festiniog visited the Romney, Hythe and Dymchurch Railway in Kent, where George Barlow, the Senior driver on the R. H. & D. R., gave Bill the opportunity of preparing and driving his regular engine, the 15" Pacific *Green Goddess*, which is a third-size replica of one of the original Gresley Als. *G. A. Barlow.*

Left Bill at the regulator of No. 4498 *Sir Nigel Gresley* with Dolly behind him on the footplate.

the Bls that first prompted the scheme, as Thompson wanted a consecutive series for the several hundred locomotives of this class that were planned. Although the scheme was complete on paper in 1943, because of the war it was not possible to implement it until 1946, so that some interim renumberings were necessary to allow newly constructed engines to take their correct place in the new list. In addition to these complications, just after the renumbering had been started, it was decided to alter the system as it affected the larger engines, and a few A3s and A4s first sported numbers in the five hundreds before settling down to those with which we are now familiar. To the author, brought up on the orderliness and simplicity of the G.W.R. numbering scheme, the new L.N.E.R. system was a great improvement, but there was considerable comment from those railway enthusiasts whose expertise enabled them to find their way through the old system, which, incidentally, had appreciably added to the difficulties experienced by Ian Allan with the production of his early ABCs.

A. H. Peppercorn succeeded Thompson in 1946, and was responsible for increasing the East Coast Route's stud of Pacifics very considerably. His first locomotive, A2 No. 525, carried his own name, and was turned out in December 1947, just before Nationalisation. Compared with the Thompson Pacifics, the wheelbase was shorter, and the result was a much neater locomotive, but like certain of the previous members of the class, the choice of names for some of them, such as Herringbone and Bachelor's Button, was somewhat unfortunate. After Nationalisation, Peppercorn stayed on at Doncaster for some time before receiving a golden handshake, and it was in 1948 that the first of his Als appeared. Using the same boiler, cylinders, and motion as his A2s, they were fitted with plain double chimneys, but the subsequent fitting of lips to them improved their appearance very considerably, demonstrating again how the chimney of a locomotive plays an aesthetic part far out of keeping with its size. Hidden behind the right-hand smoke deflector was a small electric turbo-generator that provided power for the electric headlights and for the cab. Other new locomotives, such as the Bls and Lls, were similarly fitted with this arrangement at about the same period, but this modern form of lighting did not have a universal success. In twelve months over £10,000 worth of damage was done to the generator systems in one Region as a result of misuse by enginemen, while elsewhere defects were either not reported or no one was made responsible for their upkeep. As a result of the expensive upkeep, the generators disappeared, and the 19th century oil lamps returned to their customary place on the front buffer beam instead of being perched on top of the electric lights to provide the correct headcode during daylight. To begin with, only the first Al No.60114 was named, and this was christened after W. P. Allen, the former General Secretary of A.S.L.E.F., at a ceremony at King's Cross in October 1948. In 1950, partly as a result of suggestions made by members of the R.C.T.S., the remaining 48 engines in the class were allocated names. These formed one of the happiest sets ever to be used on an L.N.E.R. class, ranging from the traditional racehorses (with nothing as unsuitable as Herringbone again) and birds, to characters from the Waverley novels, while others commemorated former C.M.E.s. The solitary Gresley rebuild, Great Northern, was joined by locomotives bearing the names and coats of arms of the other constituent companies of the L.N.E.R., and Bill was always very pleased when he was subsequently rostered to drive No. 60156 Great Central. The Als, however, never rose to the heights that Gresley's A4s attained pre-war, or were to achieve in the final days of steam express workings on the East Coast line. Even in 1965, the remaining Als were usually only to be found on freight turns, while the last of the A4s were still hard at work on the 3-hour expresses between Glasgow and Aberdeen, flattening out the gradients in a manner that often exceeds the capabilities of a 2,000 h.p. diesel.

By the end of the 1940s, therefore, the East Coast Route had a stud of 202 Pacifics already in existence or building, plus the solitary Wl 4-6-4, and in addition another 184 V2s. In spite of this vast concentration of motive power, things reached such an ebb that at one time King's Cross had nearly twice as many Pacifics as booked diagrams and even then was frequently reduced to putting V2s on express passenger workings. Various small improvements were made to the Gresley Pacifics, however, and from 1943 onwards, starting with No. 4499, Sir Murrough Wilson, they had their maximum cut-off increased from 65 to 75 per cent., which considerably improved their starting characteristics, markedly reducing the number of occasions when a driver had to go through the time-consuming effort of reversing the locomotive and setting back slightly before he could get a heavy train away properly. The few remaining Pacifics with right-hand controls, dating from the time when this was the Great Northern practice, were converted to left-hand drive, so that the driver's view of the track ahead was always the same regardless of what locomotive he was driving. Self-cleaning smokeboxes were fitted to the V2s as well, which cut down the amount of char to be dug out by the crews on disposal duties, but initially affected their steaming capabilities.

In 1951, the first of the British Railways' standard classes appeared, when No. 70000, Britannia, was built at Crewe. Although it was some time before a standard design appeared at King's Cross, the new locomotives caused considerable interest amongst railwaymen and enthusiasts while the "Britannias", in spite of their hard riding characteristics, soon revolutionised the services from Liverpool Street to Norwich. With the start of the summer services that year, 12 "Britannias", aided by three borrowed "West Country" Pacifics, worked the new even-interval services, which were faster than anything previously scheduled in East Anglia, so much so that the ten best trains between London and Norwich were faster than the top ten that the Western Region were running between London and Bristol. The introduction of these locomotives, however, was not without some upsets. It was first of all discovered that they fouled an electrification support while they were being turned on the Liverpool Street table, and there were then a number of troubles with their piston heads, Britannia herself pushing the end one off one of the cylinders on her second day in regular service, which gave one of Richard Hardy's Ipswich engines a chance to show its capabilities. These were minor mishaps, however, compared with the events later that year, which came to a head when No. 70004 William Shakespeare broke a connecting rod on October 21st while hauling the up "Golden Arrow". This was caused by one of the driving wheels shifting on its axle, and followed three more similar incidents, so that on the following day the whole class was withdrawn from serviceand stored or sent to Crewe. It was not until early December that the first reappeared in service, with the hollow axles plugged to ensure that the wheels gripped them more firmly. There were two other similar crises on British Railways during these years, which also involved the wholesale withdrawal of a locomotive class, and these concerned older designs, one of them going back as far as 1927. This was the "King" class on the Western, which suddenly had a spate of bogie trouble, and a few L.M.S. Pacifics came across from the West Coast Route to help out, while the other case involved the Bulleid Pacifics on the Southern, which urgently borrowed some "Britannias", V2s and Bls to cover the gap in their motive power. It is thus salutary to recall that the sort of trouble that has befallen the introduction of diesel and electric motive power in recent years was not unknown in the realms of steam.

It must not be inferred from this account of the introduction of new locomotive classes that British Railways were able to build all the new engines they required. The national shortage of steel resulted in annual allocations to the various industries, and in 1952 the railways were forced to halve their locomotive building to a figure of 183 new engines, while the passenger coach programme was cut out completely, although they had hoped to complete the backlog of new construction left over from the previous two years. Even the 1953 programme only comprised 306 locomotives (237 of them steam), whereas in 1950 the total had come to 414.

While these new locomotives were entering service, a number of classes that had been well known to Bill were disappearing from the scene. The last G.N. Atlantic was withdrawn in November 1950, the Eastern Region marking the occasion by arranging for the locomotive to haul an excursion to Doncaster, which then returned behind the Al, H. A. Ivatt. Five days later saw the withdrawal of the last of the Great Central Atlantics, less famous than their Great Northern counterparts, but vastly superior in the gracefulness of their appearance, which had earned them the nickname of "Jersey Lilies", after Lily Langtry, the noted Edwardian beauty. The withdrawal of No. 2918 also marked the disappearance of the Atlantic wheel arrangement from the Eastern Region, but the Brighton engines were to keep alive the lvatt tradition on the Southern for another few years. In 1951 the last Great Northern tender engine, with the exception of the Pacifics, disappeared too, when the 4-4-0 No. 62000 was withdrawn. The number of locomotives withdrawn each year was considerably in excess of new construction, the total in 1950 amounting to no less than 591.

During the early 1950s, steel was not the only major basic commodity whose shortage was causing national concern, and consequent difficulties to the railways, as well as lost revenue. There had been a chronic crisis with coal supplies ever since the end of the war, and the whole nation was working on a hand-to-mouth basis well before the end of each winter. During the near-arctic conditions of early 1947, domestic supplies of electricity were even cut off for much of the day, because of the lack of coal for the power stations. In the late Autumn of 1950, a number of train services were withdrawn to save coal, and after being restored at Christmas-time, further cuts were made in mid-January. Even such well-known trains as the "Queen of Scots" were suspended, the Pullman stock being stored just south of Knnebworth. While only selected main-line trains were taken off, some services were suspended completely, including the Palace Gates-Seven Sisters' trains, one of whose G5s had recently caused national interest when it made off with its train without anyone aboard. When the cuts were restored in time for the Easter holidays, it was announced that the object had been to save 10,000 tons of coal a week. The fuel shortages in the South of England were clearly not solely due to mining difficulties, as there was a special "drive" during December 1950 to move as much coal as possible from the Peterborough area to London, in time for Christmas. In spite of these cuts by the railways during the winter, the problem of adequate fuel supplies was still not solved, and at short notice the summer services in 1951 were suddenly curtailed so that they lasted only from July 2nd to September 9th, and even the weekly mileage was down by 11,000 compared with the previous year. Now we are conditioned to one timetable a year, it is worth recalling that in 1949 they lasted from May 23rd to September 25th, and the year before even extended into October. This particular change resulted in considerable alterations to the King's Cross locomotive workings, and as a consequence Bill did not get into the Top Link for the duration of the summer services that year, although he had started to learn the road north of Grantham again at the end of May. In 1949, British Railways' total coal bill came to £36m. for the 15m. tons they used, but the consumption per engine mile was 25 per cent. up on pre-war figures, and on the Eastern Region averaged practically 65 lbs. per mile.

The railways had reacted to the coal shortage in other ways too. On the G.W.R., a number of locomotives were converted to oil firing just after the war, an odd twist for a company which had once owed much of its prosperity to the handling of vast quantities of Welsh coal. In 1946 the idea was taken up by the Ministry of Fuel in a big way, who produced a plan to convert 1,200 locomotives, which would have saved a million tons of coal per year. By September 1947, by which time 93 conversions had been made, this grandiose plan suddenly received a set-back -the necessary oil fuel supplies were not available either. The annual running cost of these few locomotives was over a quarter of a million pounds higher than with coal, and the British Transport Commission pointed out that had the full scheme been completed, the additional cost would have been £3.5m. a year. After the expenditure of £1.5m., therefore, the locomotives were changed back, and the fuelling installations kept in good condition for a few years, while mountains of tender oil tanks rusted away at such places as Gateshead. The former L.N.E.R. were the slowest at getting their scheme going, and Bill therefore had no occasion to try out another type of firing.

The general condition of the track on the East Coast Route, which had already suffered from the neglect of the war years, was not helped by the shortage of materials, and the abnormal weather conditions also played havoc with it. The winter of 1947 brought about the general reintroduction of a 60 m.p.h. speed limit for a time, while floods also caused damage, first at Selby, and then in the summer of 1948 came the wholesale wash-outs in the Border country north of Berwick. Following torrential rain, the River Eye became a raging torrent and swept away each of the bridges where the railway crossed it, while Penmanshiel Tunnel flowed with water to within a few feet of its crown. The closure of the line for some weeks resulted in the Newcastle-Edinburgh trains being worked via Tweedmouth and Kelso. The "Flying Scotsman" went this way too, and although the timetable showed calls for water and banking assistance, some of the keener crews worked through without a halt, thus setting up a new record non-stop distance for this country of 408.6 miles. When the following summer services came round, the bridge rebuilding was still taking place and the running time of the "Capitals Limited" became 8 hours, to allow for the successive checks as the A4s brought their trains down to 5 m.p.h. to tiptoe over the girders of temporary bridges, while bulldozers scarred the adjoining hillsides. It was on May 23rd that year that this train first ran, replacing the "Flying Scotsman" as the non-stop summer service, leaving a quarter of an hour in advance of it in the down direction, and half an hour in the up. The keenness and fine work of the East Coast enginemen was again demonstrated some years later when, after another blockage north of Newcastle, one crew set out to run non-stop from Carlisle to King's Cross, which they achieved except for a momentary halt to drop the pilot driver on the relief line alongside Newcastle Central Station. In those days Bawtry Viaduct had not yet begun to provide one more demonstration of the weakness of arched construction when subjected to the effects of colliery subsidence, but there were other bad slowings, notably at Hougham and at Huntingdon, which lasted for a very long time, with consequent detriment to the running times. The great tidal surge of 1 953, which inundated the whole of the East Coast from the Tees to Dover, fortunately was without any direct effect on the G.N. main line, although other routes were very badly hit indeed.

6

As will be apparent from the description of the physical difficulties that faced British Railways in the 10 years after the end of the war, the train services in this country took a long time to regain anything resembling their 1939 standards, equally as much on the East Coast Route as elsewhere. To those who were anxiously hoping for some rise in speeds, however small, successive issues of the timetables usually brought little but disappointment. There were tantalising glimpses of the former glory too, on occasions of special runs, and as early as May 1946, Silver King worked a six coach special to Edinburgh and back on successive days. In spite of the 60 m.p.h. limit south of Hatfield, times of less than 94 minutes were achieved in each direction between King's Cross and Grantham, and on the up trip a maximum of 102 m.p.h. was attained down Stoke-the first post-war "ton", and only the seventh such run to which Cecil J. Allen was able to refer in his account that appeared in the "Railway Magazine" for May/June 1947. Ten years later the Top Link drivers at King's Cross were probably chalking up as many 100s inside a week, but there were many difficult years through which they had first to pass. Silver Fox had put up some fine running on the racing stretch from Darlington to York, achieving a time of 33 minutes pass-to-stop, and it was over these 44.1 miles that the first post-war mile-a-minute booking was introduced in the autumn of 1949. This was with the evening Glasgow Leeds train, which, in line with contemporary practice, was named the "North Briton", and allowed only 44 minutes for this stretch, which proved an easy task for the usual A3. The following summer, the "Norse man", running twice-weekly non-stop to York, was given a 188-minute booking, so that it too, came into the mile-a-minute class.

There were occasional flashes of better running, such as in October 1951, when Driver Ted Hailstone twice brought the up "Tees-Tyne Pullman" in eight minutes early, although this represented nothing better than an overall time of 238 minutes for the 232 miles. Things improved, however, over the next 18 months, so that in February 1953 he achieved a run in even time, although as long ago previously as 1947, Driver Marrable had achieved this distinction with Walter K. Whigham. That year, 1953, in the summer timetable, the up train was given a 60 m.p.h. booking from Darlington, and to my old friend Frank Mayes fell the task of firing on the inaugural run. Driver Charlie Simmons was at the regulator of Quicksilver, and from Darlington southwards they were joined by Inspector Bert Dixon and a representative from The Times. Fortified by some refreshments brought through the tender by the Pullman Conductor at Peterborough, they ran in to King's Cross six minutes early, and a fine photograph of the train appeared on the back page of the paper next day. This was Frank's first week in the Top Link, and it is of interest to recall, in passing, that during the eight days he worked no less than 2,454 miles, including three round trips to York, each of which contributed 376 miles.

The autumn of 1952 had seen the introduction of a fast morning train from King's Cross to Bradford, with a corresponding up working in the evening, which was allowed 127 minutes for the 124 miles from Hitchin to Doncaster. In the summer of 1953this allowance was cut by 14 minutes, so that it now averaged all but 66 m.p.h. over this section. Still higher speeds were required of it that autumn when a stop was inserted at Retford, but such was the slow deterioration in Eastern Region running, that by the summer of 1957 this was the only remaining mile-a-minute booking, with 103 minutes allowed for the 106.7 miles. There had been a brief rivalry between this train and the "Bristolian" on the Western Region, which was accelerated to its pre-war timing, giving it an average of 67.6 m.p.h., but nothing further came of the challenge, and both trains lapsed back to easier timings. In the winter services for 1953, the "Bradford Flyer", as it was nicknamed, had grown a Newcastle portion, running non-stop from Doncaster to Darlington, and providing a very useful businessmen's service for the North East. In the timetable revolutions that took place in late 1957, the North East "won" this train from the West Riding, and it became one of the regular King's Cross A4 workings.

After the introduction of the "Capitals Limited" in 1949, it was not until the summer of 1955 that the "Flying Scotsman" again started running non-stop to and from Newcastle, with a timing of 276 minutes in the up direction for the 268.4 miles. Unfortunately in the following winter, the Grantham stop was reinserted, and the train was promptly decelerated by 35 minutes in the up direction and 30 in the down. Worse was to come, however, in the following year, when, having regained the same summer schedules, the additional times came to no less than 42 and 35 minutes respectively, due very largely to the wholesale increase in recovery margins that dotted the East Coast working timetable. At one time it had been customary to alter the times of the "Flying Scotsman" every summer by removing a few minutes recovery time at Peterborough, only to put them back again the following winter, and an amusing exchange ensued in the columns of "Trains Illustrated", between Cecil J. Allen and G. F. Fiennes, the Great Northern Line Traffic Manager. The latter's urge for speed, which has enlivened the Western Region, or Gerry's Wonderful Railway, as it was sometimes known while he was its General Manager, really made itself felt on the East Coast Route in 1957, when there were wholesale accelerations, planned by him, Sidney Millard and Stuart Ward. In the days when we had two timetables a year, it was usually customary to introduce any faster schedules in the summer, so that crews would have the better weather during which to accustom themselves to the new workings. The 1957 speed-up, however, came in the autumn, after the summer timetables for that year had represented the saddest picture for very many years. The "Elizabethan" (as the non-stop working had been called since 1953) was accelerated in 1954 to 6½ hours for its 393 mile run, but fell back by five minutes, thus dropping it just below the mile-a-minute average, which was never to be reattained during the remaining five years for which it was steam operated. Even the "Talis man", the new high-speed train to and from Edinburgh, which was introduced in the winter of 1956 with mile-a-minute bookings to and from Newcastle, also dropped below the line. The poor showing of the Eastern Region was contrasted too by the North Eastern's efforts, where they were steadily increasing the number of bookings at 60 or over be tween York and Darlington, which by the summer of 1957 were totalling 15 a day.

This review has taken us forward for nearly nine years from the date of the New Southgate incident, and has described the conditions on the East Coast Route, with only scant reference to Bill and the part he played during this time, to give an overall picture of how things developed during his Top Link days, rather than refer to the various changes in chronological order, as they made their impact on him.

7

From Bill's diaries, 1949 seems to have been a comparatively uneventful year, with a variety of jobs and locomotives coming his way in the Express Goods Link. The turns were relatively unexacting, and he had little to complain about on the engines from the mechanical point of view, although when he got No. 60508 on March 27th, he promptly booked her with a faulty injector. He reported a Bl (No. 1203) as not steaming in February, and on November 4th No. 60134 ran hot on a turn to Hitchin. Meat specials cropped up from time to time amongst his workings, most of which were night-hours ones, it being fairly uncommon for him to book on during the day. Als, A2s, A3s, V2s, and Bls alternated with Lls, K3s, and "Austerities", and it was rare or virtually unknown for him to handle the same locomotive on two successive nights.

If 1949 had been relatively quiet, 1950 produced a lot more excitement for Bill, since for the first time he was called on to go into the Top Link for the summer workings. For most of May, therefore, he was learning the road to Leeds, and then had a week working "1252 Down", having to stop and take water at Hitchin on the Friday night as the level was too low in Langley troughs for No. 61865 to pick up sufficient water. After another seven days learning the Leeds road, he spent three weeks on the Newcastle run. When a driver is booked to learn the road like this, he is left fairly well to his own devices. A pass is issued to enable him to travel on the footplates of trains over the route, seeing how the driver operates his train, or even, on occasion, copes with the emergency that follows a dropped middle big-end, as occurred on June 14th, with V2 No. 60895 between Hett Mill and Browney. It is of course impossible to become familiar with the lines in an area such as York just on the strength of a few journeys through the station on the main line, especially when it is recalled that, at that time, the colour lights ended at Skelton Junction, and the drivers were faced with a forest of semaphores as they progressed from box to box. The drill therefore was for a driver to stop off at places such as this, and make a thorough inspection of the lines and signalling, visiting the signal boxes to ask questions if any points required clarification. Bill is a great observer of human nature, and always enjoyed looking for the differences that characterise the staff at each railway centre, getting the feeling of the place from his discussions with the signalmen and people on the platform. It is very hard to tie him down specifically on what he saw and heard, in the same way as it is impossible to get Bill to describe how he worked a particular locomotive. On these occasions his hand goes out to an invisible regulator and reversing wheel, so that the demonstration over, one is none the wiser, although given an A4 under one's feet, much more would become a good deal clearer! Each day, when he got back home or to his lodgings, he would do his homework, writing down every signal so that he built up his own diagram of the route.

A driver is never pushed to sign the route book before he is happy about it, but if he takes too long, an inspector has a word with him in his office to help him over any difficulties. It is of course, easy to memorise a route from sitting in the cab of a locomotive, especially a diesel one, but it is another thing altogether to drive a train to time at high speed over the same line under conditions of pitch blackness or fog. This ability can come only from experience, but knowledge of the whereabouts of every signal is vital from the beginning. As Bill put it in a broadcast he made just after his retirement: "It's a wonderful feeling to go right through being able to meet all obstacles with the profound knowledge you have learned and picked up." This is especially true when a blizzard strikes during the night, sweeping all the landmarks clean, with no indications at all where you are, and Bill added that to get through at all under these conditions was a wonderful feeling in itself, especially if the wires were down and it was necessary to stop at each successive box to obtain permission to proceed, on the time-interval system.

Bill's first turns in the Top Link very much dropped him

in at the deep end, as on Sunday, 25th June, he worked down to Edinburgh with No. 60029, Woodcock, on the 11.00 a.m. from King's Cross, changing over at Newcastle with the Scottish driver with whom he was to share the task of working the up "Capitals Limited" the following day. The first round trip was uneventful, but on the up journey on the Wednesday, still on Woodcock, he dropped 10 minutes between York and Grantham due to his fireman being over-enthusiastic with the small coal in the tender after the change-over, but they got in on time nevertheless. On the Thursday and Friday they had No. 60003 Andrew K. McCosh instead, and it was the engine's turn to let them down badly, as on the return trip they had to change it for No. 61860 at Hitchin. They were stopped at the column to take water because they were being diverted via Hertford, and had just got under way again when the middle piston head broke in the middle, allowing the rod to travel freely.

The locomotive change at Hitchin on 30th June was only the first of several lots of similar trouble that Bill encountered during the summer of 1950. On Saturday, 4th August, he was late off shed to work to Peter borough and back on an overnight turn, because a V2 failed, and on the following Monday, working the 9.40 a.m. to Newcastle, he had to change No. 60092 Fairway for the Darlington pilot, another A3, No. 60070 Gladiateur. On the Wednesday of that week, No. 60122 Curlew had valve trouble, which cost them four minutes between York and Darlington, while a week later the tender feed pipe on No. 60110 Robert the Devil burst while they were at Peterborough. Five days later, on Monday, August 21st, they were coming south with the 12.15 p.m. from Newcastle on No. 60063 Isinglass, but it would not steam, so Bill stopped at Peter borough and replaced it with a V2, No. 60854.

Early in September, Bill had almost a fortnight on the "Capitals Limited", as a result of some changed rosters, and going down to Edinburgh on Sunday, 10th, on the 11 a.m. from King's Cross, Andrew K. McCosh was caught by the bugbear of the A4s, a hot middle big end, and had to be replaced by a V2, No.

60938, at Pilmoor. For those who were not familiar with this particular weakness of the streamliners, it is worth recalling that, because of the enclosed situation of the middle big end, a tell-tale stink bomb device had been incorporated during the war to give the crew an early warning of any overheating, which would enable them to stop before any appreciable damage was caused by the bearing seizing. Various different scents were tried out in the bomb, varying from aniseed through violets to garlic. Inspector Harry Stevens, of Exmouth Junction on the Southern Region, told me of the unpleasant smell that pervaded the Dynamometer Car when Mallard had run hot near Gillingham during the Interchange Trials and the rueful expressions of the Eastern Region men as they explained the reasons for it. Unfortunately, drops of the fluid sometimes dropped on the track and gave rise to false alarms. An A4 had its bomb go off at Darlington one day, and a number of drivers were misled into thinking that their locomotive had run hot. The totally enclosed nature of the streamlining on an A4 meant that the big end did not get as much natural draught while the engine was running, and in addition, because of the darkness it was not so easy to inspect while the locomotive was being prepared. Gresley's conjugated valve gear also often resulted in the centre cylinder doing more than its fair share of work, especially when the pins became worn, or the levers whipped at high speed, with consequent detriment to the long-suffering middle big end. When Swindon carried out controlled tests on a V2 in early 1953, both on the testing plant as well as on the road, it was found that the indicator diagrams for the inside cylinder were at times very lopsided, with one end doing over twice the work of the other, and the two ends combined frequently producing more than a third of the total output. Various expedients were tried to overcome the trouble, a number of A4s having the inner cylinder lined down to 17" diameter instead of the usual 18½". As a result of constant complaint from the running authorities, K. J. Cook, the Chief Mechanical and Electrical Engineer, redesigned the middle big end. The new one was of Great Western pattern with a thin-lined white metal bearing, which overcame this handicap of the A4s, but even then Bill, like most other drivers, still preferred to run with the inspection doors on the sides of the casing left open to promote the maximum air-flow through the inside motion.

With the end of the Summer Services on 24th September, Bill returned to the Express Goods Link, and his wages dropped accordingly as the amount of mileage came down. On one of his weeks on the "Capitals Limited" he was paid for no less than 145¾ hours, which brought his wages up to £23 0s. 2d., plus a lodging allowance of £2 12s. 9d. These figures should be compared with the basic rate for a driver of six years standing which was then £6 18s. a week, with an additional rent allowance of three shillings in the London area, making up the £7 ls. that Bill received for the second week in October when he was on holiday in the West Country. Most crews usually looked forward to their week on the "Non-stop" because of the high rate of pay, and the challenge of trying to get through without a stop. In addition to the normal payments, each crew was given full lunch in the restaurant car, before or after they changed over, nominally at Tollerton. On the down run, the Haymarket men would come through the tender soon after the train had passed York.

By the time the two crews had exchanged information on the state of the locomotive, they would be approaching Thirsk with the speed well into the 70s, which was about the point where the Londoners picked up their belongings and made the rough journey back through the rocking tender, with the engine and track noises magnified by the water tank on their right. A turn to the right and a step down brought them to the corridor connection, where, as the door slid closed behind them, the sounds of the footplate lapsed into those familiar to the ordinary passenger. A wash in the lavatory and a change into clean clothes in a compartment reserved for the train crews quickly put them in a relaxed mood, ready to do justice to the chef's meal. They were also entitled to a free afternoon tea later on as the A4 ate up the last few miles across the gently undulating gradients of East Lothian, so by the time the brakes went on for the last time to bring them to a stand in Waverley station, they were ready to go off for an evening's sightseeing, giving a cheery wave to the Scottish crew on the footplate as they made their way to the barrier.

When the September issue of the "Railway Magazine" appeared in 1950, the only tabular log that Cecil J. Allen included in his monthly series on "British Locomotive Practice and Performance" turned out to be a run of Bill's. Timed by Mr. G. W. Carpenter on 29th April, it was on the 11.30 p.m. Saturday train to Newcastle, which Bill and Fireman Easterbrook were working with V2 No. 60889. The run was an excellent one for those days, with a net time of 77 minutes for the 76.4 miles to Peterborough, in spite of a 14-coach load grossing 510 tons. In the published account, details were given of the working of the locomotive, and mention made of the fact that the boiler had been priming in the early stages. Bill was delighted with this bit of publicity, the first he was to receive during his time on British Railways, and the details were written in the front of his diary. He did not continue this practice as the years rolled by, which was perhaps as well as there would scarcely have been room for all his published runs, even allowing for the better supply of paper, which from 1951 onwards enabled the A.S.L.E.F. diary to double its number of pages. He was, however, always very pleased to receive logs of any runs from people who had timed his efforts.

9

As already mentioned, 1951 was an exceedingly difficult year for the railways, with wholesale cuts because of the coal shortage. On the East Coast Line the Pacifics were being expected to run vast distances between shoppings, A1 No. 60136 Alcazar achieving 130,000 miles, while one of the roller-bearing members of the class, Great Central, chalked up

11,600 miles in four weeks, with A3 Robert the Devil less than 1,000 miles behind. Only in about_one in three of the round trip workings between King's Cross and Newcastle, however, were the diagrammed workings being achieved, and the Heaton A2s on the morning train from Sunderland and Saltburn to London were frequently arriving with next to no coal left. Some of the difficulties were due to the absence of a turntable at Grantham capable of handling a Pacific, since the larger of their two had been out of use since early in the previous year. A triangle was constructed during the summer, however, and when the winter timetables came in, ten Als and eight A3s were transferred there from King's Cross, together with another Al from Copley Hill. Their two A4s, however, went to King's Cross in exchange, so that shed now had 19 streamliners and Wl No. 60700. Both at Grantham and King's Cross the policy was adopted of allocating regular locomotives to the Top Link crews, and the practice of changing locomotives on most trains at Peterborough or Grantham was reintroduced, in contrast to the diametrically opposite policy of a year earlier. The result was to remove a lot of the work from King's Cross, where it had become increasingly difficult to obtain the necessary labour, which had consequently caused the maintenance to suffer accordingly.

For some time Grantham crews and locomotives had been working the "Flying Scotsman" in both directions to Newcastle and King's Cross, but they now took a hand in many more through workings. On the other hand, the only King's Cross turns to Newcastle were the "Tees-Tyne Pullman" and the "Night Scotsman", and there were another two to Leeds and back. York engines were the only ones from the North Eastern Region to get through to London, the Heaton and Gateshead locomotives coming off at Grantham and using the triangle to turn. These changed arrangements produced a marked improvement in East Coast timekeeping and morale, and the absence of Langley troughs for five months, while a subway was built late that year and early the next, did not cause too many upsets, in spite of extra stops being made for water on certain trains. The A4s at King's Cross now started to run much greater mileages, No. 60014 Silver Link topping the 7,000 mark over a three-week period early in 1952, and achieving 30,000 in four months. Reports spoke of "New Life" brought to the East Coast line, and by May speed trials were being carried out again between London and Doncaster with Ted Hailstone at the regulator of No. 60003 Andrew K. McCosh. In July it was an A3's turn to be tried on the test runs, and Ted took 500 tons behind No. 60056 Centenary to Doncaster in 154 minutes for the 156 miles. The use of No. 60056 on the special runs in July was very appropriate, since 1952 marked the centenaries of both the "Towns" line from Werrington Junction to Retford, as well as that of King's Cross itself, and an exhibition was held in the station during October. At the end of September, the "Centenaries Express" to York and back was organised by Alan Pegler, L. J. Smith and H. T. S. Bailey. With Charlie Simmons driving No. 60007, Sir Nigel Gresley, a maximum speed of 85 m.p.h. was achieved, but this was tame compared with what was to come a year later.

It was not until the summer of 1952 that Bill again got into the Top Link and he spent four weeks relearning the road north of Grantham. In the intervening two years there had been a considerable number of changes, including the colour light signalling at York, which was commissioned in May 1951. As bad luck was to have it, Bill collected the only locomotive failure on the "Capitals Limited" in the summer of 1952, when he found the middle big end of No. 60027 Merlin was hot when he took over at Tollerton on August 14th. They stopped at York and collected A2 No. 60521 Watling Street as a replacement. During the summer, Merlin was nevertheless the A4 that achieved the largest number of consecutive runs on this train, her total of 28 being followed after four days rest by another 14. On the day after the failure, Bill was working down on No. 60004 William Whitelaw when his fireman had his left arm injured when the scoop lever spun round as they ran on to Scrooby troughs. In spite of getting a nasty knock, he worked through to Tollerton, and refused attention at Edinburgh. Coming up on the Saturday, he was in a bad way, but an inspector who was on the footplate did most of the firing, and they were able to reach King's Cross on time. The fireman then went to hospital, and subsequently had his arm in plaster for quite a long time. This week on the "Non-stop" brought Bill in £27 17s. 3d., but, unfortunately for him, it was the only time he was on this working during that summer. By now, rates of pay had gone up, as, from October 1951 the top weekly rate for drivers had been increased to £8 ls. 6d. Even so, during this week, Bill had earned over three times the basic wage while working on the most highly-paid locomotive diagram in the country.

10

In the morning of October 8th 1952, No. 46242 City of Glasgow was approaching Harrow and Wealdstone station at about 60 m.p.h. on the 8.15 p.m. from Perth. For reasons that will never be known, Driver R. S. Jones missed the signals protecting an up local train in the station, and the two trains collided, with such violence that all the station clocks were stopped by the shock of the impact. Before any protecting action could be taken, a double-headed down express struck the wreckage at full speed, so that when the locomotives were extracted from the wreckage, both were only fit for scrapping, while in the tangled remains of coaches, footbridge, and permanent way, 112 people died, a total only previously exceeded by the wartime accident at Quintinshill in 1915. When the report by Col. Wilson appeared, as was not unexpected, considerable stress was laid on the advantages of Automatic Train Control, or A.T.C., which gave the driver an audible indication of each distant signal in the cab, applying the brake too, if it was at caution. The G.W.R. had started installing their own contact system as long ago as 1908, and another type, the Hudd, had been tried out on the Tilbury line by the L.M.S. in the 1930s.

Shortly after Nationalisation, British Railways announced that they were developing a new system of their own of more widespread applicability, and in 1950 the main line between New Barnet and Huntingdon was equipped with the necessary track magnets. Several of the King's Cross engines also carried the appropriate receiving gear, but a number of teething troubles ensued which caused a long hold-up. After the Harrow accident, a new impetus was given to the work, and early the following year it was announced that 50 Eastern Region locomotives were to be fitted with the now-familiar equipment with its black and yellow warning indicator on the boiler backplate, while the warning siren and all-clear bell were bolted to the cab roof. Later that year there were a number of test runs over the G.N. main line, with the Ministry of Transport observers aboard. Mallard worked a 14-coach train of L.N.E.R. stock on 25th March, Driver Burgess, with a month to go before his retirement, averaging 90 m.p.h. between Hitchin and Huntingdon. Four weeks later, Ted Hailstone had a go with B.R. standard coaches behind Lord Faringdon to test the different behaviour of the various types of stock to an emergency brake application by the A.T.C. apparatus.

It is interesting to recall that at the time great stress was laid on the high cost of equipment which only served as an additional safety device, but no account was taken in public announcements of the greater freedom to run at high speed in fog that results. This freedom must result in appreciable savings for the railways, and in an article that no one would publish in 1953, I suggested that, taking these savings into account, the use of A.T.C. on the main lines would give a return of over 10 per cent. on the investment. Only a few years later, in a radio broadcast, G. F. Fiennes was able to boast of the up "Master Cutler" being able to average almost 70 m.p.h. from Retford to London in continuous fog that reduced visibility to no more than 50 yards, although the road must have been very clear. However, to those used to running into Paddington in thick fog and averaging a mile-a-minute through the suburbs under conditions that once made my train take three minutes to traverse the length of the terminal platform, these advantages did not come as such a great surprise. Bill quickly became used to the valuable indications given to him by this Automatic Warning System, or A.W.S., as it was soon officially renamed, and one of my earliest memories of him is that of inviting my sister into the cab of an A4 at King's Cross and showing her how it worked. Indirectly, too, it was the coming of the A.W.S. which was the cause of Bill Hoole going to the Festiniog Railway in North Wales after his retirement. This arose from the appointment in September 1953 of Allan Garraway as Technical Assistant to the Motive Power Superintendent, responsible for the A.W.S. During the next two years he got to know Bill very well from his numerous footplate trips with him, and in their spare time, introduced him to the joys of the narrow gauge in Wales. In 1955, Allan was offered the job of Manager and Engineer of the Festiniog and resigned from British Railways, so that he was to be in charge of Bill at Portmadoc after the latter had retired in 1959.

11

In February 1953, my old friend Frank Mayes was promoted from the Express Goods Link to the No. 2 Link, and found himself firing for Bill during the next twelve weeks. I had first met Frank, a brawny 6ft. 2in. lad from Barnsley, when he was firing a banking engine on the 1 in 40 Worsborough Bank. Never one to be overlooked, especially during the games of dominoes or pool in Wentworth Junction box between trains, he had taken the opportunity to move to King's Cross when electrification removed the need for the banking engines. One day he found a group in King's Cross sheds eagerly scanning the new rosters, ribbing each other about the various drivers with whom they would be working in future. Frank's arrival was greeted with great mirth, and the warning that he would get a wet shirt the following Monday, as he was now to fire for Bill Hoole.

V

During the spring of 1953, Bill and Frank struck up a great friendship as a result of their work together, and Frank has been able to tell me many of Bill's driving methods and ways of working. In his own article in the January 1964 issue of the "Railway World", Frank described how, on his first trip with Bill, he was told to get into "The Seat" of No. 60010 Dominion of Canada as they left Peterborough with the down "Northumbrian", while Bill picked up the shovel and fired all the way to Stoke Summit. Bill always liked to give himself about 50 miles firing a day, to keep fit, and of course the firemen were highly delighted to take the opportunity of the resulting rest, with its experience of driving thrown in. Much of Bill's success as a driver lay in this daily work-out of his, as every fireman knew that he was not being asked to work any harder than Bill himself was prepared to. On the first occasion, Frank was really worried to see someone old enough to be his father trying to get Dominion of Canada to steam properly, and after watching the depressing activities of the pressure gauge, suggested to Bill that they should change back. Bill was highly indignant and told Frank to keep his eye on the road, promptly hanging his cap over the pressure gauge to stop him looking at it. Bill was always quick to try and relieve any tension on the footplate, and Albert Leach, who fired for him for many years, told me of another similar incident when he was worried about the water level in the boiler. As far as he could see, it was out of sight in the bottom of the glass, but Bill said he could see it all right, and just to rub in the point, promptly stood on the seat and peered down at it. Many times when things were going badly with a shy-steaming locomotive, Bill would pass his fireman a sweet, a cigarette, or a bit of fruit, saying "Try this and see if it helps". Bill also set about teaching Frank the road north of Grantham, and while waiting in a mess room between trains, or during trips home on the cushions, would suddenly ask him what was the next signal after the starter at Retford, or some similar question.

It was on one of these trips in March 1953, that Allan

Garraway first met Bill, during some trials to see whether the steaming of the A4s could be improved. At this time, of course, only a handful of them were fitted with double chimneys, these being the original four built with the Kylchap blast pipe. No. 60010, Dominion of Canada, had been fitted with a manometer to take readings of the vacuum in the smokebox, and Allan was very impressed with the way in which Bill co-operated with him, and tried to give him what they wanted. The locomotive was steaming very badly in spite of Frank's efforts, and they just managed to struggle over Stoke Summit. Having established what the locomotive would do in normal conditions, a new blast pipe cap was fitted, and two days later another test was planned, also on the 12.18 p.m. "Northumbrian". When the fitter had finished the work, there was very little time left to light her up, and when Bill signed on, the pressure gauge needle had barely lifted off its stop. This did not deter him, however, and with little more than the minimum steam pressure required to move her, he made his way down to the terminus with the blower fully open, so that when they got the "Right Away" the pressure was all right. Frank's efforts now were rewarded with much more success, and with plenty of steam available, Bill set out to show Allan what he could do. From this trip and others that he was able to make with Bill in the next few months, Allan quickly discovered that Bill's main aim in life seemed to be to get to the other end of the journey as quickly as possible. "Get the passengers there in the shortest possible time, and they'll come again" just about sums up Bill's commercial philosophy, and if it represents, perhaps, a rather too simplified approach, it nevertheless embodies the fundamental necessity of any successful transport undertaking in these days with their constantly accelerating tempo of life.

With the start of the summer timetables in 1953, the usual wholesale changes in locomotive rosters took place, so that Frank and Bill were parted, both going into the Top Link. Bill was, of course, used to such a promotion in the summer, but this time things were different as Ralph Springham had retired, and from now until Bill himself was due to retire in the summer of 1959, only illness, failing sight, or serious misdemeanour could bring his Top Link career to a close.

CHAPTER SIX

Top Link

With his promotion into the Top Link, Bill had reached as high as his youthful ambition could imagine, but if in the wildest of his young dreams he had aspired to handling the regulator of a Midland "Spinner", the A4s on the East Coast Route in 1953 offered him something vastly more powerful in the way of motive power, while their appearance, although perhaps lacking the classical grace of the 4-2-2s, nevertheless had an individuality to be found nowhere else in the country. Bill's recollections of his early days of train spotting made him very sympathetic to the "platform enders" who watched his daily comings and goings in and out of King's Cross and most of the other principal stations en route. Much of the fascination of railways and steam locomotives lies in the fact that they offer the mechanically-minded individual the chance to observe and record the performance of a powerful item of machinery in operation, capable of producing up to 3,000 horsepower when pushed to the limit. The railways also present the youngster with a system on which to display his powers of observation and deduction, working out the locomotive, carriage and crew rosters from the records laboriously entered in the flyleaf of an Ian Allan "ABC". With his cheerful disposition and love of meeting people, Bill quickly collected a large number of friends amongst railway enthusiasts, who were in any case attracted by the standards of running they were likely to be able to record when he was at the regulator. Peter Coster has described to me how he and Brian Bailey used to spend hours on the end of New Southgate platform, working out the locomotive rosters and Top Link turns. Every so often Sir Nigel Gresley, with up to 15 bogies behind her, would come roaring out of Wood Green tunnel, around the gentle right-hand curve, with the television mast of Alexandra Palace towering over the variegated-brick edifice beyond. Sir Nigel would be going a good 15 to 20 m.p.h. more than most of the other engines, and they would wave to the cheery little chap leaning out of the cab window, who looked barely old enough to be in the Top Link. Later, when he started work, Coster gravitated to King's Cross during his lunch hours, meeting the band that constituted the G.N. "Grapevine", and naturally making the acquaintance of Bill, who promptly recognised him from his New Southgate days. Coster was able to ride with Bill on a number of occasions, and later, after he had joined the London Midland Region as a civil engineer, was thus in a position to compare the work of Gresley and Stanier, the last two locomotive engineers to leave their imprint on the northern lines.

The quickness with which Bill struck up friendships with people was not confined to enthusiasts only, as I have met several high-up railway officers who in their junior days took pride in learning the hard way by firing for Bill. One of these was Allan Garraway, who after he had graduated from Cambridge and done his national service, joined the railways at Doncaster as a Grade 3 Fitter, where he set about acquiring as many workshop skills as he could, to the ultimate advantage of the Festiniog Railway. Early in the 1950s, when attached to Regional Headquarters, during his journeys up and down from his home at Lincoln each week-end, he used to take the shovel on the Bls on the through Boston workings. Allan's father was District Motive Power Superintendent at Lincoln, so the family was used to locomotives, Allan's mother coping with the washing of his shirts, only making the one stipulation that he should not get them too dirty, three moderately grubby ones being better than one that was filthy. Firing for Bill of course, produced a really wet shirt, but like other young men in their twenties, the exercise did him no harm, and he often combined an hour or two's firing with a spot of rowing on the same evening. Another engineer, now in the North Eastern Region, has told me how he used to help fire on one of the Pullmans going home to Yorkshire on Fridays, just for the fun of it. Occasionally, the Pullman conductor would bring a VIP from the train through the corridor tender for a few minutes to see what it was like on the footplate. The presence of two firemen sometimes caused surprise, but the visitor's curiosity would usually be satisfied by the explanation that it was a very important train, and he would retire to his Pullman Car again, very impressed with the trouble the railways were taking to get him home on time.

The steadily enlarging circle of friends that Bill was making amongst enthusiasts from this time onwards had the result that many more of his exploits were recorded by stop-watch experts, and an increasing number of them appeared in print. By way of explanation to the reader, I should perhaps make it clear at this point, that, although I am rarely to be seen on a train without my stop-watch handy, I do not in this book intend to quote detailed logs of Bill's running, as many of the most notable runs have already appeared in print, and references to them can be found in the appendix. ·On the other hand, certain exploits were only recorded in the guards' journals, with their times at best to the nearest half minute. Also, in a book that sets out with the object of recording one man's lifetime spent on the railways, there is little room for such details, which in any case, more properly belong to a volume of locomotive performance.

Readers will find another omission in this book, too, and this is one where I also join in regretting that the gap cannot be filled. I had hoped, to be able to describe something of Bill's driving techniques, but as hinted in the previous chapter, this has proved to be impossible. As an example of the difficulties I was up against, I cannot do better than quote Bill's account of a run from York to Darlington with the "Tees-Tyne Pullman" which David Howard timed on 9th July 1954. The train had run in to York six minutes early after being booked two minutes late passing Doncaster, but they had a tenderful of small coal which took a long time to burn through. There is, however, much more behind the story than even the timing of 36 minutes 33 seconds for the 44.1 miles indicated. The brilliance of the run was undoubtedly due to Bill, but it was his skill with the shovel and injectors, rather than the regulator and reverser, that made it possible. Knowing this, I asked Bill what the full story was, and his account was as follows:

"On the way down, Albert Leech had overdone it. We had got a lot of small coal, and on the approach to York, Albert naturally reported to me and said I would want another engine. I asked him what had gone wrong and he described it to me. He had overdone it and he had really worked hard getting this dust down, because he had had to go in and dig it out. She was really holding back, but to my mind when I looked at it, it was a really good quality fire, just becoming really incandescent, and you could do something with it. There was quite enough there for us to chew, when we did set off. When he said he thought we would need another engine, I didn't discourage him and said we'll see what we can do. We stopped, and I got down and felt round and everything was in good condition. He went back and got some sandwiches. We always got some sandwiches on that particular job - the Tees-Tyne. [This dated from an instruction issued by the General Manager of the Pullman Car Company when this train was introduced.] When he came forward, I told him to sit in "The Seat" and do his best to get to Darlington as quick as he could, and I would look after the other side. All I had to do was to watch Albert take her away, open the regulator and give her the works. He livened the fire up and all I had to do was to sit there and watch it, watch the water gradually come down to the lowest minimum, and put the injector on nice and steady, not too much, and build from there. It wasn't a case of mortgaging time and power, we had power building up. In the end Albert was going like a rocket, and I could put two injectors on. I had a wonderful fire and I didn't look at it or give it any more attention until north of Northallerton. I then just put a couple round the front and there she brought us into Darlington. Just outside, at Croft, he thought there was a P. Way and checked, but there was no P. Way and we were into Darlington in 36 minutes even then. It only goes to show, the quality of his speed south of Northallerton. It was really good. I didn't touch the fire until we were north of Northallerton, then I just had to trim it round the front. He had got so much dirt on all round the back and it really looked as if the fire was really dead, but it was just a wonderful build-up."

Bill's description is graphic enough, but he would be the first to agree that it is not the sort of account to incorporate in a manual of enginemanship as a description of how to do it. Before leaving this incident, there is an unpublished sequel that must be mentioned. Two nights later, with the same train, they had some good coal, so Bill set out to beat Albert's time between York and Darlington, and succeeded in clipping off a minute, much to his satisfaction, although he did not have the permanent way restriction with the signal check after Croft Spa that Albert en countered. The crews always welcomed the opportunity of a little extra time at Darlington, as it enabled them to get the footplate tidy and wash up, ready for a quick get-away at Newcastle. In the very early days of the "Tees-Tyne Pullman", incidentally, the train was not booked to pickup passengers at Darlington, and with no York stop either, it was on occasions passing Durham at the time it should have been running into Darlington. Having shown how difficult it is to describe Bill's technique with the shovel, I must complete the picture by trying to convey what I can of the way he drove. Prof. Tuplin's delightful account "Getting to Grantham", that appeared in the "Engineer" for March 11th 1955, might have been written with Bill in mind, and as that author has frequently remarked, making an engine go faster is only a question of giving it more steam. However, while one cannot fault this as a general principle, it does, from a practical point of view, raise two queries: how to produce the extra steam in the first place, and secondly, actually how to get it into the cylinders. Knowing exactly how to mortgage the boiler to the limit in advance of a restricted or downhill stretch is fundamental to achieving sustained high speed with a difficult engine, and the willingness of the fireman to get a wet shirt also plays a big part. Few enthusiasts have had the opportunity of firing a main line steam locomotive working really hard, and will not know at first-hand the exhausting task of moving getting on for a hundredweight of coal every two minutes from a heaving tender into the blistering firehole door. All the exertion takes place with the body bent double, and this seriously taxes the chest muscles as far as breathing is concerned. Ideally the fireman needs to rest between firing spells to help get his breath back, but at the end of a long journey this can sometimes become impossible, as he has to go into the tender between spells to get the coal forward. On a turn from Newcastle, from Peter borough southwards the fireman would usually be faced with this prospect, and similarly on a down run, the York to Darlington stretch, with its need for continuous hard steaming, could try even the fittest of mates. Bill's willingness to give his fireman a hand, especially when things were difficult, helped to ensure their co-operation, and some of his firemen, temporary or otherwise, would take pride in their ability to keep Bill provided with steam.

With Bill's supply of steam reasonably assured, it remains to discuss how he was able to apply it to maximum effect. At high speed, valve events often become very different from those intended by the designer. Bulleid's chain-driven arrangement apart, the Gresley conjugated motion is probably the most liable to give unpredictable results. Even Churchward's robust gear on the "Castles" can produce surprises on occasions, according to one account of a recent high speed run, when numerous different settings were unsuccessfully tried in an attempt to achieve the few missing m.p.h. necessary to push the speed over the "ton". We are all aware of the inaccuracies of cut-off indicators, but this account rubs in the fact that advancing the cut-off does not automatically ensure that more steam enters the cylinders. When Bill describes a run, he always reckons that he could tell from the "feel" of the reverser when the locomotive still had something more in hand.

There was one of Bill's personal characteristics that stood him in good stead on the footplate, and this was his quickness. I think perhaps that this is one of the few things about him that has changed during the years since his retirement, and it is, after all, only to be expected that a 70-year old begins to slow down compared with a mere youngster of 60. One of his former firemen has commented to me on how much quicker Bill could be on the footplate than some of his fellow Top Link drivers, many of whom carried a lot more weight than Bill's 10 stone. One of the defects of a steam locomotive is its propensity to slip, and those on the footplate always get a slight warning when this is about to occur. It is difficult to describe how one becomes conscious of this effect, but it is well known to anyone who has travelled on a steam locomotive to any extent. Perhaps it is best described as a sudden cessation of the locomotive's regular rhythm, and only lasts a fraction of a second before the driving wheels really pick up and thrash round while the cab sheets reverberate in sympathy. With Bill, though, this slight warning would be enough for his hand to flash out and close the regulator or link up the valve gear sufficiently to check the worst effects.

By the time Bill reached the Top Link, it was reasonably well known that his ambition seemed to be to get to the other end in the shortest possible time, and enthusiasts always hoped for a late start to give him an opportunity of recovering the arrears. At this time there were a number of large-scale engineering works on the East Coast line that caused considerable loss of time, and these would serve as a challenge to Bill and other drivers. Some of the restrictions were of considerable duration, like the rebuilding of Potters Bar station, and the widening of the section from there southwards to Greenwood Box, with its three intermediate tunnels. Authorised in 1953, the scheme cost nearly £2m. and involved 1,830 yards of tunnelling, and 380,000 cubic yards of excavation. The first section of the work involved widening the underbridge at the town end of Potters Bar station, which necessitated a severe speed restriction for many months. Later on, at Sandy, there was another slowing of considerable duration caused by bridge work. Other, even more severe, restrictions occurred from time to time, and I can recall one up journey on the "Yorkshire Pullman" when we passed Hitchin about 10 minutes early, only to find that the junctions at Stevenage were in process of being remodelled. All traffic was being funnelled over the slow lines and by the time we had cleared this bad check, we were no longer running early. On yet another occasion, the North Eastern Region introduced a 3-mile permanent way caution to 15 m.p.h. in connection with the laying of some of the early long welded rails, and although only lasting a few days, promptly cost all trains 10 minutes in running. At times, however, the brief absence of temporary speed restrictions would make the recovery margins somewhat unnecessary, and on one such occasion Bill said to a passenger, "If we get to Hitchin 10 minutes before time, Control can hardly keep us behind the Cambridge line train due out ahead of us", and then promptly set out to prove his point. Of course if a crew did not quite manage such an audacious move, the result would be a crawl all the way up to London, spinning out the 15 minutes on top of the normal timing. In the early days of the Type 4 diesels on the East Coast Route, the driver of my train just missed getting through Hitchin ahead of the other train, and in consequence we barely exceeded 45 m.p.h. all the rest of the way to the terminus, but nevertheless arrived on time. There is one aspect of Bill's driving methods on which I can comment, however, and this is his habit of never carrying a watch, even after he had been presented with one in March 1953 as a long service award. It was his knowledge of the whereabouts of the station and signal box clocks that enabled him to keep a reasonably good idea of passage of time as he made his way along the line. During our recorded conversations he explained his views on this subject. "If you are not using a watch you're not worried. People who do use a watch are worried stiff - those who take notice of it. I've seen drivers sweating buckets, just because they're losing half a minute in one section and anticipate losing half a minute in the next. But they don't, because they give it the works and suddenly find they have two minutes in hand and they are worried again how they are going to lose it, and what transpires then, they're trying to balance themselves all the way there and all the way home." This is Bill's point of view, but one of his firemen put it another way, "That was the trouble with old Bill, he never would carry a watch, and would always try to run ahead of time as long as the signalmen and Control would let him." On up trains, the fireman always had to be on the outlook for the clock at St. Neots on the back of the station buildings on the down side, so he could tell Bill how they were doing. Nevertheless, like many other drivers who have habitually run without a watch, Bill developed a remark able sense of time from what he observed from the footplate. The places where they passed other trains, and the state of the mail and parcels on station platforms, all signified something to him, a lot of it in all probability subconsciously.

Sounds meant a lot to him too, off the footplate, where they would be heard clearly, and he would judge the time while he was walking down to the sheds by the whistles of distant trains. When he used to live at Paddington, he would listen to the noises of the Great Central, polytan Metropolitan and Nor' Western engines in the early hours of the morning. He registered the different sounds, and was able to confirm what they were subsequently. On one of the King's Cross turns, the crew were relieved at Finsbury Park on an up freight train in the early hours of the morning, and as Bill made his way back up to Holloway through the silent streets, he would listen to the Gresley knock in the distance as the A4 shunted the train into its correct sidings. He would even detect it if they made a mistake with the shunting and had to pick a wagon up again. Then, with the train disposed of, he would hear the A4 running down light to the sheds until a distant rumble indicated it had gone on to the table to turn. Bill always enjoyed walking home after six or more hours in "The Seat", as he was glad of the opportunity of stretching his legs, but usually caught a bus down at the beginning of the shift unless he was due to sign on at an hour when they were not running.

2

Another of Bill's maxims was to forget the job as much as possible between turns when lodging away, or between the down and up journey if time permitted him and his mate to get away from the locomotive. The pair of them would wander round the town where they happened to be, finding all the museums and other places of interest to explore. Newcastle was especially pleasing from this point of view, as there is the Museum of Science and Engineering up on Town Moor, which contains numerous items of railway interest, including a section from the pipe of Brunel's ill-fated South Devon Railway, where it was intended to propel the trains by means of the vacuum created by a series of stationary engines housed in buildings such as the one still in existence alongside the line at Starcross. In another section of the museum is an excellent mural of Sir Nigel Gresley in pre-war livery, and elsewhere there are some fine ship models which naturally interested Bill too, while in the annexe at the rear is the original Turbinia which Parsons built to prove the advantages of the steam turbine in the face of Admiralty scepticism. Bill has a very generous nature, particularly when children are concerned, and he would often find an excuse for a small gift. On one occasion, when they were wandering round Doncaster, Bill suddenly discovered that Frank Mayes' wife was expecting a baby, and promptly disappeared into a toyshop, to reappear with a teddy bear for Frank to take home for the day when the new arrival put in an appearance.

Edinburgh was perhaps Bill's happiest hunting ground in between trips. The city is wonderful enough in itself, and Bill would take the opportunity of trotting any fireman of his round the sights, covering the length of the Royal Mile from the Castle down to Holyrood Palace. The crews on the "Non-

Stop" were issued with little lapel badges with the name of the train on them to serve as identification when they were off duty, and Bill was very proud of his. In Edinburgh too, these badges acted as an "Open Sesame" in many places, as the Scottish capital was immensely proud of this train. There was even one barber's in the city where Bill found he could get a free hair cut if he was wearing the badge.

Bill always considered too that the Scots were better mechanics than the Geordies, although as far as the railway side was concerned, the locomotives for the "Non-Stop" would naturally receive better attention from the fitters than an ordinary engine would at Gateshead.

One of the things Bill used to do occasionally when they were in Edinburgh was to walk across the Forth Bridge. When they arrived in Waverley, he would go up to the District Engineer's office to get permission, and then he and his mate would make their way out to South Queensferry. The bridge is looked after by two watchmen, from huts at each end. They patrol the structure and keep their eyes open for anything untoward which might occur, such as one of the timbers catching fire from a dropped cinder. When they arrived at the watchman's hut at the south end, they would be made to sign the book, paying the sum of a penny each, this being an old legal relic. It had nothing to do with the habit of many train travellers of throwing a penny out of the window, which was another even older relic, this time dating from pagan days when offerings were made to appease the water gods before anyone crossed such a wide stretch as the Firth of Forth. These formalities over, the watchman would stroll part way across with them, after contacting his opposite number at the far end by telephone to inform him about the two visitors. Bill found it very thrilling walking along the catwalks, which they reached by the various staircases running up and down the main hollow structural members.

One of the duties of the bridge watchmen is to record the amount of expansion and contraction as the bridge is affected by the changes in temperature. In the arches at the ends of the cantilevers are indicators to show the amount of expansion, which amounts to many feet in the course of the temperature variations between day and night. Other parts of the bridge expand and contract too, and I remember someone telling me about the rather alarming effect he experienced when he was doing sentry duty on Inchkeith, during the First World War. One·of the main towers is built on this small island, and certain of the main members are free to move to a limited extent on their foundations. My informant had been unaware of this until, completely without warning, the support suddenly moved an inch or so as the expansion built up to the point at which it overcame the friction. Needless to say he thought the whole bridge was about to collapse. Bill and Albert Leech once went down on to Inchkeith, not realising it was Government property. They had seen a number of men at work there, and made their way down to investigate what they were doing. It turned out that they were Admiralty workmen, and their relief boat from Rosyth had been held up. Bill and Albert gave them some sweets and cigarettes they had with them, and in exchange were presented with pocketsful of copper coins, covered with green verdigris from the salt water of the Firth around the island. They were having an interesting chat when they were suddenly alerted by one of the watchmen from the bridge, who had spotted them on the island, which was out of bounds to railwaymen. Bill and Albert hastily took their leave from the Admiralty squad, whose foreman told them he had not seen them on the island, and scrambled up the staircase to rail level once more, the weight of the copper making them appreciably heavier than they had been when they descended. Usually on these trips they would come back by ferry, and on one occasion they got into conversation with a rock climber who told them he had once gone across the top of the bridge at night as a result of a bet. His boots started to slip on the girders of the cantilevers, and he had had to continue on his hands and knees. One of the worst things was the amount of sway, at a point where there was nothing to hang on to. Although Bill is a great one for new experiences, this was one he did not seek to emulate.

3

July 1953 proved to be quite an eventful month for Bill in the Top Link, with no less than six small incidents of one sort or another. On the 4th, Miles Beevor ran its right-hand driving box hot on the down " Yorkshire Pullman", and three days later, on the Tuesday, Andrew K. McCosh dropped its brick arch coming up from Newcastle on the "Flying Scotsman". The following afternoon, on the down "Tees-Tyne Pullman", a window was smashed as they passed Finsbury Park, and to round off the week, both Seagull's injectors failed at Doncaster on the Saturday and it had to come off the train, being replaced by V2 No. 60982. The next week was somewhat better, with nothing more than a warm middle big end on Quicksilver on the Monday, and the middle small end on Lord Faringdon running hot on the Friday. It is difficult at this range to sort out the two sides of the various tales I have heard about Bill and these runs of failures that occurred from time to time. There is no doubt that in pursuit of the Hoole commercial philosophy, Bill pushed the engines he drove very hard, but at the same time there were admitted deficiencies in the standard of East Coast maintenance. Some of the failures, too, such as Andrew K. McCosh's brick arch, could hardly be ascribed to the driver's mishandling of the engine. This makes me think that at least some of the stories about Bill being hard on his engines may have been exaggerated during the intervening years as they have been passed round successive mess rooms and embroidered in the telling. Occasionally it was a hot box on the train that caused trouble, and sometimes these were due to Bill's exuberance with a fitted freight. He always speaks of the need to warm the axleboxes up gently on a freight train, even though they are now very much improved in their performance from the days when Bill and his mate would struggle out of

London with a train of grease lubricated wagons on the old Great Central. When Bill was talking to the Tees-side Centre of the Stephenson Locomotive Society, he described how they would take it easy up the bank to Potters Bar with a freight while they warmed up the boxes. When he went on to say, in a very matter-of-fact way, that if you did this, then after Hitchin you could quite happily work them up to 80 m.p.h., the meeting burst into a roar of laughter. I once commented to Frank Mayes that the guards on these trains must have had a rough ride, but he told me that the reverse was the case. Provided the sheer speed did not worry them, Bill actually laid on a smoother ride than many drivers, never braking so suddenly that the guard was in danger of being wrapped round the stove pipe as the vehicles buffered up.

Bill's 1953 turn on the "Non-Stop" came towards the end of August, his three round trips being uneventful. For the first northbound run on the Monday he had Union of South Africa, but all the others were with Empire of India. This, of course, was Coronation Year, and to mark the occasion, the name of the train was altered to the "Elizabethan", a far more exciting title than the former "Capitals Limited". This year the schedule was fixed at 6.5 hours, giving a saving of 22 minutes over the previous summer, and representing an average of over 58 m.p.h. start to stop. There was another development with the "Non-Stop", on one Saturday at least, when it was turned "Slow Line" at Cemetery Box, overtaking the queue of trains awaiting entry into King's Cross. As a result it achieved an "On-Time" arrival. The most outstanding run on this train took place on 12th August, after a defective dynamo belt on one of the coaches had been removed at Hitchin. Silver Fox, which worked more trips on this train than any other during this season, then averaged 63 m.p.h. to Edinburgh, recovering 21 of the lost minutes.

At the end of September came the first of the really high-speed enthusiasts' runs over the Great Northern line, when Alan Pegler and his associates organised the "Plant

Centenarian". Arranged to mark the centenary of Doncaster Locomotive Works, the train ran from London to Doncaster and back on Sunday 20th September, while a week later the trip operated in reverse, starting at Leeds. On the outward trip the 11 - coach load was hauled by the two preserved vat Ivatt Atlantics, Nos. 990 and 251, and although they worked up to 80 m.p.h. on the second occasion, their performance was eclipsed by Ted Hailstone on Silver Link in the opposite direction. Bill was called on to work No. 251 on both Sundays, and these workings, which marked his first connection with an enthusiasts' special, will be described in more detail in the next chapter.

From mid-August 1953, the King's Cross Top Link had been working a new lodging turn to York, working down on the 2.30 a.m. Goods, and returning on the 9 p.m. Fish train the same evening. They used V2s for these workings, rather than their regular A4s. Because of the timings, they had alternate days off, and in consequence it was not such a highly paid turn as when they worked the "Norseman" to York and back on mileage. It did give Bill and his mate the opportunity of exploring another city, and they visited the Minster, the Shambles, and numerous other places of interest. In the first week in November, when Bill was on this working, he collected only £13 17s. 5d. for the week, with 16s. 11d. expenses. This turn had its moments, however, and on the week in question, the Saturday trips were the most eventful, with a hot box in each direction, the second being on the guard's brake van.

With the coming of the summer services, the general speed limit over 120 miles of the East Coast line was relaxed to 90 m.p.h., and this gave Bill and other Top Link drivers even more scope for time-recovery. In "Trains Illustrated" for June 1953 Cecil J. Allen wrote that more consistent attempts were made to recover lost time on the Eastern Region than on any other Region of British Railways, although at times the operating obstacles put in the way of keen drivers were such that no engine or engine crew on earth could possibly keep time. He went on to illustrate this theme by two runs timed by Rodney Meadows on the "Tees-Tyne Pullman" when he had come north for a week-end with us in the previous October. Although they did not know it at the time, the driver of Merry Hampton was Bill Hoole, and even with this Doncaster based A3, it was a remarkable run. From passing Hitchin at 48 m.p.h., they were through Huntingdon in 20 minutes 26 seconds for the 27.0 miles. At that time the Pullman often had a bad road north of Newark, and it did so with a vengeance that evening, dropping 11½ minutes on schedule between there and Doncaster. Nevertheless, Bill knocked 2½ minutes off the tight 42-minute York-Darlington booking with a time of 39 minutes 38 seconds for this 44.1 mile stretch, an excellent effort with an A3, especially as it was then still devoid of a double blast pipe. Cecil J. Allen's article also contained another brief reference to a run of Bill's, again without his name being known. This was on January 5th 1954, when with Sir Nigel Gresley, he passed through Hornsey with the 12-coach 9.50 a.m. from Leeds with 17 minutes still left to complete the remaining four miles into the terminus.

Bill's long regular association with Sir Nigel Gresley started in November 1953, and although broken up by the weeks in which he worked V2s on the York turn, he nevertheless had her on 15 days in December, while the first eight turns he worked in the New Year were all on this locomotive. All told, in 1954 Bill handled her on 69 occasions, although by the end of the year she was not being used as one of the Top Link engines because of her mileage since shopping, and he was more frequently getting Quicksilver instead. The policy of allocating regular engines to the Top Link crews is well known, but there was also this arrangement of regular substitutes at King's Cross. There is no doubt that Bill developed a great affection for "No. 7", and, as far as he was concerned, there was no other A4 quite the same, although she did let him down on occasions, the most notable incident being one on April 22nd 1954. At this time, the King's Cross A4s suffered a whole series of injector troubles, which was erroneously ascribed by the crews to Doncaster Works trying to make the cones rather than buying them in from the manufacturers. The water softeners at the troughs also caused difficulties at times, and Bill described how he once got a "load of toothpaste" at Langley, while they would sometimes find the leading coaches spattered with white deposits after picking up water. In March, Bill had booked Sir Nigel with bad injectors, and on April 21st he and Jim Wilson were rostered to work the down "Tees-Tyne Pullman", with Allan Garraway keeping them company on the footplate. As usual there were checks at Doncaster which brought them in to York eight minutes late. Bill had difficulty in restarting, but once he got going, only took 37 minutes to Darlington, which recovered some of the lateness, so that they were able to pick up the remainder on the final stretch into Newcastle, arriving on time. The injectors had been giving trouble all the way, and they had only maintained the water level with difficulty. Indeed, dropping down from Durham, the only time they saw it was when it surged up in the glass at intervals. After they had stopped in Central, it was still some time before the exhaust steam injector, the only one working, put sufficient water into the boiler to make the level properly visible. It was so bad that they had difficulty in persuading the Geordie relief driver to take the engine over. Bill booked the trouble and was assured they would do their best overnight to get things right for the up trip next morning.

When Bill got down to the sheds at 8.10 on the Thursday morning, he found that they had got both injectors going, but they had not changed the cones. They worked out over King Edward Bridge without any trouble, and set back on to the Pullman coaches, which contained a number of VIPs who were travelling to London that day for some sort of NATO conference. Bill was anxious to give them a punctual run if at all possible, but they had not got very far, however, before the injectors got temperamental again, the live steam one packing up. As they passed over Wiske Moor troughs after the Darlington stop, the exhaust steam injector flew off and that was that. While Allan and Jim wrestled with both the dead injectors, trying every trick they knew to get them going again, Bill carried on as if nothing had happened, with their speed in the 80s as they sped southwards across the plain of York, and the passengers, oblivious of the difficulties on the footplate, enjoying their morning coffee. This state of affairs could not last, needless to add, but Bill was, as usual, planning ahead, so that the inevitable locomotive exchange could take place in as good a situation as possible. He warned the others he was going to get to Thirsk, and as he braked to a standstill opposite the box, the three of them started to dispose of the fire. They dropped half the grate, which spread some of the contents along the track under the cars, so that the Pullman staff thought the train was on fire. The remainder was pushed out after they had stopped, and it promptly set fire to the sleepers, which in turn ignited the oil from the locomotive's axlebox lubricators, making a black smear up the side of the streamlined casing, and raising a blister "as big as your head" in the Brunswick Green paint. While Allan and Jim were emptying the firebox, working like madmen in case the fusible plugs went, Bill disappeared. To begin with they wondered if he was taking avoiding action, but he had only gone to shout to the signalman that they would need a new engine, after which he collected a fire extinguisher from the guard to help put out the remains of the fire in the box. The excitement over, they managed to get an injector on again after the pressure had dropped, but one of the fusible plugs started to weep, showing that they had only just got the fire out in time.

They uncoupled the engine, put her in a siding, and awaited the arrival of the replacement from York. The stationmaster came up and asked Bill for full details of what had happened, and then went off with a sheaf of telegrams from the NATO delegates, telling the authorities in London that they would be late for the meeting. York had had a couple of previous failures to cope with that morning, so were only able to send V2 No.

60981 for Bill to continue with, which was only fitted with a small tender, and full of slack rather than decent coal. An inspector came with it to look at Sir Nigel Gresley, and told Bill to do his best with the V2, which, if he had known it, was rather a rash instruction to issue in that particular direction. The exchange affected, they passed York 63 minutes late but, because of a train ahead, dropped more time to Grantham, where they were stopped at the North Box. Control had the train ahead turned "Slow Line" after it left the station, so the "Tees-Tyne Pullman" got a clear road again. They were 82 minutes late at this point, but succeeded in running the 105.5 miles to King's Cross in 99 minutes, inclusive of the 15 m.p.h. slowing for the bridge reconstruction at Potters Bar, which represented a saving of nine minutes on the booked time for this section. The 27.0 miles from Huntingdon to Hitchin they covered in 22½ minutes, and by this stage it required the continuous efforts of Allan and Jim to keep the engine going. One of them would be in the tender shovelling the slack forward, while the other fed it through the firehole door, after which most of it was blasted straight out of the chimney by Bill. They arrived with very little water showing in the glass, the pressure well down, and no less than three hot boxes, the smell from which drifted across the platform at King's Cross and caused passengers to dodge the fumes.

It is a matter for debate whether Bill did right in thrashing an obviously run-down engine on such an occasion. By easier driving she might have arrived without the hot boxes, but to set against this there is the obvious psychological point that the passengers, many already late for their meeting, could not have failed to realise that the crew "up front" were doing their best to get them to London in the shortest possible time, which would do much to overlay their original annoyance at the delay. There is no doubt that even ordinary passengers soon become conscious of a rousing effort from the locomotive, as one incident which Colin Walker has described to me clearly shows. He had ridden with Bill on the up Perth Car-Sleeper one night in September 1956, during which they had touched 105 m.p.h. at Little Bytham with 18 on. In spite of a late departure from Grantham, they were into King's Cross a few minutes early, having run the 105.5 miles in 104 minutes, inclusive of a stop at Peterborough. Although six o'clock on a September morning is hardly a time at which one would expect people to be at their most appreciative, within minutes of stopping there was a small crowd of very tired-looking passengers, men and women, round the cab, with grins on their faces, expressing their appreciation of Bill and the locomotive. Colin Walker was, I think, almost more impressed by this than the run itself, and certainly Bill always thoroughly enjoyed such occasions. As he used to remark to his firemen sometimes: "We've got to put on a good job, there are hundreds of eyes watching us". Bill's comment to me after recounting the story of the injector failure at Thirsk was, "Well, we did our best: it was a poor best, but it was the best we could do", adding, in a tone of voice that provided a great insight into his character: "A very interesting day, really". So typical of Bill's whole outlook on life was this comment, that, when I was transcribing the recording months later in my living room, my wife and I both spontaneously burst into laughter as it came out of the loudspeaker! Even Allan Garraway, in one of his letters to me, commented that it was one of the most memorable days he spent with Bill.

It is, of course, one of the greatest crimes a driver can perpetrate to damage a locomotive's firebox as a result of too low a water level, which was known to the crews as "burning the boiler". When the signalman at Thirsk saw the flames licking up round the outside of Sir Nigel Gresley, he reported to Control that the boiler was burnt, and not unnaturally word got round that Bill had damaged the firebox. However, it was only one fusible plug that had started to weep, but Bill afterwards heard that the locomotive was worked up to King's Cross that evening, and was in service next day.

In the first half of 1954, O. S. Nock had two trips with Bill on the footplate, and others besides him and Allan

Garraway were taking various opportunities of riding with him to see him at work. Later that year, Bill was able to go to a Stephenson Locomotive Society meeting in London at which O. S. Nock was the speaker, and one of the questions posed by a member was whether the crew of a locomotive would stage an "act" if someone like him was travelling on the footplate. Bill considers, though, that over as long a trip as the one to Newcastle, it would be impossible to put on an act, although over shorter distances it might be done. A railway enthusiast had once introduced Bill to Driver Sammy Gingell of Stewarts Lane shed on the Southern, who shared the same delight in high speed running. Bill took Sammy to Newcastle and back on Dominion of Canada on September 6th and 7th 1954 and did his best to impress his guest from the south of the Thames. Allan Garraway joined them at Grantham on the footplate of the "Flying Scotsman" for the up journey, and the fireman was very pleased to see him, as he could help with the firing. Between them, they managed to turn a 13½ minute late departure into an arrival in London nine minutes early. Not only was it outsiders who liked to ride with Bill, but Inspectors too often seemed to take the opportunity, when ever possible, of travelling with him. Bill's kindness to everyone was very well known, and Allan Garraway told me he never heard him say any thing to the detriment of someone else. Consequently he never had an enemy, and the fact that everyone liked Bill so much meant that some of his misdeeds were squared at a low level without getting to the ears of authority.

4

It was about this time that Allan Garraway introduced Bill to the joys of the model steam railways, taking him one evening to the Central Hall at Westminster to see the Model Railway Club Exhibition. Bill was naturally very impressed with the working exhibits and was soon intro duced to Bill Carter, who for many years has been one of their passenger track stewards. His 17-year-old daughter, Ann, was helping her father as usual, and the three of them quickly struck up a friendship. Naturally, Bill soon found himself driving the various gauge models up and down the short length of elevated track on the ground floor, the trainload of small children each having two double trips before their turn was up and they got off to allow those from the front of the queue on in their places. During the peak periods there was always this queue waiting, but at less busy times Bill quickly noticed that the youngsters would not only choose their favourite locomotives to ride behind, but also discriminated between the various drivers. Once, by accident, he tapped the buffer stop at the end of the track lightly (as he had done on one occasion at Alexandra Palace in pre-war days), and the children found this highly amusing. Thereafter, whenever traffic fell off, he found it possible to stimulate interest by the occasional repeat performance. In subsequent years, Bill, with other main line drivers, shared in the duties of driving at the exhibition, writing their names on the slate provided to indicate when they would be prepared to do their turn.

Ann Carter followed her parents' vocation as a teacher, going to University College, London, which was conveniently near King's Cross, and on her afternoons off, she often came to see Bill depart for the north. On other days, she would go to his flat in Boscastle Road, and listen to Bill's stories about his experiences. In 1950 Bill Carter had commenced construction of his 5 in. gauge I vatt Atlantic, No. 3295, which was steamed at the Model Railway Club Exhibition for the first time in April 1965. Weighing 2¼ cwts., it is provided with a complete set of footplate fittings, including working vacuum brakes. Amongst the other awards it has received is a gold medal from the Society of Model and Experimental Engineers, only the third such award in the history of that body, which dates back over 70 years. Bill has watched the progress of this model since he got to know the Carters, and, since moving to the Festiniog, has visited them each year in their home at Norbury during his Christmas holiday in London. In order to give Ann her own locomotive to drive while the Atlantic was under construction, Bill Carter bought her a 5 in. gauge model of a Southern 0-6-0, which is also regularly operated at the Model Railway Exhibition. Ann does some modelling of her own, too, and, as befits the distaff side, had a spinning wheel on show at the 1965 Exhibition, together with the smokebox of a narrow-gauge locomotive, which she and her husband are building jointly. Bill's kindness and interest towards youngsters has thus meant a lot to the Carter family.

Allan Garraway was also responsible for introducing Bill to the Welsh narrow-gauge lines. On their first trip, they travelled in Allan's MG sports car to Dolgoch, on a Friday afternoon in September 1954, after Bill had worked up from Leeds that morning. On the Saturday Bill fired No. 4 Edward Thomas for two trips on the Talyllyn before they moved northwards on the Sunday. By then the Festiniog Railway had been transferred to its new owners under the Chairmanship of Alan Pegler, so they were consequently able to go into Boston Lodge, since Allan Garraway was one of the original Committee which had first met at Bristol three years earlier with the aim of getting the railway going once more, but their visit was just too early for the trial run of a train across the Cob on 23rd September. As a Liverpudlian/Cockney, Bill found difficulty with the Welsh names, and his diary records the fact that they had visited the Festinioch Railway. At that time he little dreamed that his future address would include the name Penrhyndeudraeth!

5

Bill's return from holiday on 6th June 1955 coincided with the A.S.L.E.F. strike, which lasted 15 days, although some train services were worked by N.U.R. crews who were not involved. On the first pay day after he got back from Wales, therefore, all Bill got in the way of wages was a tax refund of £2 7s. 0d. The basic rate for drivers had gone up the previous December to £9 12s. 6d. a week, and after the strike, following a Court of Inquiry, this was raised to £9 18s. 0d. Bill, of course, received a much better average wage than this because of mileage, so that during his two weeks on the "Elizabethan" that summer, he earned £32 14s. 5d. and £34 12s. 8d., plus £1 ls. 3d. expenses each week. Indeed, his income tax came to £7 18s. 0d. on the second week, which was as much as a man would earn weekly in his first year of driving up to December 1954. From the running point of view, the first of Bill's weeks on the "Elizabethan" was not good, as they had to stop to take water with Kingfisher at Huntingdon on one up journey and at Doncaster going down next day. The second week with Seagull was better, and they got through without any incidents. On one of his rest days in August, Bill made the "Britannia's" acquaintance, going down to Norwich on William Words worth with the "Broadsman", and coming back with Oliver Cromwell at the head of the "Norfolkman". He thoroughly enjoyed the trip, having a go with the regulator as well as the shovel but his personal conclusions were that though the "Britannias" were good for the Norwich turn, he doubted if they would have stood up to the hammering the V2s got during the war. Two years later, Bill was able to make some more foreign footplate trips, this time on the Bulleid Pacifics between Waterloo and Salisbury.

It was in November 1955 that Bill probably achieved the highest speed of his career during a run on the up "Tees-Tyne Pullman". Sir Nigel Gresley was in particularly fine condition, and Bill gave it the works descending Stoke Bank. Unknown to him, however, the Civil Engineer ing people had installed a Hallade Recorder in the last coach as part of their routine three-monthly recordings. This French device was used by our railways for something like forty years to determine the condition of the track, and it has only been superseded in quite recent months by the use of the track recording car which measures the actual irregularities in the track directly, rather than their effect on a coach passing over it at speed. A clockwork motor drove a 9-centimetre wide roll of translucent paper through the Hallade at a speed of a millimetre a second.

There were four styli that provided continuous traces on the chart. Three of them were worked by pendulums and indicated the transverse and vertical movements of the coach, as well as the amount it rolled. The fourth trace was normally a straight line, but there were kicks in it at intervals, when one of the engineers in charge operated a button on the end of an electric lead. Equipped with goggles, he spent most of the journey with his head out of the window, pressing the button as they passed each milepost or other readily identifiable location, such as station platforms and points or crossings. It was customary to press the button twice in quick succession at the mileposts, but only once at the quarter, half, and three-quarters. At the end of the journey, the chart was annotated with details of the train, locomotive, and coach used, and the speeds were worked out over each full mile and marked on the chart too. Other details were put on as well, such as curvature and speed restrictions, while places where the movement of the coach was excessive were suitably marked for the benefit of the people concerned on the track. Dyeline prints were then made, and sent out to the various District Engineers for their attention.

On the "Tees-Tyne Pullman" run with which Bill was concerned, the marks indicating the passage of the mileposts got closer and closer as they descended Stoke, until the subsequent measurements indicated a maximum of 117 m.p.h. At such a speed, however, there would be less than eight millimetres between the marks for successive quarter mileposts, and the kicks themselves were something like a millimetre wide anyway. Even if this record of the speed was based on as much as a single mile as it appeared on the chart, it was unlikely to be very accurate, and I have seen a Hallade trace later at little over half this speed that gave speeds over successive miles as 72, 75, and 72 m.p.h., on perfectly level track. Bill was certainly travelling fast, faster probably than the 112 m.p.h. achieved officially 3½ years later on the "Golden Jubilee Special", but the accuracy of the figure must remain in doubt. The engineering people were probably delighted to have the opportunity of seeing how their track withstood this very high speed, but it was some time before the Motive Power Department's attention was drawn to the occurrence, so there was a lapse of several months before King's Cross shed started looking for the culprit. As it happened, on the day concerned, Bill had been covering another driver's turn, so the suspicion did not fall on him to begin with. At about that time too, the Western Region had started fitting the "Kings" with double blast pipes, and were claiming some outstanding speeds with them, advantage being taken of the fact that certain sections of their main lines were not subject to any maximum speed limit whatsoever. Although the claim of 114 m.p.h. for King Richard III on the descent to Athelney has since been queried, there is no doubt that the East Coast people were feeling anxious about the safety of Mallard's world record. Anyway, by the time Bill was "on the mat" for allegedly achieving 117 m.p.h., the incident was being talked about in all the mess-rooms, and word of it had reached the Western Region. This, coupled with the time that had elapsed, and the questionable accuracy of the method of recording the speed, enabled Bill to get away with a telling-off, and the curt instruction not to do it again.

It was not only the Civil Engineer who would have been perturbed by such a high speed in normal service, as the signalling on the East Coast Route was not designed for running of this sort. In pre-war days, double block working had been adopted for the streamliners, but this arrangement was not, of course, in use for the "Tees-Tyne Pullman" in 1955. Even with his quickness of action when he sighted an adverse distant, Bill's high speed efforts occasionally resulted in his slightly overrunning a signal. He always liked to tease his fireman when making a sudden stop of this sort, sitting there in "The Seat" with his hands pressed together as if in prayer, and the occasional incident promptly got exaggerated during its progress from mess-room to mess-room. One of the few that I have managed to authenticate was on a Cambridge train one evening, first stop Welwyn Garden City. Bill was trying to regain the time lost by a late start, and consequently had to brake hard as they approached the. signal controlling the turn-in from Main Line to Slow. He overran the signal by a few yards, and my informant, a senior locomotive engineer, told me he could not recall a driver coming to a stand, reversing, and setting back with a train so quickly. Another time, in 1954, a thick fog suddenly came down as they were climbing Stoke on Humorist, and the fogmen were not in evidence until they passed Newark. At Barnby Road, Newark, Bill did not see the home signal in time and stopped well past it, which earned him a Reprimand. The coming of the diesel era later caused the whole question of the signalling distances on the East Coast Route to be gone into very carefully, and Bill was involved in some test runs to find out the limitations of the old arrangements.

As already described, the "Hoole philosophy" aimed at getting to the other end of the journey as quickly as possible. Intermediate stops did not really fit in with this, and Bill's occasional failure to make those booked for his train landed him in trouble from time to time throughout his passenger driving career. At other times, for good measure, he put in some extra ones, not shown in the timetable. Put this way, these incidents sound rather amusing, but I know what my reactions would have been if I had been one of the 27 passengers for St. Neots who got over-carried to Huntingdon when Bill was driving the 12.1 p.m. from King's Cross on January 31st 1949. This earned Bill a Caution, as had his failures to stop at Potters Bar with a down Royston train in 1943 and at Harringay with the 7.12 a.m. for Letchworth three years later.

Bill's love of railways generally took him to see all the various exhibi tions that were on anywhere in London. One that he found particularly interesting was that held at Willesden Junction at the end of May 1954 in conjunction with the International Railway Congress. It will be recalled that it was this international event that prompted the building of the only multi-cylinder design of British Railways, No. 71000 Duke of Gloucester, named after the President of the

Congress. The locomotive was on display at Willesden, and naturally interested Bill, who found no one about when he got there, somewhat before the official opening time. Being anxious to learn more about her, and being in uniform, he made his way underneath, and was examining the layout of the inside motion and roller-bearing axleboxes when he suddenly heard a voice asking him what he thought he was doing. The person in charge of this exhibit, who turned out to be the L.M.S. Shedmaster from Peterborough, had arrived, and was inspecting the locomotive before the arrival of Sir Brian Robertson, who was due to open the exhibition. When Bill had explained what he was doing, he was promptly asked to describe what he could see of the underside, for the benefit of the Shedmaster, who had never previously set eyes on the locomotive. This incident was very typical of the way Bill would get into unusual places, and indeed one of his superiors has described his ability to talk his way in anywhere. He never knew him fail in an attempt, and added that where he had not been at one time or another was not worth knowing.

6

With the 1956 winter timetables, the East Coast authorities introduced the "Talisman", a new afternoon Anglo-Scottish express, leaving the two capitals at 4.00 p.m. and taking 6 hours 40 minutes for the journey in each direction, with one stop at Newcastle, where engines were changed. The crews immediately set about showing what they could do, and Cecil J. Allen travelled north on the Monday, returning next day. The 7-coach trains were made up partly from new standard stock, and partly from the twin-articulated firsts from the pre-war "Coronation", all of them painted in the new maroon livery with which we have now become familiar. Compared with the "Coronation's" schedule of 237 minutes from Newcastle, the "Talisman" was allowed 265, but on his first round trip Cecil J. Allen estimated the net time for the up run was only 236 minutes. This fine running was achieved by a Gateshead crew on Sparrow Hawk, and included a maximum of 92 m.p.h. at Essendine.

Although the up "Talisman" working was a Gateshead one, their first lodging turn to London since pre-war, the down train was worked by the King's Cross Top Link, and within two months of its introduction, Bill was to make the newspaper headlines, with what became known as the "New Barnet Bomb Incident". This, however, was on his third northbound run on the train that particular week, and to keep in chronological order I must describe the first of these three journeys, which took place on Guy Fawkes' Day. The fireworks on the East Coast Route that evening stemmed from the fact that owing to a mishap with some empty coaches, the express left King's Cross 23 minutes late. Bill was at the regulator of Miles Beevor, and he immediately set about regaining the lost time. So well did he do this that he rolled into Newcastle six minutes early, although as he was only one minute early at Durham, the recovery margin over the final stretch must have helped this achievement. Thus he had run the 268.3 miles in no more than 239 minutes, the first time since the war that the journey had been completed in under four hours. Four days later the train left King's Cross punctually, this time with Bill driving Falcon, and they were still somewhere south of Finsbury Park when the telephone rang in the Station Master's office at King's Cross. The caller, who insisted in remaining anonymous, said there was a time bomb on the train, and although the authorities immediately suspected a hoax, they would not risk ignoring a message such as this.

On the footplate of the A4, Bill and Les Hammans were getting to grips with their load, and after the initial slog through the tunnels, had picked up speed on the drop down to Wood Green, ready for the long climb to Potters Bar. In the gloom of the late November afternoon Bill suddenly noticed the Oakleigh Park starter go to danger just as they passed it, and commented to himself that the signalman must have been rather quick putting the lever back. At New Barnet, however, all the boards were on, and he was called forward to the box, where the signalman put his head out to tell him he had a bomb aboard the train. Bill's immediate reply was typical, "We could do with two of 'em, mate", but the signalman told him that the "Flying Squad" were on their way, and they had to get the passengers out on to the platform. The police arrived in force, and inspected everything thoroughly, even searching the coal in the tender as well as the passengers' luggage, so it was not until they had stood for 25 minutes that they got the "all clear". The signalman pulled off the boards, leant out of the box, and called down to Bill, "You're right away to Newcastle". Fortunately Falcon was in good condition, and Bill succeeded in reaching Newcastle on time, so that some useful publicity was made of the incident by the railway authorities.

This bomb scare involved Bill in his first television appearance, as he was asked to take part in the I.T.V. Panel Game "Tell the Truth" the following October at the Hackney Empire. After the compere had talked about Bill's exploits on the "Talisman", he and two stooges walked on the stage, one at a time, each announcing "My name is Bill Hoole". One of these stooges was another small man, a Civil Servant from Nottingham, and the other an Electrical Salesman from Hounslow. The panel of two ladies and two men then asked the three of them some questions in turn for a few minutes, after which they had to vote on which was the real Bill Hoole. Although the stooges could invent their replies, the proper Bill was supposed to be reasonably truthful, although he was told he could use a certain amount of licence. For instance, the question "What happens if I pull the communication cord?" provoked the reply "Without a good excuse it would set you back five quid". When the voting came round, the Salesman got two, and Bill and the Civil Servant one each, so that the three of them only shared £75, instead of the £100 which they would have got if the real Bill had not got any votes. The compere asked the members of the panel why they had voted in the way they did, and the lady who had cast hers for Bill said that she had done so because she thought he had looked a bit neglected! Her sympathy thus cost him a third share in £25. His calm confidence gave him the ability to talk easily, and he was the natural choice whenever the B.B.C. or I.T.V. people asked the Eastern Region for a practical railwayman to take part in a programme, so that he also appeared on "Railway Roundabout" and "Lucky Dip" as well as other features.

7

Space does not permit an account of all Bill's exploits in the Top Link, so we must content ourselves with just some of the more outstanding stories that I have managed to collect. Much to my regret I was only able to make a few trips behind him myself, and never travelled with him on the footplate while he was on British Railways. Unlike Bill's London friends, who could reckon on seeing him at least once a day at King's Cross, his visits to the North East were less frequent. Also, while the Londoners had many opportunities to ride behind him down to Peter borough or Grantham and back, either during the day or overnight, on most of the occasions when Bill passed through Darlington, his next booked stop was London, 232 miles away. I remember very well, though, my first service run behind him, on 11th January 1955, when he and Albert Leech were working the up "Tees-Tyne Pullman" with Quicksilver. The bright sun did little to dispel the cold or melt the patchy covering of snow as I stamped my feet on Darlington platform that morning, torn between the rival wishes for a punctual arrival of the train so I could warm myself in the Pullman car, or the chance of a late start that would provide the impetus for some time recovery. It was the latter I actually got, and delays in County Durham made us 15 minutes late away from Darlington. From my window seat on the right of the second car I watched the shadow of Quicksilver's exhaust arcing up above the locomotive on the snow-clad cutting sides as we blasted our way over the Tees at Croft, and up to Eryholme, accelerating to 65 m.p.h. on the 1 in 391 bank. Then we quickly reached the 80 mark, and took Wiske Moor troughs at this speed, where the initial fine spray on the windows turned to a freezing deluge as the tender overflowed. By Thirsk we were doing 88, and speed barely fluctuated by more than a mile per hour until steam was shut off for the slow passage through York, passed in 35 minutes 33 seconds. More fine running followed, with the usual slowing to 40 for Selby, and the end of the first hour from Darlington found the brakes going on for a 20 m.p.h. relaying check just before Shaftholme Junction. The York and Selby slowings included, we had thus covered exactly 69 miles in the hour, a remarkable bit of running. Unfortunately more checks ensued, but we did get a good run down Stoke, where, as usual with this train, I had to make the awkward choice between timing our progress or enjoying the excellent lunch provided by the chef. The stop-watch won, as our speed increased to a maximum of 98 m.p.h., the fastest I had recorded to date, eclipsing by 1 m.p.h. that achieved by Ted Hailstone on the down "Plant Centenarian" eighteen months earlier, but still 2 m.p.h. less than the magic of the "ton". Two days later, when I was returning north, Ted on Silver Link worked the down Pullman up to 99, but it was not until the "Golden Jubilee Special" that Bill clinched things for me, with his maximum of 112 m.p.h.

Another run I had behind Bill was on the first Sunday of the Summer Services in 1957, when he worked thenew 2.15 p.m. Edinburgh train down to York. Sunday travel on the East Coast Route was very slow at that time, and this new service represented the first move towards faster trains, although the diversions occasioned by engineering work usually enabled travellers to enjoy more of the English countryside than their tickets would normally have permitted. On this occasion, however, we were not diverted, other than from the Fast to the Slow line and back at intervals. Bill did not take some of the turnouts with quite the caution laid down by the rubrics, and on another trip when this occurred at lunch time, there were mutters in the restaurant car when the soup got spilt.

In spite of the two spells on the Slow line, and some signal checks, we only took 198 minutes 36 seconds for the 188.1 miles, or 176 minutes net. I had spoken to Bill before leaving King's Cross, and he had broken off our conversation when he saw that one of the washout plugs on the bottom corner of Sir Nigel Gresley's firebox was weeping. Getting his spanner from the cab he gingerly tried to tighten it, cheerfully warning me to stand back, as he had known these plugs to fly out when touched, although I am not certain how much of this was for effect. When we stopped at York, I made my way up to the engine again, to find Bill showing his fireman, Trevor Brown, some of the unusual features that could be seen from the cab since it was his first visit to that fine station which had resulted from Hudson's half-boast, half-command, "Let them all come to York".

Jack Boston, living in North London, was fortunate enough to make a number of footplate trips with Bill. One such run was on the down "Fair Maid" on Guy Fawkes' Day 1957. Jack met Inspector Goodhand at King's Cross and while they were waiting for the locomotive to arrive, a message was sent down to say that the locomotive would be late as it had had some trouble with a brake hanger. Here was fate repeating itself exactly a year after Bill's record-breaking run on the "Talisman". On that cold, blustery morning, however, the clock only showed eleven minutes after the booked starting time of 7.50 when they got the "Right away", and Bill immediately set out to recover the arrears. They roared into Gasworks Tunnel with 45 per cent. cut off and full regulator, the sparks from the newly-fitted double chimney of Andrew K. McCosh bounc ing off the roof. By Hornsey they were doing 60 m.p.h., and small lumps of coal had started to follow the sparks out of the chimney, one of the latter bouncing up Jack's sleeve, which caused him to take some rather frantic avoiding action. By the time they passed his home adjoining Greenwood Signal Box, speed was 66 m.p.h., but they then had a slight signal check to contend with, which spoilt the climb to Potters Bar. Through

Hitchin they were doing 92, and in spite of the rather run-down condition of the locomotive, worked up to a maximum of 107 by Arlesey. The vibration at high speed was very bad, and proved too much for the cracked glass of the steam-chest pressure gauge, which promptly fell out, one of the pieces piercing the back of Bill's right hand and drawing blood. This produced a number of Anglo-Saxon four-letter words until he had extracted the offending sliver, but as they rolled through Peterborough he was cheerfully wiping his hands on the usual cloth, and, turning to Jack, remarked casually, "Not bad for an hour". This was only a slight exaggeration too, as they had taken 50 seconds over the even 60 minutes for the 76.4 miles. More delays ensued, with two more signal stops, separated by a maximum of 91 at Hougham. Trouble caught up with them after Doncaster, however, as Shaftholme Junction had accepted a ballast train off the line from Knottingley, which then failed to put in an appearance. Since this box was not provided with an outer home signal on the branch, all the signalman could do was to keep his boards on and wait for the recalcitrant train to appear when its work on the track was completed. This took no less than 9½ minutes, for some of which they were joined in the distance by an up express as well. Bill and Inspector Goodhand got out of the cab, going forward to look at a new overbridge being built, which also gave them the opportunity of answering the call of nature behind a suitable hedge, a luxury normally denied the crew of a steam locomotive on a long non-stop booking. After the ballast train had appeared, they got going again, with maxima of over 90 before Selby as well as after York. On this latter stretch Jack Boston drew Bill's atten tion to the position of the pointer on the scale of the reverser, which was cheerfully indicating a cut-off of a few per cent. in reverse gear. They finally stopped at the colour light controlling the platform turnout at Darlington in 213 minutes from King's Cross. Not only were they ahead of schedule again, but their net time for the 232 miles worked out at 190 minutes. When they finally stopped in Newcastle a few minutes early, Bill turned to Jack and said "There you are, it's easy. We could do it in four hours".

That evening they came back on the 10.55 p.m. sleeping car train from Newcastle, and Andrew K. McCosh had by now developed a bad blow from the centre cylinder gland. A freight too had caught fire near Selby, which held them up badly, and then a steam hose broke. Nevertheless they tried to regain what time they could, and after a maximum of over 90 down Stoke, were making good time over the racing stretch after Offord when they suddenly sighted Tempsford distant on. Down went the brake handle, and the regulator was quickly shut, but they nevertheless slid a coach length past the home signal. Bill's only comment, wiping his hands as usual, was "Hope they are all asleep". These delays prevented a punctual arrival at King's Cross, but Jack was certainly not disappointed with his round trip.

The last trip Jack had with Bill, a few weeks before he retired, started off on a down freight, and leaving Peterborough they failed to lift any water at Werrington Troughs. As Bill passed Tallington box, he popped the whistle, and leant out of the cab making a drinking motion with his hands. The importance of this message was quickly passed along the line, so that when they reached Essendine the road was set for them to go inside where they could take water. On this occasion they returned on the up " Northumbrian", and Bill announced to the Inspector that he was going to give Mr. B. another 100 down the bank, which he duly achieved, although Jack's stop-watch only recorded 108 m.p.h. compared with the 112 showing on the speedometer. They were eleven minutes early through Peterborough, where Dick Roberts was photographing them, with the result shown in this book. Bill promised Jack another 100 near Tempsford, and speed was just working up into the high 80s when the injector failed. There were immediately a lot of incantations on the footplate, but more practised efforts, in the shape of a few taps with the hammer, got it working again, but the incident robbed them of the opportunity of another "ton".

It must not be inferred from these accounts that Bill's efforts at regaining time were always crowned with success, even when he got the road. With the up "Elizabethan" he was once trying to pick up time after 80 minutes delay had been caused by a derailment at Drem. Bill took over the train at Newcastle, and they only got a moderate amount of water at Wiske Moor and Scrooby. At Muskham, however, he took the troughs fast, scattering water in all directions, with little more than a trickle getting into the tender. They consequently had to stop at Grantham for water which lost them more time than had been gained by exceeding the speed limit over the troughs, but during the stop he discovered that the scoop was damaged. From Huntingdon onwards they were getting short of coal too, but with the last climb over, Bill came down the bank from Potters Bar so fast that the Stationmaster at one of the stations sent word in to King's Cross, where an official was dispatched to remonstrate with him. When he reached the engine, however, he found Bill in con versation with a well-known member of the Eastern Region Board and during the time it took to pay his respects to him, Bill quietly sidled off, thus escaping the immediate consequences.

Bill even exceeded the speed limit with the Royal Train on one of the occasions that he worked it. The Queen was travelling down overnight to York on Sunday 3rd June 1956, and there was some new stock in the train which had not been tried out at speed on the G.N. Line. The loading gauge in Stoke Tunnel is rather tighter than elsewhere, so, to be on the safe side, a speed limit of 5 m.p.h. was imposed. Bill had Sir Nigel Gresley for this working, and an inspector accompanied him on the foot plate. As the schedule was a very easy one, Bill passed Corby Glen in good time and braked gently almost to a stop as they rolled over the top and into the tunnel. The brakes were just coming off and there would consequently not be any sudden noise to disturb anyone who was asleep on the train. The blocks were warm too, so a quiet rub as they ran through the tunnel prevented any acceleration down the 1 in 200. The inspector consulted his watch as they ran into the tunnel, and said nothing as they made their way slowly through the darkness, listening for the changing echoes that would indicate when they had reached the far end. The quiet clanking of Sir Nigel's motion suddenly softened as they emerged into the starlitnight, and Bill was congratulating himself on his effort at managing it nicely without any assistance from a watch or a speedometer. He was, however, promptly greeted by the remark "You've done it again - the limit was 5 m.p.h., not 6". They had evidently taken only five minutes to traverse the half-mile tunnel instead of the six minutes that would have been needed if the speed had been kept absolutely to the limit, but Bill considered that the inspector was probably missing his sleep and refrained from any comment. Although he had often worked the stock for the Royal Train down from Highgate, this was the first of Bill's Royal Train workings proper, and he also handled two "Deepdenes", the first of which was on October 1st 1955, when Bill worked the train to Leadenham on the line from Barkston to Lincoln. Three years later the Duke was in Newcastle, and Bill worked his train back with one of the English Electric Type 4s, No. D206. Inspector Bert Dixon came with him and was somewhat anxious throughout the trip, as it was the first occasion on which the Royal Train had been worked by a diesel on the East Coast Route. This was before the Queen had been stuck at Audley End when a Type 2 diesel-electric failed, or those concerned might have been more anxious still. On some of the occasions when Bill worked the Royal Train, Dolly went down to King's Cross to see them off. Platform 10 was completely closed, but she was able to get on to No. 8, and see things perfectly from there.

Kenneth Leech was another who made a number of footplate runs with Bill. The two of them first met at the late W. J. Reynold's suggestion on the occasion of the London, Tilbury and Southend Centenary, when they both watched the departure of the special trip behind the restored No. 80 Thundersley from Bishopsgate on 11th March 1956. The most interesting of Kenneth's four journeys with Bill was on 27th May 1957 when they had two A3s in the course of a round trip to Grantham. Going down they had Sandwich in excellent external condition on the 467-ton "Northumbrian", but something was very wrong with her steaming as the boiler pressure was down to 195 lb/sq. inch at Belle Isle and even lower by Finsbury Park, by which time the water level was also down to half a glass. They struggled over the summit at Potters Bar doing 45 m.p.h. with only 135 lb/sq. inch left on the gauge, and time was already being dropped. Bill and Inspector George Harland both had a go at firing to try to see if they could improve matters, but they were able to do little about it, and the train rolled into Grantham five minutes late, although they had regained one and a half minutes since Peterborough, Stoke Bank notwithstanding. They hooked off, and retired to the shed to try and find out the cause of the trouble, which appeared to be due to the saddle joint of the smokebox drawing air.

For the return trip on the "White Rose", Sandwich was discarded in favour of another King's Cross A3, Prince of Wales, which they found at Grantham. They prepared her with great care, the fire especially, and the safety valves were lifting at intervals as they set back on their 410-ton train, which had been delayed further north. As he opened the small ejector to create the vacuum, Bill carefully listened and watched the gauge's movements, since a keen observer could often detect a bad steamer from the indications given by these two items. Locomotives that suffered from chronic shortage of boiler pressure on the road would have the quantity of steam passing through the small ejector increased to ensure that the brakes did not leak on too quickly as the pressure dropped. Everything seemed normal, however, but once under way, their ability to maintain a full glass of water and a reasonable boiler pressure disappeared, and they were unable to exceed 40 m.p.h. by Stoke Summit, although they did reach 85 down the other side. Nevertheless they recovered half a minute to

Peterborough, and that station saved them another 15 seconds, so they were only 7¾ minutes late as they set off on the final stretch to London. After a 15 m.p.h. slack at Sandy, they had 185 lb/sq. inch in the boiler and three quarters of a glass of water, but by Three Counties, although the pressure was only 5 lb/sq. inch lower, the water level was almost out of the bottom of the glass. With the hard slog up to Knebworth ahead, they did well to recover time, going over the top with 150 lb/sq. inch on the gauge and the water nearly out of sight. Even the downhill stretch to Hatfield did little to raise either the level or the pressure, but they successfully cleared Potters Bar summit and even a slight signal check at Holloway could not prevent an arrival two minutes early. On the up trip too, Bill had taken the shovel from Dennis Ehn, but this was by no means with the object of showing him how to do it, but to give him a rest and at the same time to encourage him by demonstrating that even a fresh approach could produce no better results.

The last trip Kenneth Leech had with Bill was on 22nd June 1959, shortly before he retired, and with Sir Nigel Gresley on the up " Northumbrian" from Peterborough. They reached 91 m.p.h. through Tempsford with their 11-coach train, and at Biggleswade a smell of burning on the footplate was tracked down to an incandescent cinder that had hit the leg of the passenger's boiler suit. It turned out that the drop grate had tried a do-it-yourself effort, and what fire remained was thin enough to dance in the draught until the cause had been spotted and appropriate remedial action taken. With a minimum of 70 m.p.h. up the bank to Stevenage, the 8½-minute late start had been recovered, and they had time in hand. By Potters Bar they had no less than 25 minutes left for the 12.7 miles into the terminus, but they were then checked at every signal from Hadley Wood onwards, finally coming to a stand at Finsbury Park for 20 minutes. It thus took them as long to cover the final 11 miles as it had to cover the preceding 65½ miles, a disappointing end to a fine run.

Bill's diary for that day included the entry "Kenneth Leech

on fire" but it was some years earlier that another footplate. incident occurred which resulted in Bill finishing up soaked to the skin. On 21st May 1955 he and Fireman McLoughran were working Gannet on an early morning train to Grantham and back, and on the return trip one of the gauge glasses broke at Arlesey. To make matters worse, the ball valves did not operate, so they were bespattered with shattered glass, scalding water, and steam. Bill "dropped the handle", closed the regulator and dampers, while McLoughran got the injectors on to lower the boiler pressure. After covering one hand to protect it from the immediate effects of the steam, Bill dived quickly into the roaring white cloud, feeling for the shut off cocks to close them. This done, they were again able to see what they were doing, and after sorting themselves out, carried on with the remaining gauge for the rest of the trip, although both of them were soaked to the skin. The incident cost them 10 minutes. Another time, in the early days of the A.W.S., the "All-clear" bell sounded in the cab as they passed through Hitchin, but after ringing for the normal two seconds, failed to stop, only grating into silence as they got to St. Neots, 20 miles further on, during which time Golden Fleece had been sounding more like a fire engine than an A4 as far as its crew were concerned.

During his footplate journeys with Bill, Kenneth Leech took a number of photographs that graphically convey Bill's attitude on the footplate, his gaze centred on the track ahead, but nevertheless relaxed in his pose while he nonchalantly flicks the ash from his cigarette out of the open cab window. From the fireman's seat too, Kenneth Leech was able to take some fine shots of the track ahead, framed on the left by the foreshortened outline of the A4s that remains indelibly imprinted on the memory of anyone fortunate enough to have travelled on the footplate of this famous class. In return for the runs he had had over the East Coast Route, Kenneth Leech was able to get Bill a trip on a Western Region locomotive on one occasion in November 1957, after he had visited Chippenham, and the Bristol driver let Bill take over the regulator of the engine, Farleigh Castle. The up "Merchant Venturer" was running 25 minutes late, but when Bill set about regaining time the regular driver stopped him, much to his disappointment, but it did at least mean that there was no danger that Tregenna Castle's record on the "Cheltenham Flyer" would be eclipsed.

Another of Bill's great friends was Norman Harvey, who has, I think, been able to chronicle more of his runs in print than any other writer. Sam Gingell had introduced the two of them in 1956, and thereafter Norman became a very assiduous recorder of Bill's more notable performances, many of which have been published in the columns of the "Railway World". When Norman heard of the plans for this book, he immediately offered me his full assistance, and kindly provided me with a copy of the notes from which he has addressed many railway meetings on the subject of Bill, sometimes taking the original along to add extra interest to the evening. The appendix owes its origin to Norman too, who provided much of the information it contains from his own files.

One of the most interesting of the runs Norman recorded was, I always think, the one on the down "Flying Scotsman", on 30th May 1958. With their 11-coach load, they set off from King's Cross with Al Great Central. In spite of Ken Pettinghall's efforts with the shovel, the boiler pressure fell to 150 lb/sq. inch at Knebworth, and then both injectors started being temperamental, finally packing up at Yaxley. Like other main line men, Bill realised early on that he would be unlikely to get the locomotive through to Newcastle, so decided that the time spent changing engines at Peterborough would be repaid. He accordingly whistled up as he passed Tempsford, indicating to the signalman that he wanted another engine. There was another trick that could be played on such an occasion though, and that was to pick up as much time as possible before Peter borough, and, helped by the recovery margin, run in to stop in the station eight minutes before they were booked to pass through. This earliness had had the signalman at Holme rather puzzled, and he leant out of his box tapping the watch on his wrist. He obviously wanted to make sure that the driver of a train running early really did want a replacement engine, so Bill gave another three crows on the whistle, and as the "Flying Scotsman" came to a stand in the platform at Peter borough, V2 No. 60869 was standing alongside, ready for the change over. Ken got his shovel and equipment off the Al while Bill wound the reverser back and eased open the regulator to compress the buffers ready for the shunter to uncouple. The Peterborough fireman, after getting the headboard off, had now joined Bill on the footplate, while Ken was getting the low-down from the driver about the V2. Bill collected his gear and crossed over too, stowing them away as the Peterborough men quickly set off with the Al to New England sheds. The points slithered over, the subsidiary came off, and Bill got the first feel of the V2, as with cylinder cocks blowing, she ran forward and then set back on to the train. A quick couple-up by the shunter was followed by his shout of "Blow Up", and the hiss of the V2's blower and the clank of Ken's shovel on the firehole door were joined by the splutter of the ejectors recreating the vacuum. At the rear of the train, the guard was alternating anxious glances between his watch and the vacuum brake gauge. As its pointer quivered off the stop and started to rise, he gave the brake its quick regulation test by depressing the handle. Satisfied by the antics of the needle, he stepped to the door again, whistled and waved his green flag. On the engine, Bill was craning his neck for the "Right Away", and as soon as he had got it, made a quick check of the starter and promptly started the task of easing their 374-ton load out of the station. Only six minutes had elapsed since they had stopped, so that even allowing for the locomotive change, they still had two minutes in hand.

The V2 was in good nick, but due allowance had to be made for the state of the fire. There was plenty of coal in the box, but in the time available, the Peterborough crew had not been able to get it to burn through, so they dropped a couple of minutes to Stoke, with a minimum of 58 m.p.h. at the summit. Down the other side they reached 84 at Claypole, but had to contend with a permanent way caution and a bad signal check in the Dukeries. Helped by a generous recovery margin, they were eight early through Doncaster, although a bad caution over a viaduct outside lost them some time. Selby then stopped them momentarily, and finally they were checked by signals passing through York. Speed was in the seventies most of the way to Darlington, and with one 80 in the Croxdale dip and another through Chester-le-Street, they ran in to Newcastle in 200 minutes 32 seconds from Peterborough, 191.9 miles away. They had thus gained another two minutes on schedule, to add to the early start from Peterborough. It was most fortunate that Norman was able to log this exceedingly interesting run, which not only demonstrated some typical Hoole techniques, but provided another excellent example of the abilities of the V2s.

Another run of Bill's that has been published by Norman Harvey is remarkable, as during it Bill succeeded in running the Darlington to York stretch in exactly 35 minutes, thus equalling with steam the fastest schedule to appear in this country's timetables prior to 1966, the short-lived "Deltic" timing of 75.6 m.p.h. on the up "Tees-Tyne Pullman". Bill's run was on the 5.5 p.m. from Newcastle with Seagull, the run being timed by D. F. Howard. Their maximum was 97 through Alne. The diesel schedule was later eased to 36 minutes, but the "Deltics" have, of course, shown themselves capable of beating even 33 minutes when pushed. (The fastest I have heard of was 29½ minutes, but that is another story!)

8

As already mentioned, the King's Cross Top Link had a number of express goods workings, of which the most well known was "266 Down", the King's Cross-Niddrie train. In the 1956 winter timetable this train was substantially accelerated, being booked to run non-stop to Skelton Sidings, York, for its first examination, the 189 miles constituting a record non-stop run for a British freight service. A year later, with the wholesale revision of the East Coast passenger services referred to previously, the principal fast freights were altered too, and the "Scotch" Goods came forward to a 3.5 p.m. start, being turned "Slow Line" from Tallington to Corby Glen to allow the "West Riding" and "Afternoon Talisman" to pass. At the same time two more express freights, both usually V2-hauled, were given longer non-stop bookings, the 2.55 a.m. also running through to Skelton, and the 4.30 p.m. as far as Selby. The "Scotch" Goods was usually worked by the crew's own A4, and knowing that two of their colleagues were on the "Talisman" behind them, it was not surprising that they often took the opportunity of running early to try and keep ahead of the express.

The stop-watch brigade does not normally have the opportunity to log the performance of fast freights, so that many of Bill's efforts on "266 Down" have gone unrecorded. There is, however, one account of a run with this train which has been referred to by none other than G. F. Fiennes, the Great Northern Traffic Manager at that time. Although no driver's name is mentioned, one cannot fail to imagine that Bill was responsible, but, to be Irish, if he was not, there is no doubt that he would have wished he had been. The train was 23 minutes late away because of some last-minute repairs required on the locomotive, and as Mr. Fiennes put it, "The driver knew that unless he got his skates on, the 3.40 Leeds (the 'West Riding') and the 'Talisman' would catch him before Peterborough, and the 4.50 before Grantham. By Hitchin he had got his train well on the swing and ran the 27 miles from Hitchin to Huntingdon in 20 minutes." As these fitted freights were strictly-speaking limited to 55 m.p.h., this was somewhat overdoing it, and a hot box developed on one of the wagons, forcing them to stop and put it off at Peterborough. Control decided to hold them there while the passenger trains were allowed past, and to return to Mr. Fiennes' words, "When the signal came off, nothing daunted, he set off after them and caught the 'Talisman' at Retford. Probably that is the only time that I shall ever see on the Express Freight Sheets the entry

"266 Down, five minutes' delay at Grove Road waiting for 'Talisman' to clear." For such an authority to make public runs of this sort, with its infringement of some of the limits, shows clearly how highly they thought of the morale and abilities of the East Coast crews at that time.

Bill also tells a few stories of this train which could be an exacting working from the crew's point of view. If some bad weather ever coincided with a trip for which an Al was provided, it could be touch and go whether they would get through without running out of coal. On these occasions they were very glad to get through Durham with just sufficient in the firebox for the last few miles, and sometimes the relief driver had only enough steam pressure left in the boiler to get the light engine on to Heaton Sheds, where the engine on this particular working was stabled. One day on this train Bill had Dick Doran riding with him, and another passenger, Mike Langdon, in the brake van. They had a load of small coal in the tender, and Bill realised it was doubtful if they would get through. The engine was inclined to do some spark throwing, and they were stopped three times before Doncaster by fires starting on the floor boards of the same "Conflat", which seemed to have a propensity to collect the red-hot cinders. On the last occasion they got the crew of a light engine on the adjoining line to put the fire out withtheir slacker pipe. With these extra delays, the coal situation became worse still, but they just managed to make Newcastle. The load of this train was limited to 50 wagons, all of them for Scotland, and it would be a hard slog, especially up Stoke, since the total weight would come to something over 750 tons. With this behind the tender, they were lucky to go over the top at more than 35 m.p.h., and the fireman would then be able to sit down for a welcome breather over the easier grades that follow as far as Newark. Out of King's Cross it was not quite so hard going, as Bill believed in leaving London "as casually as you could, to enable the boxes to warm up gradually, which permitted you to get cracking later" (i.e. averaging 81 m.p.h.

for nearly 30 miles on end). In spite of Mr. Fiennes' story, hot boxes were not common, certainly much less frequent than they were in the early diesel days when anyone could get high speeds with a freight train, just by moving the control lever round an inch or two too far. (The maximum I have ever heard about was 20 odd between Stockton and York.) There was one other very important incentive with "266 Down" to reach Newcastle early. They were booked to be relieved on the freight line outside the Central Station at 10.30 p.m., which was closing time. Bill was never a great drinker, but he had every sympathy with any fireman who wanted a quick pint or two after 260-odd miles of hard work in the full glare of a Pacific's firebox. Whenever possible, therefore, he tried to run in early, letting his fireman drop off as they travelled the last short distance with their flanges squeaking on the sharp curves and turn outs, so he could get to the station buffet with time for a couple of pints before "Last Drinks" was called.

9

Bill always liked working the up "Tees-Tyne Pullman" as it formed a nice morning's work and enabled him to get home for dinner. He and Dolly were very fond of the theatre, especially musical comedies, and they would often go to one of these when Bill was on a morning turn such as this. Dolly would travel down to town early to buy a stool in the queue for the gallery, and then did her shopping and jobs, before meeting Bill when he arrived. After a meal and some window-shopping, they would then take their place in the queue in time for the evening show.

In Bill's later Top Link days, with their two daughters married and off their hands, he and Dolly were able to go abroad for their holidays, helped, of course, by the free passes they could obtain on the foreign railways. In July 1956 they travelled up the Rhine, crossing from Harwich to the Hook on the S.S. Arnhem. There they boarded the motor yacht Serenity for the river journey, spending the first night at Cologne and the second at Koblenz. The trip was a great success, but at one point the yacht was nearly overcome by the lure of the Lorelei or another of the goddesses of the Rhine, as one of the wire ropes holding the rudder snapped. Fort unately the Tranquility, a sister yacht, quickly got a tow rope to them, so they were not swept very far down stream in the rapid flow of icy water, while red flags hoisted on the banks warned other shipping to keep clear. The next year Bill and Dolly went even further afield, taking to the air for part of the journey. In mid-October they travelled from Victoria to Paris, arriving in the middle of a strike which made them very late. They were only just able to get a meal before making for the 8.30 p.m. train from the Gare de Lyon, which took them southwards overnight and during much of the next day as far as Barcelona, where they arrived at 2 p.m. After a day recovering from the journey, they visited a distillery, Sitges beach and the fountains, before watching the Shrimp dancing until 2.00 a.m. On the Sunday, they went by air to Majorca, finding the noise in the small twin-engined aircraft ear-splitting. On the island, they visited the various places of interest during the following week, and Bill records in his diary their enjoyment of the prickly pear they purchased at Genora. The week over, they reluctantly made their way to the airport again, and returned home by the same route they had followed on the outward journey, having a clear day in London before Bill reported to Top Shed once more to work the 8.20 a.m. to Doncaster.

10

This account of some of Bill's more outstanding runs has taken us well forward in time, almost until his retirement in July 1959, and much more could be written about his exploits with steam locomotives. In 1955, however, British Railways' Modernisation Plan was announced, and with it, the intention to change over to diesel and electric motive power. After ordering a number of different diesel designs by way of a pilot scheme, it was quickly realised that there was an urgent need to get diesel traction into operation as quickly as possible, so that time did not permit a full evaluation of the different locomotives before embarking on the large scale production of certain of the types. As far as the G.N. Main Line was concerned, the first express diesels they were to receive were five of the English Electric Type 4 diesel-electrics of 2,000 horsepower. Delivered during the late summer of 1958, they were used between King's Cross and Newcastle on the existing steam schedules. Even then, the basic design of these locomotives was some 10 years old, going back to the Southern trio of 1-Co-Co-ls, which in turn had considerable similarities to the L.M.S. twins Nos. 10000/1. Their inability to deliver more than 1,500 drawbar horsepower or thereabouts, made the Type 4s inferior to an A4 in good condition and with a fireman prepared to work hard. They were never theless the most powerful single units then available, although the East Coast Route authorities had realised the need for more horsepower and ordered 22 of the "Deltics" from English Electric, which were not only 65 per cent. more powerful, but a great deal lighter. The "Deltics" were based on the private venture prototype that English Electric had built in 1955, and which, first of all, had been in service on the London Midland main line out of Euston. After the East Coast people had decided to purchase their 22 similar locomotives, the prototype was transferred across to the Eastern Region, which enabled them to gain some very valuable experience before large-scale deliveries commenced. During the last few months before he retired, Bill thus had the opportunity of trying his hand at driving this new form of traction, and put up some remarkable perform ances, although, like many of us, he found the diesels lacked the romance of steam.

Bill's first acquaintance with diesel traction began in June 1958 when he received the following summons to attend the Diesel Training Course at Ilford:

"Will you please note you will be required to commence your Diesel Training Course on Monday next, 16th June 1958.

The course, as you are no doubt already aware, will be of three weeks' duration, the first week being theoretical at Ilford Training School, the second and third weeks being practical training at the Shed and on the road.

Your schedule for the next five weeks will be:
Week commencing 16th June, Theory at Ilford
,, ,, 23rd June, Rostered working
,, ,, 30th June, Practical training
,, ,, 7th July, Rostered working
,, ,, 14th July, Practical training

Your Rest Day for next week will be taken on Saturday 21st June. On Monday 16th June you will be required to report at the School (Aldersbrook House, off High Road, Ilford) at 12.0 noon. You will then have lunch and the afternoon session will finish at 5.0 p.m. On the following days the course will be from 9.00 a.m. to 5 p.m. Lunch, etc., will be provided and overalls will not be required.

You will not be required to sign on or book off duty when at Ilford, or submit tickets, but you will be allowed (on Monday excepted) a total of two hours a day for travelling purposes.

You will pay your ordinary fare between King's Cross and Liverpool Street and an allowance of a shilling per day will be entered in the paybill for this."

Bill found the school very interesting, and quickly became very anxious to try the new form of motive power out on the road. The last week of the course started with a practical test at Hornsey on the first of the Type 4s, No. D201, and on the next two days they travelled down to Peterborough and back with this locomotive, the various trainees taking it in turn to handle the controls. On the Thursday the actual driving test took place, and on the Friday Bill successfully passed the full diesel examination at Hornsey. During the following week he worked his normal turns on steam locomotives, which included the "Elizabethan" with Golden Fleece on the Friday and Saturday, when he had a footplate passenger for the journey. This was Arnold Quick, the Chairman of the North East Essex Transport Committee and subsequently treasurer of the Essex County Cricket Club, who was accompanied by Chief Inspector Bert Dixon. All of them finished up at the North British Hotel that evening, which was somewhat more luxurious than the usual standard of overnight accommodation that Bill frequented on this lodging turn. During the trip, Arnold Quick had been standing in the front of the corridor on the tender as they passed over Scrooby troughs. Unfortunately the tank had overflowed, drenching him to the skin, and he had to dry himself out in front of the firehole door.

On the Saturday, Bill worked back to London again, but by now they had given up the impossible task of trying to operate the "Non-Stop" at week-ends, and calls were made at Newcastle and York with a correspondingly slower timing. Coming down Stoke, Bill suggested that Arnold Quick should have a go with the shovel, but after five minutes, during which the pressure gauge steadily crept backwards, Bill removed the shovel from his guest's hands with the comment: "If you carry on much longer, then we shall come to a dead b ... halt". When they arrived back in London at 5.30, Mr. Quick decided to have an early dinner in the Savoy before catching his train home to Clacton. The A4s are reasonably clean engines to ride on as steam locomotives go, but few footplate passengers were in the habit of going to that hotel after a journey from Newcastle. Arnold Quick's appearance consequently caused some surprise for the Floor Waiter, who came up and asked if he was in the right place, this was the Savoy Grill Room. As a result of this trip, Arnold Quick invited Bill and Dolly to Clacton, and they spent one of Bill's rest days there with his family at the end of August.

Bill's first solo diesel runs were on 28th and 29th July, when he took D206 to Peterborough on the "Heart of Midlothian", the journeys proving uneventful, as did the next one with D207 on Friday August 1st.

A month passed before Bill was rostered with a diesel again. This and his next trip with them were both disappointing. On September 2nd D206 lost him eight minutes at Spital because of a faulty relay contact, and two days later the fire alarm started on D207 at Decoy, which caused them another similar delay, and in addition the train heating boiler was out of order on this second run. Over the remaining four months of the year, the incidence of diesel turns was very irregular, but on 6th January 1959 it was a diesel's turn to suffer from Bill's efforts, rather than vice versa.

Bill was working the 11.20 p.m. down to Newcastle with D207, and there was heavy snow during the grim journey, which upset the signalling so much that they were continually being called forward by signalmen against signals at danger. At Arksey, signal No. 17, protecting the turnout for the down loop, was at danger and they stopped, sounding their horn to tell the signalman. Then through the falling snow they saw a green light being waved from side to side, the recognised calling-forward signal. Although they should have used the telephone to check with the signalman, the practice of passing signals under such conditions had become so much a feature of the run, that Bill eased the controller round and set off along the line. They had only gone a few yards, however, before a thump from behind them indicated that one of their bogies was off the line. Immediate steps were taken to protect the train, and Bill then discovered that the green lamp was not one being waved by the signalman but was an optical illusion caused by a man walking down the side of the track, swinging in his hand a Tilley lamp, the base of which was painted green. They made the person concerned do it all over again so that others could see what had happened, and having shut the diesel down, they were relieved at 6.10 a.m., nearly nine hours after they had signed on. Then came the usual round of report writing and so on, but in view of the unusual circumstances that led to the derailment, Bill was let off with a Verbal Caution in place of the original Reprimand. The derailment caused more than the usual amount of difficulty for the breakdown gang too, not only because of the shocking weather conditions, but due to the fact that British Railways at that period had no cranes capable of lifting one of the Type 4 diesels, not even one end at a time. As a result they had to use jacks and packing to get D207 back on to the rails.

From mid-January onwards, however, Bill was involved with the prototype "Deltic", after it had been transferred to the Eastern Region. On Sunday 18th he travelled down passenger to York, and at 7 a.m. the following morning made his way through the yards to collect the blue and yellow monster, which had worked across the Pennines from Newton-le-Willows, where it had been overhauled before being transferred. They worked the locomotive slowly up to Hornsey in easy stages, trying out the clearances at various places en route, and did not arrive until 4 p.m.

Next day was spent at Hornsey Shed, where Chief Inspector Bert Dixon, Driver Perce Edwards, and Bill were thoroughly shown over the locomotive by the English Electric people. The "Deltic", with its 3,300 h.p., was clearly a much more potent piece of machinery than a Type 4, but Bill's sense of humour was well to the fore as he was shown round by the English Electric representative who always travelled with it. Catching sight of the maximum speed notice inside the cab, he is reported to have com mented with a twinkle in his eye, "Wot, only 90 m.p.h. ?" This maximum speed was clearly too low for the performance standards the Eastern Region were contemplating, and after a very brief stay in London it travelled north once more to have the gearing on the electric motors altered to permit a speed of 1 05 m. p.h. After this change had taken place, each of the King's Cross Top Link drivers was taken out on a trip by Bill or one of the other two who had been trained on her by the English Electric people, and the operation of the locomotive explained. As far as Bill was concerned, these runs occupied the second half of February, being mainly to Doncaster and back.

The G.N. Line management were extremely interested in their new machine, and Cyril Palmer, the Motive Power Officer, rode with Bill to Doncaster and back on the 18th February. The following Monday, however, there was an even larger party aboard, as G. F. Fiennes and C. N. Morris joined Cyril Palmer on the 9.5 a.m. working to Doncaster, to find out at first-hand what the locomotive was like. On March 4th came the first of the test runs with the "Deltic" that involved Bill, and on the next day Bill's diary recorded the various speeds they had achieved, but unfortunately he failed to note the size of the load they were hauling. The next time Bill got this locomotive was on 16th March, when he worked it down to Newcastle. The prototype "Deltic" was built to a somewhat generous loading gauge, and the tighter clearances in the North Eastern Region resulted in her being banned north of York for ordinary purposes, as she was not allowed to use any of the platform roads at Darlington or Newcastle, the test runs starting and finishing at Greenfield, Gateshead. Nevertheless the performance of this new type of locomotive on the Eastern Region was exciting general interest, and Bill was interviewed in a B.B.C. News Broadcast about it. By this time they were trying her out with a load of nearly 550 tons, and on the up trip they ran from York to passing Hatfield in half a minute under 2½ hours, their net time being 145 minutes for the 170.4 miles. It is interesting in retrospect to note that on the guard's journal for the trip the steam supply for carriage heating was not satisfactory, a difficulty that continued with the production versions. Later they tried her on freight stock, hanging a 50 wagon coal train weighing no less than 1,146 tons behind her for a trial run from Doncaster to Ferme Park, timed at an average of 60 m.p.h. They did not succeed in managing it, as two wagons ran hot and had to be put off at St. Neots and Welwyn Garden City. However, when the production versions entered service several years later, their rosters on passenger turns were sufficiently intensive to prevent any use being made of them on freight workings. Amongst the Platform Enders, the

"Deltic" got christened the "Ice Cream Wagon" because of its livery, which resembled the colours of the vans which at that time were common in London. Before his association with this locomotive ended, Bill drove it for two more test runs. One of them was with a 4-coach special filled with permanent way staff, a speedometer being installed in the front vehicle, so they could see how fast they were going. Starting at the north end of Huntingdon station, they were doing 40 m.p.h. by the time they cleared the platform, and took no more than 16 minutes for the 27.0 miles to Hitchin, an average of just 100 m.p.h. Bill was allowed to run faster than the normal speed limits, and the object of the trip was to demonstrate to the engineering staff the sort of performance that their track would have to withstand in the future. At this time too, the long welded rail programme was just getting under way, and up to that time, the stop watch addicts had not yet seriously had to face up to the dilemma that they encounter nowadays, when the mileposts are invisible.

The most exciting run with the "Deltic" was when a series of stopping trials was being carried out. The object of these was to see how the signalling on the G.N. line would have to be altered to cope with the speeds that were being contemplated. The most dramatic of these were carried out by waiting until they flashed past a selected distant signal and then, using this as a marker, making a full emergency brake application. Double block working was in force on this occasion, and as they raced down Stoke Bank on the return run, they reached the full 105 m.p.h. permitted for the locomotive as they came up to Lolham distant. As they passed the signal, Bill put the "Whoa-er" down and the brakes went on fully throughout the 10 coach train, but it was not until the stop signals, which were kept at danger for this test, had disappeared well behind them that they finally came to a stand, just over 6,200 ft. beyond the distant. In normal practice, however, the driver would start to brake as soon as he sighted an adverse distant, rather than waiting until he actually passed it, but this test run showed how close the margin was, here as elsewhere. I know too, from footplate trips of my own over the East Coast main line, how drivers used to dislike this particular set of signals, some of them regularly shutting off as they approached this point, with everything ready to make a full brake application if the distant (a colour light), which was not very visible in daylight, was showing yellow. The high speed that the "Deltic" had achieved was all the more notable because of a 25 m.p.h. relaying check through Corby Glen.

At the end of April, Bill got involved in another series of stopping trials, this time with Type 4 No. D206. The object of these was to try out the effects of adjusting the rate at which the brakes on the locomotive were applied as a result of the deadman's pedal being released or a caution indication on the AWS going unacknowledged. Compared with a steam locomotive, a diesel has more braking power, and with a loose-coupled freight train, there is thus the possibility that the locomotive could almost have stopped before the rear wagons buffer up, which would mean they were still moving at their full, unchecked, speed. It was most important to be able to reach a satisfactory compromise between the dangers of an excessive "click" of this sort, and of making the brake too slow acting to give sufficiently short stopping distances at high speeds. The trials were to be carried out at Bottesford on the Grantham-Nottingham line, and as the King's Cross crews were the only ones trained on the Type 4 diesels, it involved one of them spending a week at Grantham. Bill was very interested in the prospect and squared things with the local branch of the Union so that he could take part.

No. D206 was taken down light on the Sunday to Grantham, and the first two days were passed in a series of static tests, but the excitement started on the following day. One of the reasons for the particular choice of the site was the presence of a large dump of freight stock awaiting scrapping, so any damage that was caused to the vehicles did not matter. The trials were all carried out at low speed where the effect of sudden braking is most dangerous with unfitted stock. After making up a suitable train they would potter along at the desired 5, 10, _15, or 20 m.p.h. to the required point where Bill would either release the deadman's pedal or the AWS magnet between the rails would apply the brakes. The technical people would take the required observations during and after the stop, after which Bill would sort out the wagons that were too damaged and replace them with some more out of the adjacent sidings. Certain of the results were extremely spectacular, and after one or two trials, the guard elected to watch what was going on from the lineside rather than travel in his van. This was as well, because in the final test everyone in the cab had to put their feet up on the front bulkhead to brace themselves for the shock as the wagons piled into the nearly-stationary locomotive. By the time the concertina effect made itself felt at the end of the train, the shock on the guard's van was so great that one of the doors to the end verandahs was wrenched off its hinges. Bill claims that the impact was sufficient to move the diesel engine on the frame, but this is, I think, driver's licence, and the tests concluded without having to exchange locomotives, although on the Friday they had to adjourn to Lincoln for a while to refuel. The last tests were on the Saturday, and in the evening, Bill worked No. D206 back light from Grantham, booking off at 9.15 p.m., his wages for that week coming to £25 6s. 0d. as a result of the overtime worked. Although the intricacies of the equipment were naturally beyond him, he was most interested in the tests themselves, not to mention the opportunity of indulging in some paid train wrecking.

There is no doubt that in the few months with which he was associated with them, Bill derived a great deal of interest from handling the diesels, but I am certain he would soon have found them very dull had he driven them day in and day out. He has commented about their impersonality and the degree of remote control involved, while the very nature of this form of motive power means that anyone can obtain the same power output, regardless of his skill. Bill has said that if Dolly knew the road she would have been able to drive one, and do her knitting at the same time, but I do not know whether the design panel could have been persuaded to fit each cab with row counters, like the intriguing one that always has to be hurriedly rescued and put out of the reach of any young children who go into her kitchen. This comment of Bill's, is, of course, typical of his sense of humour, and no one appreciates more than he the exacting task of driving the "Deltics" regularly on the present-day East Coast schedules.

11

By 1959, Bill's remaining days on the Main Line were rapidly drawing to a close, but few drivers could have had a more exciting last few months than he did, with the running of the Stephenson Locomotive Society's "Golden Jubilee Special" on Saturday May 23rd, as will be described in the next chapter. After that, his last 6½ weeks were all spent on steam turns up and down the main line. Bill's forthcoming retirement was looked at with great regret amongst the railway enthusiasts, and many of his particular friends took their last chance of riding with him, which also kept the King's Cross Inspectors busy. He also went to Durham School on the morning of June 10th, to talk to the boys before working home on the 3 p.m. from Newcastle, and was presented with an inscribed cigarette case. He also had his final interview with C. N. Morris, his District Motive Power Superintendent, at Great Northern House.

While there was regret among the enthusiasts at Bill's retirement, this event, I gather, caused a certain amount of relief in official circles at King's Cross. In his latter years, he was liked as a person by Foremen and Inspectors, who respected his confidence on a locomotive, and the text book job he could turn out when he wanted to do so. There is no doubt that many of Bill's efforts, such as that with the "Talisman" after the Bomb Incident, were the cause of great satisfaction to the authorities, but some of his more exuberant efforts, when tearing round the place for no apparent reason, sometimes caused people a lot of trouble, and he often could not resist playing to the gallery nor the encouragement of his admirers. There were consequently many of his supervisors who were relieved when he retired, although they were sorry to see the last of him as a person. It was his personality, therefore, that had enabled him to get away with more than many other drivers would have done, and I am certain that had it not been for this, he would not have finished his days on British Railways as a main line driver, and this book would not have been written. Many other drivers in their turn have served the railways equally as well over the years without getting into trouble to the extent that Bill did, and while several of them have also become well known in enthusiasts' circles, it was again Bill's personality, as much as his deeds, that attracted his group of admirers and friends.

Bill's 65th birthday was not until July 27th, 1959, but he had some holiday entitlement to take that year, and his last run was thus on Tuesday 7th, which happened to be an occasion on which he was rostered to work the "Elizabethan". The day before, he and Alf Hancox had taken Merlin on the first stage of the non-stop journey to Scotland, and as the same locomotive was speeding its way southwards across the Plain of York, Bill left their reserved compartment for the last time and made his way forward on to the footplate of the A4. Merlin was in good nick, and only the bare routine exchanges were necessary with the Scottish crew before they collected their gear and went back through the tender, leaving Bill in charge. Alan Pegler was on the train that day to take a last trip with Bill, while as usual, on such occasions, many of those along the line who knew him were ready with a last wave or a farewell whistle from their locomotive to wish him well in his retirement. Soon they were slowing for York, passing the usual vast number of steam locomotives in the depot to their right, on which the diesels had by then scarcely made any inroads. Green colour lights and illuminated route indicators beckoned him under the majestic sweep of the station roof, which half way through echoed to the beat of the exhaust as Bill tugged the regulator open again to pick up speed once more. The rumbles of Naburn and Selby bridges passed behind them, and soon they were easing to 50 through the centre road at Doncaster and continuing southwards between the acres of sidings and other railway installations. Alf broke off from his work with the shovel and injectors so as to take water at Scrooby and then Trent, latching the scoop in the raised position as they passed the gravel pits with their rotting hulks of barges. The tracks were now opening out on the approach to the foam-covered river itself, the diagonal bracing of the twin viaducts producing its dazzling patterns out of the cab-side windows, and then their wheels thumped across the spaces in the London Midland level crossing just beyond. From Newark up to Stoke the engine was worked hard, which kept Alf firing more or less continuously until the summit was reached, but he could then take his seat and hang on while Bill let her rip down the other side. Everything was set for a final "ton", but suddenly a distant was spotted at caution and the regulator closed. The brakes were applied for water at Werrington, and then used to check speed right down for the slow passage through Peterborough. Clear of the low overall roof, so different from the spaciousness of York, Merlin erupted into life again, her exhaust becoming suddenly more purposeful as she lifted the train up the sharply inclined reverse curve past the power station to the bridge across the Nene.

They were now on the most familiar stretch of all as far as Bill was concerned, with all its old well-known landmarks that he had first got to know 15 years before. After the brickworks, the riding of the A4 became that little bit worse as they dipped down on to the fen between Yaxley and Holme, the two tracks, between the sedge and the birch thickets, opening out from the usual six feet to spread the load over a greater width of the soft black soil that regularly swallows up the materials tipped in by the engineers. Huntingdon slipped past, and, the Offord restriction over, Alf remembered to catch a last glimpse of the St. Neots clock as they sped through. They dived under the bridges at Sandy before catching a glimpse of the blaze of colour from the station garden. Biggleswade, with its blue-brick cuttings, and the steepening gradients sent Alf back into the tender more frequently to bring forward the coal required to keep the locomotive going on the fast slog up to Stevenage, and Hitchin echoed to the roar of Merlin's exhaust, the beat becoming more distinct now as the speed dropped off up the 1 in 200. Four tracks became two, and the haunting sound of Merlin's chime whistle reverberated in the cuttings as they ran through the Welwyn Tunnels and out across the lofty viaduct at Digswell. From Hatfield up to Potters Bar came the last bit of hard steaming, and then Alf could sweep the coal dust off the footplate and wash up as Bill came down the bank, still finding it slightly odd to be apparently running wrong road through the old tunnels as far as Greenwood, since the altered track layout had only come into use a few weeks previously with the opening of the three new tunnels. New Barnet, New Southgate, Wood Green, Finsbury Park, and Holloway sped past, all with their memories, but speed was being progressively reduced, until finally they were dropping down the bank for the last time through Copenhagen Tunnel, to draw slowly to a stand at Belle Isle Box. The restrictive track layout of the terminus had once more halted the "Non stop" almost within sight of the terminus, but the signal quickly cleared, and with a blast on the chime whistle they were swallowed up in the darkness of Gasworks Tunnel, Bill regulating his speed by the gas lamps on the wall. Before emerging they sounded a final whistle to warn anyone crossing the tracks outside the terminus, and they were out into the daylight once more, twisting their way over the junctions past the signal box. The porters were already in position as the train made its slow way along Platform 4, while Bill alternately eased Merlin's brake handle downor raised it to invoke the sharper hiss of the large ejector, aiming as usual at stopping by the footbridge halfway along the platform. Then, with the use of a little more steam, they continued the last few yards, the "Elizabethan" coming gently to a stand just clear of the buffer stops, by the small group waiting to saytheir farewells, which included Dolly and Irene, as well as some of his friends and a B.B.C. interviewer. The brake handle went right down, the lingering sigh of the inrushing air stopped as he turned off the small ejector with a quick twist of his wrist, and Bill's main line career was at an end - "On Time".

CHAPTER SEVEN

Enthusiasts' Idol

Nowadays we take the operation of frequent rail tours very much as an accepted part of the enthusiast's calendar, and yet, 10 years ago, the total number of trains of this sort that had ever been arranged in this country was fewer than would now be projected in a single month. Indeed, in the Coming Events columns of the "Railway Magazine" for September 1965, no fewer than 19 projected tours were listed for that month alone, a total, however, that proved to be too ambitious and uncoordinated, since lack of adequate support caused the cancellation of several ventures. The East Coast Route has been associated with rail tours almost from their inception, at least as far as the Railway Correspondence and Travel Society is concerned, who took the opportunity of arranging a special train to Peterborough and back in pre-war days behind the Stirling single, No. 1, which the L.N.E.R. had restored in connection with their publicity for the new stock built for the "Flying Scotsman" in 1938. As already mentioned, the Eastern Region organised the "Ivatt Atlantic Special" in 1950, and this was followed the next year by the privately-sponsored "Centenaries Express". It was not until 1953, however, that Bill became involved with any of these special workings, when he was chosen to drive the Ivatt Atlantic No. 251 on the "Plant Centenarian".

The "Plant Centenarian" was the most ambitious venture that Trevor Bailey, Alan Pegler, and Les Smith had so far organised, and in some respects it is still unique in that it was the only occasion when two locomotives have been privately brought out of retirement to work a special train. The engines concerned were No. 990 Henry Oakley, the prototype Ivatt Atlantic, and No. 251, the first of the more famous large-boilered versions. Henry Oakley had been withdrawn in pre-war days and was on display at York Museum, so had to be hauled out of there on 21st July and sent to Doncaster for overhaul, together with the Stirling "Single", the event being marked by sound and television broadcasts. No. 251 had similarly been scheduled for exhibition at York after withdrawal, but lack of space had prevented her going there, so she had been kept at Doncaster after restoration to her original external condition. This operation had resulted in the removal of her water scoop and superheater. The boiler she was carrying at the time was not changed, and the only alteration made was to remove the superheater and replace the chimney in its original position, further back on the smokebox. When the locomotive was prepared for working once more, this caused some difficulties, since, if the boiler was left in that particular state, too high a proportion of the firebox gases would have gone down the superheater flues, where they would not have been particularly effective in giving up their heat to the water. Dummy superheater elements were therefore fitted in the flues, and although steaming was somewhat tricky, the locomotive performed excellently. In order to spread the costs of the restoration work, the organisers decided to run the train on two successive Sundays, the first starting from London and the second from Leeds, a move which also enabled the large number of enthusiasts living in the North of England to take part a great deal more easily. Alan Pegler subsequently also made use of No. 251 on a number of other excursions he arranged, paired this time with a former Great Central "Director".

The outward journey on each occasion was behind the two Atlantics. On the first Sunday this was direct from King's Cross to Doncaster, where those taking part were able to spend 1¾ hours looking round the Works.

Then came the return trip, this time with Silver Link in charge, and for the first time on such a special train, a really high speed was attempted down Stoke, but unfortunately the magical 100 was not achieved. The following week the train started at Leeds Central at 8.45 a.m. and ran to Doncaster where it stopped for just over 1½ hours while people looked round the works. It then continued to London, travelling via Lincoln to Grantham, as the main line was blocked by engineering operations. Just under an hour was spent in London before Silver Link again took over for the return trip by the same route as that followed on the outward journey. Some of the preparations necessary beforehand have already been described, but a series of trial runs were organised in order to test out the old locomotives, and get the crews used to handling them. Early on in the summer of 1953, No. 251 made a number of trips between Doncaster and Lincoln or Scunthorpe, and, together with Henry Oakley, worked a 434-ton empty stock train to Lincoln early in September. At the London end, Allan Garraway had a lot to do with the preparations on the locomotive side, and one of his first jobs was allocating suitable drivers to work the specials.

He was very pleased to find that the turns being worked by Ted Hailstone and Bill were such that they could be rostered for the job, and on the Wednesday and Thursday before the first special run, the two locomotives with these drivers were turned out to work the 5.00 p.m. King's Cross-Peterborough. Word got round the grape-vine that they would be running, and numerous enthusiasts turned out to see them, although the eyes nearly popped out of the heads of some of the spotters who were not in the know, when the pair of Atlantics emerged from Gasworks Tunnel to set back on their train. They were not the only ones to be surprised too, as someone in the King's Cross signal box rang up Top Shed to enquire which train the second locomotive was for, so unusual was the use of a pilot engine on the G.N. Main Line. On the first occasion Les Smith and Trevor Bailey rode on the two engines, and the Thursday evening saw Richard Hardy on No. 990 and Allan Garraway joining Bill on No. 251.

Sunday 20th was a fine sunny day, but cool enough to show up the exhausts of the veterans as they lifted their 11-coach load up the bank out of King's Cross. Accommodation was in open coaches, with kitchen cars marshalled between them, and in the centre came the 1938 Buffet Lounge Car built for the "Flying Scotsman", with its ladies' powder room at one end. Jim Wilson was firing for Ted Hailstone, and Albert Leech for Bill, and the trip to Doncaster went well. After a minimum of 42 up to Potters Bar, there came the 5 m.p.h. restriction over the bridge work, but the train covered the 27.0 miles from Hitchin to Huntingdon in less than 31 minutes, in spite of being turned slow line at Paxton. Water was taken at Peterborough, after a maximum of 73 m.p.h. at Holme, and the minimum over Stoke was 48 m.p.h. Nothing outstanding, but nevertheless a run that delighted all those taking part, as well as the numerous lineside photographers, now a usual feature of rail tours, but at that time completely unexpected. The two Atlantics were in spotless condition, with their steel- and brass-work shining in the sun. There was a large crowd awaiting them at Doncaster, with the T.V. cameras among them, and everyone surged round the two locomotives. Albert Leech has told me how Bill turned to him and said "Come on, let's leave Ted Hailstone and Jimmy Wilson on 990 to enjoy themselves", while the two of them slipped across the rails to the shunter's cabin for a wash and change. Ted transferred to Silver Link for the return journey, and attained a top speed of 96 m.p.h. down Stoke, which in 1953 created quite a sensation. With three permanent way checks, they ran the 156.0 miles to King's Cross non-stop in 147 minutes 7 seconds, an excellent performance, especially as Jimmy Wilson had fired for over 300 miles by the time they arrived back at the terminus.

I travelled on the "Plant Centenarian" the following Sunday, and because of the difficulty with connections from Middlesbrough, had to join the train at Doncaster. O. S. Nock started at Leeds, however, and recorded a rousing climb of the 1 in 100 up to Ardsley, with a slight accel eration beyond Beeston from a minimum of 30 m.p.h. Doncaster was swarming with enthusiasts, and the Stirling eight-footer had been brought out from the works to stand in the bay platform alongside the two Atlantics which remained in the station while the passengers toured the "Plant". Bill and Albert were still on No. 251, but although Ted Hailstone was to work north with Silver Link on the return journey, he was not on No. 990, and his place was taken by Alf Cartwright and A. Barker of Copley Hill. Chief Inspector Sam Jenkins rode on Henry Oakley, and Bill's old A.R.P. colleague, Inspector Bert Dixon, joined him on No. 251. Coming from Leeds, the crew of Henry Oakley made an exhibition of their footplate, and during the hour or so spent at Doncaster, the cab was constantly full of admirers, which prevented them giving the fire much in the way of attention. There was another excursion for London that day, headed by the Al, Foxhunter, but as it was booked to take water at Lincoln, Control decided to hold it at Doncaster while the "Plant Cen tenarian" took precedence, the blue Pacific, also with an Inspector aboard, standing in the centre road until the two green Atlantics, aided by a rear-end shove from a J52, had rolled their train over the curves and away southwards through the misty morning. Bill, of course, would not normally have known the road via Lincoln, but for this occasion he learnt it in 2½ days early in September, assisted by the arrangements made by R. H. R. Garraway, Allan's father, who was D.M.P.S. at Lincoln from 1941 until he retired in 1954. Henry Oakley's steaming now started to give trouble, as a result of the visitors at Doncaster. From the footplate of No. 251, Bill could see right into the cab of the smaller engine in front, even being able to pick out the downward movement of the pressure gauge, while the rueful faces of her crew indicated that they were in difficulties. No. 251 was going well, however, and Bill was able to open her up to take a larger share of the work while No. 990 was pulled round. The sun cleared the mist as the special ran through Lincoln, enabling the superb views of the cathedral to be enjoyed to the full by those aboard, although by now lunch was being served throughout the train. From Doncaster the fare was only 55s. 0d., and for this everyone was provided with afternoon tea as well as lunch. The lunch menu included such topical items as Creme Klondyke, Poulet

Roti a l'Atlantique, Cauliflower Double-Headed, although some doubt was expressed by the East Coast fanatics about the inclusion of that particular vegetable, and Meringue Ivatt. Both engines had to take water at Grantham, which necessitated a 5-minute stop, during which a solid semi-circle of photographers blocked the up and down main lines at the south end of the platforms.

The organisers had invited a number of notable visitors on this trip, including the two Misses Ivatt, daughters of the locomotives' designer, and Sir Ronald Matthews, the last chairman of the L.N.E.R. They were travelling in the Beaver-Tail Observation Car from the pre-war "Corona tion" which was attached at the rear for the up journey, together with their own restaurant car marshalled ahead of it. A typical Pegler touch was to arrange for the conductor from the Royal Train to take charge of their luncheon arrangements, and special permission was obtained for him to wear his full-dress uniform, normally reserved for Royal occasions only. The highlights of the previous week's running were being talked about on the train, in particular the fine effort by the Atlantics in topping the 70 mark, and everyone was hoping that the second trip would at least equal the first in excitement. With a steady acceleration up the 1 in 200 to Stoke, the train reached 42 m.p.h. and then quickly accelerated down the other side, crossing the 70-mark just beyond Corby Glen. O. S. Nock was calling out the speeds for the official guests as they sat at lunch, and the tension steadily mounted as speed crept slowly upwards. 78 was reached by Little Bytham, and then finally at Milepost 91 the full 80 was attained. As this speed was called out, Alan Pegler signalled to the Conductor, and a loud report inside the car signalled the opening of the first bottle of champagne, the two vat Ivatt sisters being the first to have their glasses filled to enable them to drink the toast to their father. Peterborough was reached in 31 minutes 31 seconds from Grantham, a most creditable performance for a train weighing 445 tons gross, since it involved a start-to-stop average of 55½ m.p.h. No. 251 took water at Peterborough, alone this time, as Henry Oakley had picked up a supply at Werrington troughs, and was expected to do so again at Langley. The 76.4 miles from Peterborough to King's Cross were run in 89 minutes 34 seconds inclusive of the 10 m.p.h. permanent way slowing at Potters Bar, one to 20 m.p.h. at Fletton, and another to 40 at Welwyn. Over the 27.0 miles from Huntingdon to Hitchin, the locomotives averaged just over a mile-a-minute, but speed fell off to 41 m.p.h. up the long climb to Stevenage. No. 990's boiler pressure falling well back as the dirty fire made itself felt. When the crew on Henry Oakley dipped for water at Langley troughs they found that the scoop did not work and consequently had to take it easier thereafter, finishing up with very little water left. The schedule had allowed 92 minutes for this stretch, so that the slightly late start from Peterborough had been turned into an early arrival.

Bill's connection with the special ceased at King's Cross, of course, but for those on the train the excitement of the day was not yet over. The observation car was removed by one of the station pilots, and then Silver Link backed on to the train. This was my first introduction to the way in which Top Shed could turnout the locomotive for a special train, and I remember how vividly I was struck by the way in which the front coupling links and buffers had been burnished, the latter finished in quadrants. The chargehand cleaners at Top Shed, Dick Ball and Bob Frost, with their gang of Poles, had done an excellent job, so that her appearance, and that of the two Atlantics, impressed everyone considerably, and I imagine that they recalled to Bill's mind the standards achieved in his early days at Walton and Neasden. At least one Great Northern cap badge was being sported by a member of the station staff at King's Cross too that afternoon.

Ted Hailstone got the 410-ton train away from King's Cross in the drizzle with only a trace of a slip, and it was exhilarating to climb up to Potters Bar at 58 m.p.h. before going slowly over the underbridge widening. Hatfield was taken at 79, so much over the official limit that out of kindness to Ted the speed was deleted from my published log. 90 was reached at Hitchin and we shot down the bank to reach 97 at Three Counties. After falling off to 92 at Milepost 40 we again touched 97 through Biggleswade, but the full 100 was not quite achieved. We nevertheless beat the "Coronation" schedule from Hitchin to Huntingdon, which was ample satisfaction for those aboard, and averaged 90 m.p.h. for 22 miles. Some more outstanding running took place after we had passed slowly through Peterborough in 70 minutes 39 seconds from King's Cross. 79 was reached after Tallington, and the special went over Stoke at exactly 70 m.p.h., a magnificent effort for a train weighing over 400 tons. The average from Werrington to the summit was no less than 73 m.p.h., and while the "Deltics" now frequently manage to achieve figures 15 m.p.h. higher, for 1953 it was an eye-opener indeed. The running of Silver Link on these two Sundays really started enthusiasts talking about high speeds on the East Coast Route once more, and as far as special trains were concerned, this was to culminate in Bill's run six years later with Sir Nigel Gresley on the "Golden Jubilee Special".

2

For Bill and the others who had been on the two Atlantics hauling the first "Plant Centenarian", there was a very interesting sequel nine months later. On the first Sunday, Mr. Simpson, the A.D.M.P.S. at King's Cross, had taken one of the passengers, an admiral, through the corridor tender during the descent of Stoke bank. The naval visitor was so thrilled with this visit that he asked Ted Hailstone what would be an equally interesting experience for him. Ted suggested a trip in a submarine, and in consequence a party made its way down to Portsmouth Dockyard on 13th July 1954 to climb aboard H.M.S. Auriga. Besides Ted there were Inspector Bert Dixon, Bill, the two firemen, Jimmy Wilson and Albert Leech, Trevor Bailey and Les Smith, while Alan Pegler was unable to join the party. They went by car and had to be aboard by 8.00 a.m. so that the submarine could clear the blockhouse a quarter of an hour later. They were piped aboard and met her young Canadian Skipper who told them they had the freedom of the ship. If they wished to try their hand at anything, they were only to ask the member of the crew concerned, an invitation which naturally appealed to Bill, who promptly had a go at everything except the Asdic.

Until 11.00 a.m. they cruised on the surface, but after that they dived, going deep as well as running at Snorkel depth. As soon as they had got clear of Portsmouth Harbour, all the crew discarded their uniforms, with the exception of the captain, and even he was in some very old kit. Once they were submerged too, the watch off duty lay down, as usual, to help conserve the air supplies. Bill had a go at balancing the vessel, and quickly discovered that one man walking from one end to the other altered the trim quite appreciably, which had immediately to be corrected. Later on they fired some practice torpedoes off the Isle of Wight, and when the exercise was over, they were all entertained in the Ward Room, which Bill thoroughly enjoyed. An amusing incident occurred towards the end of the day when they surfaced. Due to the usual slight leakage of air from the bottles while the ship was submerged, the pressure inside had arisen above atmospheric, and as the hatch was opened, the sudden release of this pressure caused a drumming in their ears. The hatch in a submarine is not very large in diameter and a naval acquaintance informs me that even admirals have been known to get jammed in them at times. One of the party, a very much bigger man than Bill, stuck and blocked the way up, at the same time being partially deafened by the depressuri sation. The others gave a hand to push him through, but as he could not hear what they were saying nor see what was going on below his waist, he thought they were trying to take his trousers off. They got him safely through, however, but to avoid any repetition he stayed on the bridge for the rest of the voyage. The visitors were provided with cups of tea to drink while they were up there, and the wind was so strong that the sugar was blown out of the basin as the sailor carrying it arrived on deck. Both Bill and Albert Leech have described the trip to me, and it was clearly a highlight for all of them, Bill's summary of it all being "The Navy did us grand."

3

Special trains for railway enthusiasts can broadly be divided into three main classifications. The first consists of using an unusual form of motive power over a main line, as with the Ivatt Atlantics on the "Plant Centenarian", while on the second type, the branch line addicts explore such of the railway byways as still exist, the choice of motive power on these occasions usually being dictated by the ability of the bridges and track to support the locomotive. Rail tours on which really high speeds have been scheduled have been very rare indeed, and have, of course, to be confined to the main lines. The second train for enthusiasts that Bill drove did not really fall into any of these categories and much of its interest centred round the use of some very old East Coast stock. While rail tours frequently made use of ancient locomotives, the railway enthusiasts usually look after their own comfort and insist on modern coaching stock, although of course the two preserved Caledonian coaches have been used on numerous occasions north of the border for short journeys, usually behind the Caley single-wheeler No. 123.

The Westminster Bank Railway Society organised the special from King's Cross to York and back on Sunday 3rd April 1955, to enable those aboard to visit the Railway Museum and the Motive Power Depot. Going down they travelled via Lincoln as the level crossing at Newark was being relaid, but the engineering work had finished by the time of the homeward journey, and they were the first train to use this short new section of track. Bill had accordingly spent four days learning the road again via Lincoln for this trip. No. 60103 "Flying Scotsman" was turned out for the special, and behind her tender was a load of eight coaches, one of them dating back to 1903. This was a former East Coast Joint Stock clerestory vehicle, No. SC3620E, and passengers travelling in it reported that it rode surprisingly well. Besides this vehicle there was an L.N.E.R. Buffet Car, and one of the "Coronation" observation saloons, while the remaining coaches were of Great Northern origin, dating back as far as 1907. Their schedule in the down direction was a fairly easy one, but because of permanent way checks they arrived a few minutes late, the heavy rain on the journey fortunately giving way to bright sunshine for the visits at York.

Three hours later they set off back, and although no really high speeds were planned, Bill naturally intended giving the passengers a good run. "Flying Scotsman" was still operating with her original single chimney at this stage, and few of those taking part would have dreamed that she would be restored to L.N.E.R. livery again eight years later when Alan Pegler bought her from British Railways. Down from Stoke, Bill whipped her up to a maximum of 95 m.p.h., but they had an unfortunate sequel, as the tail lamp blew out, and they were hurriedly brought to a stand at the next box so that it could be relit. The delay cost them twelve minutes, but Bill regained a couple of these, reaching King's Cross only ten minutes late. There were other occasions that particular winter when lamp troubles caught up with Bill. On one of these they lost eight minutes at Cromwell when the headlights on Wild Swan blew out.

During one of our recording sessions, after talking about the Westminster Bank Special, I asked Bill what the reaction of the average railwayman was to the activities of the enthusiasts, especially where special trains were concerned. He told me that, to begin with, when trains were organised without any particularly unusual features about them, they thought that the enthusiasts must be an extraordinary group of people to be prepared to pay for a trip that the railwaymen were called upon to carry out as a normal day's work. Fairly soon, of course, special features of one sort or another were introduced, like high speed, unusual locomotives, or an unusual route, and they could then see more point in the trips. They nevertheless think that enthusiasts are a "Load of nuts with steam to let off", but it is accepted that they do it for a hobby. The railway industry is probably unique in having this attention from amateurs, and Bill pointed out that one would not expect a group of people to take over the books of a bank for the weekend, just for the fun of it. He thought that the staff generally had caught some of the enthusiasts' interest for these special trains, and to use the expression made famous by a certain well-known politician, were now equally as "Bonkers" on the subject.

4

The Stephenson Locomotive Society's "Golden Jubilee Special" on 23rd May 1959 will undoubtedly go down in history as the most spectacular steam trip ever to be run in this country, and its success depended on months of careful preparation by the Society as well as the Eastern Region. With the arrival of the first express diesels the previous autumn, it was obvious that the days of the A4s were now numbered, and the idea was mooted of a farewell high-speed trip over the East Coast Main Line to coincide with the Golden Jubilee of the Society. Suitable sympathetic ears were found at Great Northern House, the idea was agreed in principle, and detailed arrangements were begun. Now that Ted Hailstone had retired, Bill was the obvious choice to drive the train, especially as he was a member of the Society. Similarly Sir Nigel Gresley was an obvious choice of locomotive, not only because of Bill's association with it, but because of carrying its designer's name. The first move therefore came in November 1958, when No. 60007 was sent through shops at Doncaster for a general overhaul. In normal service it took an A4 something like six weeks to reach optimum mechanical condition for high speed running, but it was customary to send the engines earmarked for next year's "Elizabethan" for overhaul during the winter, so that all the minor defects could be located and rectified before the arduous non-stop running commenced. By choosing Sir Nigel as one of those to be allocated to this service in 1959, therefore, two birds were killed with the one stone.

Much debate went on between Society officials and the railway people about the details of the trip, and in particular the speeds they would be allowed to reach. As maxima of 100 m.p.h. were fairly common then on the descent from Stoke (in spite of the official 90 m.p.h. limit), something slightly higher was hoped for, but a certain King's Cross driver, not unconnected with this story, decided privately that the opportunity might well be taken to see whether Mallard's record could be broken. Negotiations went on throughout the winter, and after the Civil Engineer had given permission for the normal speed limits to be relaxed over certain sections, it was suddenly realised that the only diesels likely to be around for the next couple of years were limited to 90 m.p.h. Clearly the image of this new form of motive power might take a denting if a 20-year-old steam locomotive were allowed to beat them hands down as far as speed was concerned. There was thus a strong school of official thought that held the view that the special should be limited to a maximum of 90 m.p.h., but persuasion from the Society enabled this to be overcome. Agreement was thus reached that on the return trip a maximum of 110 m.p.h. was to be permitted down Stoke, although nothing more than the promise of a "high-speed run" was mentioned in the announcements of the trip that appeared beforehand in the Society's Journal. There were further relaxations of the normal speed restrictions, too, on other sections of the trip, which on the outward journey was to be routed from Grantham via Lincoln.

The sun was shining on the Saturday morning when Sir Nigel Gresley came down through the tunnel and set back on to the 8 coach train in Platform 5 at King's Cross. Open stock was used for the train, with a buffet car in the middle, which was the only vehicle that was not either a new one or had been newly painted. Every seat was taken, so that the 271-ton train load was increased to 295 tons gross. On the footplate with

Bill were his fireman, Alf Hancox, Chief Inspector Bert Dixon, Alan Pegler, and Cyril Palmer, the Motive Power Officer of the G.N Line. A public address system had been installed, with loudspeakers in each coach, and a microphone on the footplate, where Cyril Palmer was to have given a running commentary throughout the trip. The noise was such, however, that he had to retire to the tender corridor, and Alan Pegler relayed the details back to him. This was a most unexpected feature of the 'I run, and everyone on the train was delighted to be able to hear frequently about the way in which Bill and Alf were working the locomotive. Some consternation however, was caused when it was found that the locomotive's speedometer was reading slightly high on the down trip, and with the promise of 110 m.p.h. on the return journey now public, those on the footplate were left in no doubt about the speedometer's error when we got to Doncaster. So clear was the address system, that the sound of the A.W.S. bell could be heard throughout the train, as we passed each successive distant. Peter Handford had installed his recording gear too, in the leading van, with the stereophonic microphones, well protected against wind noise, standing just inside the open windows. The results of these recordings, superbly edited as usual, have now been released in the form of mono and stereo Argo Transacord records with Bill's portrait on the back of the sleeve, although one regrets that it is a picture of Mallard and not Sir Nigel Gresley that dominates the front. One's greatest difficulty with this record is finding opportunities when the volume of the record player can be turned up sufficiently high without causing widespread complaints from the neighbourhood, a problem that Bill did not have to contend with when he and Jack Boston travelled to Princes Risborough to hear the recordings played back three weeks after the trip.

With two blasts on the whistle, Bill got Sir Nigel Gresley away from King's Cross without a slip, and we were quickly through Finsbury Park. The engine was blowing off as we approached Oakleigh Park, so there was plenty of steam available for the climb to Potters Bar, all of which we covered with the speed just over 60 m.p.h. With a maximum of 70 m.p.h. down the other side, we were through Hatfield in 20 minutes 3 seconds, and passed Woolmer Green just over five minutes later, before taking water at Stevenage troughs three miles further on. After Stevenage we were promised the first really high speed section, with the normal 90 limit raised by 10 m.p.h. for our benefit, but we did not quite achieve the full hundred according to my continuous stop-watch recordings, although other recorders have claimed such a speed. There is no doubt that it could have been managed, but the error in the speedometer was not then appreciated, and for some distance Cyril Palmer was announcing the speed as 100 m.p.h., so Bill was not anxious to overdo things early on. After using 25 per cent. cut-off and full regulator through Hitchin, Bill eased Sir Nigel back, and the highest speed was achieved with only 15 per cent. cut-off and half regulator, as had been the case with Silver Link on the "Plant Centenarian". The 27.0 miles from Hitchin to Hunting don took exactly 18¾ minutes. There was no relaxation of the usual speed limit across the Fen between Holme and Yaxley, and a 30 m.p.h. permanent way caution at Fletton made our time through Peterborough 69 minutes 24 seconds.

Clear of the station restriction, we were unable to pick up speed as quickly as usual because of a permanent way restriction and some adverse signals, the sound of the A.W.S. hooter being relayed over the loudspeakers in the train. After Werrington Junction, however, Bill really got down to it, and an outstanding climb of Stoke ensued. I had gone forward to take some cine shots of the locomotive out of the leading coach, and it suddenly became clear that the speed was showing no signs of falling, so I hastily changed from my camera to the stop watch. Speed had reached 79 m.p.h. at Tallington, and after 80 at Essendine, we touched 83 between there and Little Bytham. With a minimum of 80 just before Corby Glen, we actually accelerated over the final stages of the bank to clear the top at 82 m.p.h., a magnificent effort on Alf

Hancox's part, as Bill had been using 40 per cent. cut-off and full regulator over the concluding stretch. Boiler pressure was down to 210 lb/sq. inch by the summit, but with half a glass of water still left. Speed down to Grantham was restrained, and Bill braked to a stop in the station in 96 minutes 59 seconds for the 105.5 miles. As the train came to a stand, doors flew open and the passen gers flooded out on to the platform to run forward and see the engine. The stop was only booked to be a momentary one, however, just to pick up a pilotman for the road via Lincoln, so Bill whistled loud and long and eased the locomotive slowly forward, which sent people scurrying back into the train.

After this the remainder of the down run was very tame, as no high speeds were possible via Lincoln. It did, however, give Cyril Palmer the chance of introducing Bill, who talked briefly to everyone on the train over the loudspeakers. To provide background material for use in his commentaries, Cyril had prepared some lengthy notes on Bill, and shortly before his sudden death early in 1965, he very kindly sent me a copy of them, together with some more of his recollections about Bill, dating back to the early days of their acquaintance, 30 years previously. When we reached Doncaster our reception was tremendous, and Peter Handford's recording conveys something of the excitement as Bill brought Sir Nigel Gresley slowly to a stand in the platform. Alan Pegler presented Bill with a clock to mark the occasion, and then Bill and Alf quietly climbed down on the far side of the train and made their way across the tracks, unseen by most of those taking part, leaving Harry Steel, the driver who relieved them, to do all the hand shaking. The special was due to spend all but five hours at Doncaster, during which time Sir Nigel Gresley was worked down to the motive power depot where Bill joined her later that afternoon to prepare her for the return trip, in the meanwhile following his usual advice of forgetting the job and coming back fresh.

From 5.00 p.m. onwards, as the time approached for

the return journey, Doncaster station was thronged with passengers and sightseers, watching the traffic and speculating on whether the special would catch up the "Queen of Scots" which passed through behind an Al half an hour before we were due away. So many people were thronging around the cab that it was impossible to manage a word with Bill before we were away two minutes late. This was the sort of incentive he really wanted, although he told me he wished it had been ten rather than two. Four miles from the start we reached 70 m.p.h., and after the 40 restriction over Bawtry Viaduct, touched 80 before Retford where we had to slow to 65. Up the 1 in 200 to Markham we accelerated to 72 m.p.h., and Sir Nigel treated us to a display of sparks as we shot through the short Askham Tunnel before accelerating to 80 through Dukeries Junction, after which Bill let the speed fall off as we took the twisting lower section of the bank. Beyond Newark we had to contend with an additional slowing to 28 m.p.h. that had been introduced the day before when one of the first sections of long-welded track started to show signs of instability. Coming at the bottom of the long climb to Stoke, this added to the task facing the locomotive and its crew if they were to give a good account of themselves on the descent from Milepost 100. Bill had carefully studied Duddington's world-breaking 1938 run with Mallard and had come to the conclusion that it would be possible to beat this with Sir Nigel Gresley given the impetus of a faster run through Grantham than the 70 m.p.h. usually allowed. Mallard had, of course, started from rest just north of Grantham, and had been driven hard up the bank, accelerating from 24 through the station to 75 m.p.h. at the summit. Bill had already done something like 117 m.p.h. down the bank with the usual 70 restriction through Grantham, and with 80 permitted for the special train, it was a question of simple arithmetic to work out that 117 + 10 = 127, which was one more than Mallard. So, for at least one person aboard the train, the idea of setting up a new World Record for steam traction was not entirely out of the question. Albert

Leech has told me how he was with Bill the night in March 1955, when the French electrics topped the 200 m.p.h. mark, and Bill commented to him that he reckoned that Quicksilver, their regular engine at the time, could do that too. Albert is of the opinion he would have had a try, had it not been for the fact that it was a fish train they were hauling back from Grantham that night, and they got badly checked all the way!

By Barkstone we were doing 70 m.p.h. and had increased this to 75 m.p.h. at Grantham, a speed which was held to the summit, with an excellent firework display from No. 60007 as we shot through the tunnel. Excitement in the train was intense, and a wave of clicks from the massed stop watches greeted the passage of each milepost, while those on the other side of the train were making their estimates of the speed by furiously counting the number of rail joints in 40 seconds, a task that can be appreciated by any listener to Peter Handford's record. On the footplate Bill turned to the officials present and said "Are we going to do it? You've got two minutes to make up your minds". Acceleration was very rapid down the bank, with 99 reached before Corby Glen, and 1 09 by Little Bytham five miles further on. Speed was still rising steadily and Bill could feel that Sir Nigel still had plenty in hand, while Alf Hancox was keeping the boiler pressure well up. Bill intended to keep going hard until someone stopped him, and with another seven miles of racing ground ahead was confident of achieving something really outstanding. With 400 passengers behind them, however, the risk was more than anyone in authority could allow, so with the speed well up to the maximum allowed by the Civil Engineer, Alan Pegler, who, as a member of the Eastern Region Board, was personally responsible for seeing that the limit was observed, signalled to Bert Dixon, who moved across and tapped Bill on the shoulder as an indication to ease off. Cyril Palmer could tell that Bill was thoroughly an noyed as he in turn signalled across to Alf, who packed up his firing efforts and the boiler pressure fell off quickly in consequence. By my milepost recordings, taken over a full three-quarters of a mile (the shortest distance over which even a tenth-second stop watch is sufficiently accurate), we nevertheless reached 112 m.p.h., an official post-war record for steam traction. We were still doing over 90 at Tallington, and brakes then came on for the permanent way restriction at Werrington. From Corby Glen to Tallington the 12.3 miles took only 7 minutes 6 seconds, an average of 104 m.p.h.

After this the passengers on the train relaxed, and the buffet car became a convivial centre of discussion about the trip so far, and the suggestion was even made that we might as well throw our stop watches away as we would never see the like again. It was as well that no one took this too literally, as beyond Offord we suddenly realised that speed was rapidly increasing once more, and there was a dash to the right-hand windows. Up at the front Bill was indulging in one of his typical bits of artistry, and Alf, with no need to watch for the clock at St. Neots, was ably supporting him, after having already fired for more than 250 miles that day. From 90 m.p.h. at Milepost 50, Bill steadily worked the speed up on the mile-and-a-half of 1 in 300 down, at the foot of which we were doing 98 m.p.h. The acceleration continued, however, until just beyond Tempsford we finally touched the full 100 again, this time on level track. This represented a magnificent effort by the locomotive, and was all the more impressive because it was so unexpected. The excitement now was really over, and after a minimum of 78 through Stevenage, the rest of the trip was taken comparatively easily, so we rolled into King's Cross in 137 minutes 38 seconds from Doncaster, just over four minutes early, an actual average of 68 m.p.h. start-to-stop for the 156.0 miles. Few railwaymen can have had the opportunity of taking part in a more exciting day's driving than Bill did on the 23rd May 1959, and at King's Cross the locomotive was surrounded as flash bulbs went off one after another, while Bill was hauled out to stand on one of the front buffers and pose alongside the headboard. There still remained the one regret, though, that Mallard's record was still intact, but whether Sir Nigel Gresley could have beaten it on that occasion had Bill been allowed to try will remain a subject of debate for many years to come. Bill, however, is still convinced that "With our technique and her abilities, Mallard's record would have gone by the board". In one very important respect, however, Sir Nigel was far better than Mallard, and Silver Fox, for that matter, which reached 113 m.p.h. on the "Silver Jubilee" on 27th August 1936 - she completed the trip in perfect condition and was available for work next day, whereas the others both had hot middle ends. Indeed, within the next week Bill had had her over the 100 mark again with Jack Boston on the footplate, as described in the previous chapter. The outstanding success of the "Golden Jubilee Special" was a tribute to the Eastern Region, the Stephenson Locomotive Society and lastly to the two enginemen most involved, Alf and Bill. Steam power on the East Coast Route could not have had a more fitting grand finale.

5

Now, at the end of 1965, only a handful of A4s remain, and those are still at work in Scotland, although Sir Nigel Gresley penetrated as far south as London on 23rd October, while working a Gresley Society special from Manchester to Paddington. The last time one worked into King's Cross, however, was 12 months earlier, when the R.C.T.S./S.L.S. Joint Committee organised the "Jubilee Requiem". The original suggestion for a farewell to the A4s was that the last working locomotive in the class would haul a special train from London to Newcastle, returning to Doncaster, where a "Deltic" would take over for the final run back to King's Cross. The A4 by then would inevitably have been in poor condition, so that her performance would have been but a shadow of its former glory. The alternative was to take the Eastern Region authori ties up on their suggestion of making it the last A4 working into King's Cross, the normal ban on steam south of Peterborough becoming absolute thereafter as far as any remaining A4s were concerned. Thus it was that the Union of South Africa steamed out of King's Cross for Newcastle on Saturday 24th October 1964 at the head of an 8-coach train packed with enthusiasts.

Every seat in the train had been applied for twice over, but among the 450 taking part was Bill, who had been invited along as a guest of the Joint Committee. My duties as Publicity Officer for the Stephenson Locomotive Society took me to Newcastle to welcome the arrival of the down train, which was badly delayed by a broken rail near Grantham. While I was talking to Hally Brown and Jack Boston, our Chairman and President, I caught sight of a black-faced figure approaching, who seemed familiar. On looking up it turned out to be Bill, who had been giving a hand on the locomotive, bringing coal forward from the tender for the fireman's benefit. Unused to any speeds higher than 20 m.p.h. on the Festiniog, he had lost his new uniform cap early on, and was correspondingly more dirty by the time he had returned to his reserved seat in the train. The only water troughs remaining in operation were those at Scrooby and Wiske Moor, so the special was booked to call at Peter borough in each direction for water. To help ensure a good supply on the down trip, Bill had assisted by winding on the tender hand brake as they ran over Wiske Moor troughs, an old trick reputed to make the scoop take a little deeper bite into the water. After he had got washed, Bill took Hally, Jack and myself up to see the museum at Town Moor, and a couple of hours later, we all boarded the train for the return trip. I was only going as far as York, and spent most of the time introducing the press to various people on the train, but managed to note that Union of South Africa was running in the 80s south of Northallerton.

Sitting on the opposite side of the gangway from Bill for most of the journey was Cyril Palmer, also a guest of the Joint Committee, and at various points en route he would lean across to Bill and recall some past event when Bill had done something at that particular spot, such as passing a signal or exceeding the speed limit. Bill confided to me later that, although he knew Cyril had been aware of certain of these incidents at the time, he was under the delusion that he had forgotten them, and had been rather embarrassed when he had not only reminded him of them, but of others as well.

On the concluding stages of the run the train reached a high speed down Stoke, but authorities differ as to whether the "ton" just was or just was not attained, since darkness and the long welded track made recording difficult in spite of the home-made searchlights some people had provided. The Newcastle-York stretch had been run in under schedule at a mile-a-minute average, and water was taken there too during the stop. With more schedule-beating later on, they were allowed to leave Peterborough before booked time and continue up the main line instead of being turned slow road from Fletton to Yaxley to allow a scheduled train to overtake. Bill would dearly have loved to get hold of the regulator again, but they compromised by letting him fire for a short spell, before they ran in to King's Cross 20 minutes early. On the concluding stretch Bill and Alan Pegler were both on the engine, and the latter told me how the 5-year gap vanished as they found themselves both once more on an A4 running into King's Cross. Bill thus had the satisfaction of knowing he had contributed towards this last ever journey to London by one of the A4s, while many of his old friends were delighted to see that he was looking as young as ever in spite of the five years that had elapsed since his retirement.

CHAPTER EIGHT

The Festiniog

The present flourishing state of the Festiniog Railway is the result of a long but successful battle against seemingly impossible odds. This narrow gauge line in North Wales, dating back to 1832, was described a hundred years ago as "the most wonderful railway in the Kingdom". During the latter half of the 19th century, as one of the main outlets for slate from the quarries at Blaenau Ffestiniog, it enjoyed unparallelled prosperity and fame, and contributed many innovations to railway practice, including the first iron-frame bogie coaches and the famous Fairlie double locomotives. With the decline of the slate trade in the 20th century, however, the railway fell on evil days, and in 1946. services were suspended and the whole undertaking left to rot and rust. The luxuriant vegetation, fed by the rains for which North Wales is noted, quickly stretched out to try and obliterate all signs of the narrow-gauge rails as they wound up through the woods above Cei Mawr. The closed railway had applied to the Ministry of Transport for an Abandonment Order, only to be told that the Minister had no powers to grant it, so that the creditors were unable to sell the rails and rolling stock to pay off the heavy debts with which it was saddled. Over several years a number of unsuccessful efforts were made to revive the Festiniog, and these were latterly spurred on by the success that had resulted from the formation of the Talyllyn Preservation Society in October 1950. Their narrow-gauge line, further south along the Welsh coast, had continued to operate during the lifetime of the owner, Sir Haydn Jones, and after his death, a holding company was formed, controlled by the Society and the executors of Sir Haydn's estate. Nearly a year later, on 8th September 1951, there was a meeting in Bristol, called by Leonard Heath Humphrys, and it was from this that the Festiniog Railway Society was formed. There were, however, considerably greater difficulties facing this Society than those that the Talyllyn had successfully conquered. These were not only physical, like the steadily encroaching tide of vegetation, but legal and financial as well. The Festiniog Railway Company was set up by Acts of Parliament, and therefore its constitution can similarly only be altered by submitting an appropriate Private Bill and getting it passed through both Houses of Parliament. Then there was the problem of the overdraft, which amounted to over £10,000. The way out of this seemingly impossible situation was provided by the assistance of Alan Pegler, who, over a period of eighteen months, was able to purchase more than fifty per cent. of the Preference and Debenture Shares, and thus take over control of the Company. A new Board was set up, with him as Chairman, and like his fellow directors, he had personally to own 300 shares in order to satisfy the statutory requirements of the Festiniog Railway Acts. The remaining shares that had been acquired were placed in the Festiniog Railway Trust, so that three-quarters of each class of stock are now held by the Trust, which ensures a degree of continuity for the enterprise. The new Board, after making a settlement with the bank, officially took control of the assets on 24th June 1954, and set about the task of searching for their railway once again beneath the undergrowth. There was no cash in the till, but stout-hearted support came from the Festiniog Railway Society, which was formed into a limited company, nominating one member to the Railway Company's Board, in exchange for a similar nomination to their own Board by the Railway. Over the years, the Society has contributed no less than 300,000 man-hours of volunteer labour to the running of the railway, and cash contributions exceeding £20,000. It was to this environment that Bill transferred himself as an employee when he retired from British Railways, and, as previously mentioned, he had already been associated with the enterprise as a volunteer.

The new management's first step was to get something moving on the line, and this was the Simplex petrol locomotive which dated from World War I. Its armoured ends were found to be very useful for bulldozing the bushes growing on the line, but the trees that were rooted on the track had to be sawn off, and their stumps hauled out with the aid of chains. In this way, progress continued, so that in January 1955 a platelayer's trolley reached Moelwyn Tunnel, hauled by one of the former Welsh Highland trolleys with its rebuilt engine. The aim was to run a passenger service in the summer of that year, and much work was required to be done, including the rebuilding of Prince with its new boiler that had providentially arrived just before the railway closed down. Bill Hoole spent a week-end at Portmadoc in March, and then another 10 days there in May as part of his holidays for that year. It was during this longer stay that he drove the Simplex quite a lot on track-clearing work. The passenger service was scheduled to start on 23rd July, and Bill again went down for a week-end at the beginning of the month to help with the frantic last-minute preparations. After Colonel McMullen had given the Ministry of Transport's official approval to the operation of the service, it started as scheduled between Portmadoc and Boston Lodge, and the official opening by Miss Janet Jones, the Welsh Tourist Queen, took place on the 29th. In the evening of 2nd August, amid great interest from all those working on the railway, Prince steamed across the Cob, nine years after the last steam locomotive had run on the Festiniog. Three days later she entered regular service, and until September 1956 every passenger train on the railway was handled by this diminutive 0-4-0, one of the first pair of locomotives ever built for the narrow gauge, with its large saddle tank that always looks like an overgrown horse blanket. When the service ceased at the end of the summer, it was found that there had been 22,000 passenger journeys, so that there was clearly considerable potential custom in the area. The summer of 1955 was notable too, in that Allan Garraway resigned from British Railways to take over the post of Manager and Engineer of the Festiniog Railway Company, after having been associated with the revival ever since the Bristol meeting in 1951.

For the summer of 1956, the Festiniog had been opened up as far as Minffordd, which provided a connection with the Western Region Cambrian Coast trains once more. Bill went down first in February, and during the weekend that followed the start of the public service on 19th May, he drove Prince for four round trips between Portmadoc and Minffordd on the Saturday. This was the first time he had handled this locomotive, which became a particular favourite of his, and on the Sunday he cleaned its tubes and washed out the boiler. This did not occupy the whole day, however, and some of the remainder was spent on making trimmings and fitting them to Taliesin, the first of the double engines to be overhauled, the Vulcan Foundry people undertaking the work at Boston Lodge. After trials on 1st and 2nd September, this locomotive went into service on the evening of the 4th, and the Festiniog could once more boast a working example of Fairlie's patent form of articulation, its two chimneys emitting their characteristic exhaust beats as the thrust of the cylinders caused the bogies at either end to nose their way along the track. Bill missed seeing the locomotive at work that year, as by late November, when he went down for a week-end again, the summer service was over for 1956, and the total number of passenger journeys had nearly doubled, to practically 39,000.

On 12th November 1956, Taliesin worked a train up to Penrhyn, the next loop above Minffordd, with the General Manager of the Western Region aboard, and this point was to serve as the terminus for the next year's summer service, which started at Whitsun, after a warm-up over Easter. Bill had five days' holiday in the week before Whitsun and went to Portmadoc to spend three days driving and firing Taliesin, during which Major General Llewllen Wansbrough-Jones, the Secretary-General of the B.T.C., performed the official opening for that season. Bill found it somewhat unusual to be separated from the other member of the crew by the humped-backed double firebox with its twin firehole doors on the south side. This footplate arrangement meant too that if he had a volunteer fireman, there was no chance of keeping an eye on the state of the two fires. Bill paid another couple ofvisits to Wales that year for week ends, and joined in the satisfaction of knowing that the largely volunteer run line had again beaten its previous year's record, with getting on for 54,000 passenger journeys. Before the season had ended too, Prince had battled up to Moelwyn Tunnel, which was now plugged halfway through with a mass of concrete to prevent the escape of water from Llyn Ystradau, which forms part of the C.E.G.B.'s pumped storage scheme at Tanygrisiau.

In 1958 the passenger service worked through to Tan-y-Bwlch, as it has continued to do ever since, the spacious station, originally the mid point of the line, serving as an admirable temporary terminus until such time as the extension to Blaenau Ffestiniog is completed. Bessie Jones, the wife of Will Jones the platelayer, donned her Welsh costume once more, and now greets the arrival of each train, before dispensing refreshments from the counter in the old station waiting room beside her house. If this book were a gastronomic guide, I would be able to recom mend her scones which she bakes every morning after getting up at five a.m. Bill again went to Wales three times that year, the second being for his holidays when he took Dolly for the first time, since the possibility of the two of them emigrating there was then being discussed. They spent 10 days on a general tour of North Wales, but on the last day Bill's diary records that Prince was derailed at Boston Lodge, so he clearly looked in on the Festiniog for part of the time. His last visit to the Festiniog before he retired was in November 1958, but eight months later, on Tuesday 28th July 1959, Jack Boston drove Dolly and Bill from Potters Bar to Boston Lodge, and the following day Bill joined the Festiniog's payroll.

2

By 1959 the Festiniog had got their railway well and truly working once more, with the regular summer service coping with 60,000 passenger journeys over almost the full length of the line which remained workable. It was obvious too that a lot of consolidation would be necessary before the "Great Leap Forward" would once again provide through running over a deviation route to Blaenau Ffestiniog. The Festiniog Railway were thus anxious to take on more permanent staff who could carry out operating duties in the summer, and during the winter would be available for any other work that cropped up. There was the rather large snag, however, that they were unable to afford much in the way of wages, and the idea was therefore mooted that Bill might be interested in joining the railway for a small wage to eke out his pension of 50/- per week. His total pay in the last but one full tax year on British Railways had been £1,225, so there was clearly going to be a big drop in Bill's income. There was a limit, however, to what he could be paid before he started to have his state pension reduced, but the railway were able to make him and Dolly the promise of a house, one of those the railway owned and which they were told was about to be vacated by the tenants. Bill had no real hobbies other than his work, and, being still active, would have had to find some other form of employment had he remained in London. There was the possibility of finding work as a janitor somewhere, or he might have had to take on the job of an outside porter at one of the terminal stations, as Sammy Gingell has done at Victoria. The Festiniog offer was much more attractive, although it meant that Bill and Dolly would have to give up living in London with all their friends and their married daughter not far away, and move into a very quiet part of the countryside where English was by no means the usual language spoken.

When the time came for them to move north, another snag arose, as the house that they had been promised did not fall vacant. As a temporary expedient, it was therefore arranged for the Hooles to share No. 1 Boston Lodge with Fred Boughey and his family, which was naturally not a satisfactory permanent arrangement. Fred is an instructor at Birkenhead Technical College, and right from the early days of the revival he had been in charge of the repairs to the passenger stock, offering to spend most of his weekends and holidays there, if they would provide him with somewhere for him and his family to live during their visits. The provision of adequate stock has been a matter of considerable importance as the annual traffic steadily increased year by year. After all the available vehicles remaining from the railway's previous incarnation had been very successfully restored to working order, they cast further afield, and the former Lynton and Barnstaple Railway coach that had served as a hen-house at Snapper since 1935 was bought, dismembered, and the pieces triumphantly transported to Boston Lodge, later to appear as the "Snapper Bar".

Bill found it somewhat difficult to accustom himself to the narrow gauge after the main line. The "Hoole philosophy" may have been all very well with the resources of Doncaster Works to back him up with locomotives, and a track that had repeatedly showed its ability to withstand speeds 20 m.p.h. or more over the normal limit. In 1959 on the Festiniog, things were not only very different from the main line, but markedly different from what they are on that railway seven years later. On a short narrow-gauge line, a driver has to know the condition of almost every rail joint, and instead of having all the early preparation of engine carried out by fitters and fire lighters, he has to do it himself. What's more, there are no convenient clocks in the woods beside the line and Bill still does not carry a watch. It was not easy to resolve the accommodation for the Hooles and Bougheys on the Festiniog, and the sudden introduction of such a famous newcomer might well have produced difficulties, but Bill's disarming manner, his perennial smile and cheerfulness, and his willingness to help as much as he could, soon made him an inseparable part of the Festiniog scene.

3

An enterprise like the Festiniog has to maintain an unending publicity drive even to retain its present level of passenger traffic, which will be appreciated from the fact that over 80 per cent. of the passengers who filled in a traffic census form during three days in July 1964 were making their first journey ever over the line. 1963 provided an admirable oppor tunity for more than the usual amount of publicity, as it marked the centenary of steam power on the line, and for the Centenary Week in May there were special efforts to provide a Victorian touch to the line. Everyone entered into the spirit of the thing wholeheartedly, and Bill celebrated by growing a magnificent beard which he topped by a bowler hat. The result rendered him almost unrecognisable until the familiar voice and smile emerged from the undergrowth.

Living alongside the ·works, Bill helps keep an eye on what is going on there, which is a most important function, as it is regrettably true that items such as whistles have disappeared. Members of the Festiniog Railway Society may wander round the Works, however, after seeking permission from one of the staff present, and Bill is always ready to encourage any bona fide visitor, even if this at times entails distracting him from what he is supposed to be doing. He looks after the issue of the various items from the stores too, and in the course of the season gets through no less than two gallons of Brasso which is bought in bulk for Bill to put into small cans for the footplate staff to use. Bill also makes himself responsible for seeing that the engine for the first turn is lit up in time each morning, more often than not doing the job himself.

Until the summer of 1964, the motive power position on the Festiniog was tight, with only two or three engines available to work the two locomotive rosters at the height of the summer, and Bill worked regularly on Prince or one of the Fairlies, the second of them, Merddin Emrys, having been restored to traffic in 1961. The arrival of Linda in 1962, hired from the Penrhyn Quarries, helped considerably, but the following year she was purchased outright, and this was coupled with the acquisition of her sister engine, Blanche, so that from 1964 onwards, the locomotive position became very much easier. With a total of over 150,000 passenger journeys, the operating task that faces the railway during the summer months has become a very considerable one, and the construction of some completely new passenger coaches has been a great help. In the summer of 1964, Bill became 70, and the Board decided that he should not regularly work such long hours in future. With more staff and more locomotives, it also became possible to adopt regular manning, and although Bill was offered Blanche he felt he would prefer to stick to Prince, which, as the smallest and oldest of the Festiniog stud, was normally rostered as spare or odd engine. Nevertheless during that season he worked some very full days, while others have commented that if they can do what he did when they are 70, they will be very pleased. In September 1965, too, when the Royal Engineers were engaged on their 3-week exercise on the Festiniog, Bill was getting up at 4.00 a.m. to enable him to open the Works by 4.30. There is no doubt too that his ever-ready help for any volunteer and his interest in the Festiniog pay dividends in attracting and maintaining interest in the railway among his friends.

4

Although I had watched the Festiniog revival with great interest from a distance, it was Bill who sold me, or perhaps my wife, the idea of spending our 1964 holiday in North Wales to see something of it at first hand. Bill had come to Middlesbrough early that year to talk to the Tees-side Centre of the Stephenson Locomotive Society, and during his week-end with us, immediately captivated the whole family. We travelled down to Harlech on Saturday 25th July and on the following afternoon the six of us made our way to Boston Lodge, where we found Bill in his old overalls titivating the paint-work on the footplate of Prince, while on the next road Allan Garraway wrestled with a somewhat inaccessible cock that had broken on Linda. Merddin Emrys had taken the Sunday train up to Tan-y-Bwlch, and while we waited to see it return and cross the Cob, Bill showed us round Prince and the Works. The children loved the diminutive size of Prince, although our 3-year-old, after proving that even Valspar does not dry in five minutes, was heard to remark "Where is the little engine you said you would show me?", which only goes to prove that everything is relative. After a good look round, followed by a frantic dash to watch the Fairlie heel to the curve past the Works on its return trip with the down train from Tan-y-Bwlch to Portmadoc, we were then escorted up the flight of stone steps and through the long passage of No. 1 to the kitchen, to meet Dolly and experience the first of much hospitality we were to receive there during our stay in Wales.

The following Monday was Bill's 70th birthday, and as it turned out, Prince had to be rostered for a double trip to Tan-y-Bwlch for the whole of that week, hauling the first train up in the morning at 10.40, as well as the non-stop "Y Cymru", leaving the Harbour station at 3.00 p.m. We decided to make our first journey on the Festiniog on the latter train, and this decision prevented us seeing the welcome that greeted Bill o:r.. his first trip past Boston Lodge, where an all-steel band had been assembled to mark the occasion. In the afternoon we found Prince at the head of five coaches in the Harbour station, and chose to travel in the leading vehicle, which was one of those from the Welsh Highland, the unglazed windows in the doors proving somewhat draughty as we pottered across the Cob, while low clouds robbed us of much of the grandeur of the view to our left. After shutting off for the curve at the far end, we were all rather astonished by the vehemence of Prince's exhaust as Bill opened her up for the 1 in 80 gradient, which marks the start of the long continuous climb to Tan-y-Bwlch. The locomotive's fire was very thin, too and in conse quence gave rise to the characteristic loud humming sound on the latter part of the journey, so that by the end of the trip we rather wished we had travelled further back in the train, particularly as Bill was using the locomotive's "Elephant Whistle" rather more than usual for our benefit. Many will be familiar with the 7½-mile journey, but first impressions are often the most lasting, and I personally will never forget that journey along the line. My memories, though, centre less on Bill, than on the line itself, and the view away to our right that opened up with every successive rail length as we rumbled past Minffordd and on to the dry stone embankment beyond, giving us the first glimpse of Harlech Castle away to the south beyond the Dwyryd Estuary. The first really tight rock-hewn cutting followed, and with it a section of track where the rails had been reversed, so that the rumble of the carriage wheels suddenly became a clatter, its intensity doubled by the proximity of the cutting face to our windows. Then we were through Penrhyn, with the sister of Merddin Emrys' regular driver in Welsh costume on the crossing gates, and up the long open stretch to Cei Mawr. From the right-hand side of the train we could appreciate the full 62-foot height of this amazing dry-stone structure, as Bill eased off to take the sharp right-hand curve on to it. Beyond we were into the woods, the line twisting and turning through rocky cuttings and over dry-stone embankments, the trees hiding much of the precipitous nature of the hillside below us. This was to be demonstrated even more markedly later on as we ran past Plas, the former home of the Oakley family, where from the train you can see almost straight down the chimneys.

Beyond Plas comes Tyler's Curve, the sharpest on the line, and speed was slackened right down to a crawl as the train rumbled around it, enabling us to catch the all-too-brief glimpse of the Vale of Ffestiniog, with the Oakley Arms below and the village of Maentwrog away across the valley. Then Tyler's Cutting hid the view, and Prince started barking once more as we turned back on our tracks to continue round the long horseshoe that lifts the line to Tan-y-Bwlch. It was not until some days later that I could appreciate the lie of the line on this section, when I watched the progress of another train from the rocky vantage point at the south end of the passing loop at that station. On this second occasion, Linda, at the head of its green and ivory-liveried coaches, could be seen twisting and turning amongst the woods as it made its way steadily up the long continuous grade that was so vital for the operation of the gravity slate trains in former years. On our first journey, however, Prince's bark occasionally became hesitant and then stopped altogether, our train coming gently to a standstill for a short while. Unable to put my head out of the window to see what was happening I assumed that we had halted for a "blow-up", but it turned out that there were some sheep on the line ahead, and Bill had to stop to let them get out of the way. (Later during my visit I was to hear some other stories of Bill and sheep, but they will have to remain untold until the passage of time renders the statute of limitations operative.) From the less-wooded sections of the line, we could see a plume of steam in the trees opposite which marked the position of Merddin Emrys standing at the head of the 3.35 down in Tan-y-Bwlch station, waiting for us to clear the long section from Minffordd. We reached Whistling Curve, the long right-hand one that took us around the base of the horseshoe, and Bill roused the echoes with Prince's Elephant Whistle to warn the staff at Tan-y-Bwlch of our impending arrival. Then we rumbled across the cast-iron girder bridge over the Gareg road into the final cutting, and took the left-hand loop. Norman Gurley collected the single line-staffs as we ran in alongside the waiting train, which had begun its downward journey before we came to a stand at the north end of the long passing loop.

Safety considerations on this line of tight clearances and long vertical drops have always necessitated locking passengers into their compartments, and by the time we had been let out, Prince was taking water under the tank. As some of the passengers crowded round the cab, Bill leaned out and asked my wife if he could borrow her children. The family were duly installed in the tender, to the detriment of their white socks, and given a ride as the locomotive made its way down to the bottom points, to come up again on to the other end of the coaches. I am certain that in his love for children Bill sees himself again as he was when he spent his holidays on the platform ends at Liverpool 60 years ago. Dolly commented to my wife afterwards that Bill has even been known to desert some V.I.P. if a child comes along to ask him something. The 3.00 p.m. up was booked to spend 35 minutes at Tan-y-Bwlch to allow the previous train to clear Minffordd, so there was still time to investigate Bessie Jones' refreshment room and make our first acquaintance with her scones. Then the whistles were blowing, and, helped by Norman Gurley, the guard checked the passengers' tickets and locked us into our compartments for the downward journey, which was to prove a quieter experience than the one in the opposite direction. Three quarters of an hour later we ran in around the curve of the Harbour station at Portmadoc, and our first round trip on the Festiniog was over, but three of the children were once again treated to a ride in the tender as Prince ran round the train and then shunted the stock into one of the sidings parallel to the platform road.

During the full summer service, there is an admirable evening train up the line on certain days in mid-week. Although it attracts some custom from local trippers after they have had their evening meal, it is especially popular with the volunteers and other members of the Society, most of whom patronise the Buffet Car for the journey. During the summer of 1964 the former Lynton and Barnstaple coach was on this working in its rebuilt guise as the "Snapper Bar", and I made several delightful journeys in it, once turning Bill out of No. 1 to come and point out some of the landmarks to me in comfort. Throughout the war when petrol rationing cleared most of the traffic from the North Devon roads, cycling came into its own, and many times from my home in Barnstaple I made my way along the Yeo Valley, looking out for the remains of the Lynton and Barnstaple Railway during the course of our blackberrying or whatever else was the object of the family expedition. If I had been told that 20 years later I would have been riding on the Festiniog in the hen-house then reposing at Snapper, I think I would have been forgiven for treating the statement with some degree of incredulity. Nevertheless the unique opportunity of drinking draught beer in a railway buffet car can be highly recommended as a way of passing the evening. At Tan-y-Bwlch the volunteer firemen aboard always stroll up to the locomotive as soon as possible after arrival for a quick look at the pressure gauge and the state of the fire, to see how well the fireman on duty has managed, and considerable rivalry ensues in consequence.

5

Through the kindness of Alan Pegler and Allan Garraway, I was able to spend a full day with Bill during my stay in Wales, most of it perched in Prince's diminutive tender to see something of the way in which, at the age of 70, he occupied his time. He was still rostered for the same double turn as he had been working on his birthday when I arrived at Boston Lodge at eight in the morning, to find that he had already lit Prince's fire, using the pile of sticks that had been drying out on the footplate since the previous evening. He was hard at work polishing the brasses as I strolled up, and shortly afterwards the whistle of the 8.15 from Portmadoc General station echoed across the Glaslyn estuary. As the 3-coach train came into sight, a mile away, the locomotive could be identified as a Collett 22XX 0-6-0, one of the few former G.W.R. locomotives still at work in North Wales during the 1964 summer. This train was Bill's cue to leave the job of cleaning, and get down into the pit to lubricate the motion. With the narrow gauge there is very little space between the tracks, and it is not possible to get above the motion on Prince, so Bill has to do most of the preparation by feel, with his arms above his head. He has made all the trimmings himself, and knows that with 25 squirts from the oil can in each box, they will last all day, although he usually tops them up at lunch time to be safe. The oiling took about 20 minutes, and while it was in progress Bill had kept his ear open for the sounds of the water circulating in the boiler as it warmed up. Occasionally the fire goes out and an ominous silence then descends on Prince in place of the comforting gurgles that indicate all is well. At 8.40 Bill emerged from underneath, shut the dampers, turned the blower off and put the hose into the open cover on top of the tank. The tank sufficiently full, he got down, washed the worst of the dirt off his hands in the water lying in the hydrant pit, and went in to breakfast. I joined Bill and Dolly in No. 1 while they ate their meal, Bill following his boiled egg with toast and marmalade.

Breakfast over, Bill went upstairs to shave, wash and change. When he reappeared he collected his cap from one of the pegs inside the front door and we walked down the steps and through the opening on our left into the Works yard, to find Richard Hanlon hard at work on the job of getting Prince's cleanliness up to Festiniog standards. For Richard this was the last day of his fortnight's work as a volunteer fireman for that year, and although he would have liked to spend longer on the railway, the cost of his lodgings had to be taken into account. He had just finished in the sixth form of his school at Derby, and would be going up to Sheffield University the following October to read zoology, so the budgeting of his pocket money had to be, of necessity, a matter for careful thought. After our day together, I met him again the following morning, when he told me with great delight that some volunteers who were expected had not turned up, and he had therefore been given another week's work by Allan Garraway, during which the company would pay for his lodgings. His delight at the prospect was only slightly tinged with the difficulty he faced of finding somewhere to stay in Portmadoc at the height of the holiday period. While the cleaning work was going on, the postman dropped the mail in to No. 1, before going over the hill to deliver the post to Bill's next-door neighbour, Bertrand Russell. Dolly came out with Bill's letters, and he glanced through them before asking her to take them back to read at lunch time, but there was one letter for the Harbour which was put on Prince to take across the Cob in due course.

Prince has no cocks on the cylinders, although there are some on the steam chest, and Bill therefore likes to give her a good warming up before she moves. The front end was thus soon enveloped with clouds of hissing steam, and then Bill slowly set her back an engine length so that Richard could shovel some coal aboard from the wagon on the next road. Bill meanwhile started filling the oil cups on the outside rods, and after doing one side, set the locomotive back unfalteringly exactly one quarter turn of her 2ft. 1½in. wheels, to bring the other rod to its bottom dead centre. Although the first train was not due out of Portmadoc until 10.40, it was not long after 10 when Richard collected the electric staff, and we eased our way out on to the main line, to make our way slowly across the Cob, Dolly overtaking us in the bus for her daily shopping expedition to the town. As we made our way across, Bill pointed out the strengthening work carried out the previous winter by the River Board, which had necessitated the removal of the overhead telephone wires across the Cob, and the new plastic-covered cable could be seen lying along the top of the wall on the seaward side. Halfway across we passed Allan Garraway in conversation with Norman Pearce (the head of the Signal and Telegraph side, as well as being Deputy Chairman of the Society), and exchanged a brief greeting with them.

There was still a fair bit of work to be done at the Harbour Station before the first train could depart. We ran in to the platform road, and Alan Heywood reported to Bill on the progress of the coach oiling, while John Dobson, who was to be our guard for the morning, came along and told us to collect coach No. 23 and add it to the other four vehicles already sitting in the platform, as there was an extra party coming down from Tan-y-Bwlch on our return trip. During these operations, Bill commented to me that they had to be careful with the brake in the station when creating vacuum for the first time, as the condensation could result in their spraying the passengers with sooty water, a pastime not to be encouraged. With our train made up, we retired through the third road to the water tower by the buffer stops, to top up our tank. A wagon of coal was also standing there for use if necessary, and in the last few minutes before we finally coupled on to our train, Richard finished the job of polishing the brass on Prince, concluding by stowing the can of Brasso in the locker in the tender, and finally raking out the ash pan just before we started.

We were away on time, and as we rolled out on to the Cob, Richard put three shovelfuls of coal on to the fire, one in each back corner of the box, with the third just under the door. Bill worked the firehole door between each shovelful almost in traditional Great Western fashion, the narrow opening from the cab back into the tender causing quite a time to elapse between successive shovelfuls. Bill meanwhile had got the injector on to fill the boiler up, as they do not like to get too much water in before starting, to avoid any chance of priming. As a result, our boiler pressure fell back from 150 to 140 lb/sq. inch as we crossed the Glaslyn estuary. Another three shovelfuls of coal went on before Pen Cob, and with a blast from the whistle, Prince took the curve beside the Works where Merddin Emrys now occupied the pits, being prepared for the second turn. Bill pushed the regulator well over and brought it back slightly again, so that our bark became fiercer as we started the 6½-mile climb. There were no passengers to signal to us at Boston Lodge Halt, so we carried on under the new road bridge, Prince's exhaust becoming deafening from my exposed position on the tender. We went up past the cemetery, and while Bill whistled, Richard was looking ahead for the colour light protecting Minffordd Level Crossing, which is looked after by Lottie Edwards, widow of a former member of the Railway's permanent-way staff. Lottie is extremely popular with the volunteer fraternity, many of whom lodge in her cottage hard beside the line. So well known is Lottie's Cottage, that, as someone looking at the 1 inch Ordnance Survey Map remarked, it is even marked on that august publication by the initials "L.C." ! Many of the train crews have, over the years, tried to creep up unheralded to the crossing, and then scare Lottie through the roof by leaning on their whistles outside her living room. This practice has, however, been foiled by the provision of a bell in her cottage, which is now actuated on the approach of a train by track circuits, although this does not prevent the device being known as "Lottie's Treadle" from the original form it took. We whistled the signal off and with a passing wave to Lottie at the gates, took the right hand line to stop at Minffordd station, 9½ minutes out from Portmadoc, Prince's safety valves lifting as we came to a stand.

Richard left us to collect the miniature staffs for the section ahead (Minffordd-Penrhyn and Penrhyn-Tan-y-Bwlch) with the screw-in tickets on their ends, which were used at that time when trains were to cross at the upper terminus. We were away again with a full glass of water and 150 lb/square inch in the boiler, Richard firing another two "rounds" before Penrhyn, with another above the level crossing, the exhaust note of the engine altering markedly as Bill opened the firehole door for each shovelful. The blast from our chimney was dislodging water from the trees arching across the line after we had crossed Cei Mawr and had taken to the woods, but steam was soon shut off for the slowing to 5 m.p.h. for the P.W. caution marked by a yellow flag alongside the track. Clear of this, Bill collected a fly in his eye, but it did not trouble him unduly as we continued up the bank, the gloom of the woods showing up my reflection dancing in the rear cab window as it vibrated with the locomotive's exhaust. We continued past the tank where wagons of sea water used to be emptied to provide brine showers for the inhabitants of Plas, while the mounds of dead rhododendron cuttings on the lower side of the line provided an indication of the extent to which they had encroached during the "lost" years before 1954. Tyler's Curve, and we were heading westwards now, Bill pointing out to me the lineside gate made of old boiler tubes, and the place where the skeletons of sheep can often be seen in the spring, close beside the line where they have come to take refuge during the winter snows. Beyond was Whistling Curve, where Prince's whistle sent warning ahead of our coming, and then we caught the brief view right through the short Garnedd Tunnel, which lies half-a-mile on the other side of the station. 24½ minutes after leaving Minffordd, we were braking to a standstill on the right-hand loop at Tan-y-Bwlch. Richard uncoupled smartly, and we drew up at the water tank before the first passengers had alighted. As usual, Bill gave a youngster in an F.R. cap a ride down to the bottom points, where the lad worked them for us after climbing down from the tender. Bill made him do the job properly, insisting on him waving us forward in the correct manner after the points had been changed and the locking bar pulled home. Then we ran forward again to couple on to the Observation Car, while Richard walked along to collect the enginemen's "perks" from the Buffet Car - a bottle of orangeade for himself, and coffee for Bill and me.

On the way up, Richard had put about 28 half-shovelfuls of coal on our fire, but although this was not exactly hard work, the bucking locomotive and tender made it more a test of balance rather than stamina. Allan Garraway has materially improved the riding of Prince and the two Penrhyn engines by fitting telescopic shock-absorbers on their tenders. On Linda and Blanche there is a pair connecting the locomotive and the tender too, and it was most interesting to watch their operation one evening when I rode down with Allan on the last train from Tan-y-Bwlch. Having a qualified locomotive engineer as General Manager (the post to which he was promoted when the passengers reached the 100,000-mark) certainly helps to ensure that the mechanical side of the Festiniog receives its fair share of attention, and the riding of the passenger coaches has similarly improved, in spite of the very restricted space available in the region of the bogies.

The trip down was easy, with little need for anything more than careful control of the brakes, but at Penrhyn we were hailed by some passengers and drew to a stand beside the station buildings, now used as a store by the Co-op. Leaving the station, a white and brown dog in the adjoining field barked furiously at us, racing along the fence and then struggling through a hole in it to continue beside the track, frighteningly near our wheels. There is a footpath that crosses the line here, and we were anxiously on the lookout for some children who were putting stones on the line, which could easily damage the springs of the locomotive. A little further on the line passes a house on the right with two large monkey puzzle trees in its garden. This marks the point where down trains can be sighted from Portmadoc, and now looking in that direction, we could make out two lots of steam in the distance, one from a Festiniog engine at the Harbour and the other from British Railways. After Boston Lodge Halt, we got a quick wave from Dolly in her kitchen window as we took the curve, and with steam on again we crossed the Cob to reach the Harbour station where Linda with Allan Garraway, now in his overalls, was waiting to take over the next working of the stock. As it was Friday, Bill went into the office to collect the pay for those over at the Works, so we ran as a bullion light-engine back across the Cob, with Richard at the controls as is Bill's custom with every volunteer. Back at Boston Lodge, Richard climbed down to work the points, while Bill drove Prince into the yard and on to the pits. He screwed the handbrake hard on, checked the condition of the fire, and we retired to lunch after distributing the small cylindrical pay tins, Dolly providing an excellent meal of cold ham and fried potatoes for us both, while Bill went through his morning's post at leisure.

By the time we came out again, an hour or so later, the heavy cloud that had kept the morning weather short of the best was beginning to lift, and although Snowdon was to remain cloud-capped all the afternoon, the covering lifted off Moelwyn as the sun came out. Richard was back at work before us, cleaning the fire and ash-pan, but as we strolled up to the locomotive, there was a tiny wisp of smoke arising from the sleeper box at the side of the yard used to hold the coal slack. One of the hot cinders had rolled against it and started the wood smouldering. As quick as anything Bill spotted it, and a smart word to Richard had him roundfrom the other side of the engine to deal with it before any major fire developed. It was very interesting to see how sharp Bill's normally quiet voice became when something needed doing in a hurry. Bill then refilled the displacement lubricator, catching the water draining out in a shovel to avoid making a mess of the cab, and reminiscing about the time he had been scalded when the lubricator contents on an "Austerity" had blown out on him during the war.

The afternoon trip was very similar to the morning one, but this time we had the benefit of the sunshine as we ran across the Cob in time to tuck ourselves out of the way against the water column until Merddin Emrys had left with the 2.15. The double engine had coaled and watered at the Harbour station rather than returning to Boston Lodge, and while she ran round her train, I rode on her alongside Driver Evan Davies, while Bill and Richard sat on the low wall on the seaward side of the Cob and admired the view. Promptly at 2.15, Merddin Emrys was away for Tan-y-Bwlch, the low slung "bug-boxes" at the front of the train rocking as they took the sharp curve out of the station. The knot of holiday-makers who had come to see or photograph the departure faded away, and all was quiet until Linda arrived back half an hour later with the train we were to take up non-stop. Allan Garraway departed across the Cob, Linda's steeply inclined cylinders twirling her massive scarlet cranks outside the frames that almost completely hide her wheels. Prince took her place at the end of the train, and Richard went to collect the green and red "Y Cymru" headboard. He settled it firmly into place on the lamp bracket at the foot of the chimney, which was crowned with a ring of water droplets glistening on its smoky rim. Packed with holiday-makers, we were away on time, and thirty part-shovelfuls of coal were all that was required to get our train non-stop to Tan-y-Bwlch, the last three being of dirt as we neared the terminus to deaden the fire down for the return journey. The fire burned thin by Plas Halt, and started its familiar buzzing, but we cut 2½ minutes off our 35-minute schedule for the trip to Tan-y-Bwlch, Merddin Emrys again starting its down train out of the loop there before we came to a stand.

We took water and ran round once more, to wait on the bottom end of the train until Merddin reached Minffordd and we were free to follow. To quench our thirsts, Richard and I had an orange squash each from the Buffet Car, while Bill preferred lemonade, but he then disappeared into Bessie Jones' to reappear with an ice cream for each of us. A passenger got Bill and Bessie to pose for a photograph alongside Prince and Richard settled the headlamp on the bracket on top of the tender back, its standard gauge size making it grotesquely large in proportion to the narrow-gauge centenarian on which it was perched.

The 3.35 down was clearly making good time, and we got away slightly early, dropping easily down the bank in the warm afternoon, and easing to 5 m.p.h. over the permanent way caution where Will Jones exchanged greetings with us from the track side. Beyond Pen-y-Bryn Halt, the distant Cob came into view, with the sun glistening off the sea beyond it, silhouet ting Linda as she steamed across at the head of the 4.30 up. Bill braked our speed well down as I switched to the telephoto lens on my cine camera and steadied myself to record the distant inter-play of sun and steam. Then we were running into Minffordd, Richard leaning out of the tender to snatch, from the hedge alongside, the green flag that gave us entry into the right-hand loop, to await the arrival of Linda, now transformed into a purposeful 4-coupled tank engine from the distant ant-like object of ten minutes previously. We exchanged staffs, and made our way down past the haymaking in the field above the cemetery, Bill remarking that it was the first year they had used a tractor rather than horses for the tedding, but even then the hay was being loaded by hand on to waggons. Passing under the road bridge, Bill whistled for the guard, and Alan Heyward appeared in the window of the leading van, shaking his head as an indication that there was no one to alight at Boston Lodge. Just over four minutes later we were running into Harbour Station, and once more Bill Hartley's voice greeted us over the loudspeakers extolling the virtues of the Festiniog record, an exhortation which, as far as I was concerned, was now wearing rather thin, having heard it four times that day already.

The stock was put in No. 2 Road, and with Richard in charge we returned across the Cob. The clouds were dropping on Moelwyn once more away to our left, as the horses and cattle grazed on the banks of the Glaslyn, the surface of whose water was broken by the concentric ripples of rising fish, while swans sailed their majestic way along on the seaward side of the Cob. The Pen Cob signal swung from left to right of its post and we eased in to the yard once more, coming to a stand on the pits. Bill screwed the handbrake on again, leant across the cab to drop the side dampers of the ash pan, and entered 34 in the log book - Prince's mileage for the day. Richard was meanwhile swinging the smokebox open and easing the hot bar off its supports with a shovel to facilitate the job of emptying the smokebox of char, before cleaning each of the tubes. Bill and I strolled in to No. 1 for tea, with Dolly holding court once more, as she did for the 21 visitors who called in the course of Bank Holiday Monday that year. More friends would almost certainly look in later in the evening after I had left for home, while the other engines coming in for the night would push Prince up alongside the hedge under their kitchen window, the shimmering air rising from her chimney as it was drawn by convection through her still-warm boiler. Later still the reflections of the patterned waters of the Glaslyn would take on the purple and pink hues of the evening sky, while the clouds behind Moel-y-Gest would glow with the gold of the setting sun.

These Merionethshire evenings must seem a great change for Bill and Dolly after a life spent in the bustle of London, and they must find the loneliness somewhat strange, unlike Will and Bessie in their house at Tan-y-Bwlch who have known the roar of the winds through the pines on dark winter nights above the deserted tracks for almost a lifetime. Quiet though it is at Boston Lodge in the winter, there are still the working parties and other visitors, the "Sun", "Daily Mirror" and "Observer" to be read more leisurely, and letters to be written to more distant friends, awaking memories of events long ago on railways whose names and liveries have long since vanished from the scene. For Bill, the Festiniog must provide a link with so much of his past, the close association of its staff and the condition of its locomotives all belonging to an age that has now disappeared on the main lines, swallowed up in their fierce competition for survival. For Dolly, there is the reflected pleasure that Bill still finds in living out his life that has for more than 60 years centred itself round the steam locomotive. Their years in Wales have brought her much admiration for the way she has come to enjoy their isolation in a half-alien country. For those who have known the Festiniog in the last six years, it is impossible to imagine the scene without Bill's cheerful smile and Dolly's ever-ready welcome.

We will all, I think, echo the words of one of the King's Cross officials when Bill retired: "There are no characters left now, only drivers." For few others can there have been the satisfaction of having got so much out of steam power, but perhaps Bill's own words best sum up his life: "It amazes me that people believe me, it amazes me what I've done, and it amazes me that I've got away with it."

Engineman Extraordinary indeed.

Appendix One

ACCOUNTS PUBLISHED IN RAILWAY PERIODICALS OF BILL HOOLE'S LOCOMOTIVE PERFORMANCE

Notes:-The reference is to the start of the article that contains the account or log of the run concerned.
There will be duplication of information between different accounts of the same run, and no attempt has been made to indicate which of the accounts gives most information.

Ref No	Year	Month	Magazine	Page	Section	Date of Run	Train	Locomotive	Recorder	Comments
1	1950	Sept.	Railway Magazine	623	King's Cross-Peterborough	29th Apr. 1950	11.30 p.m. ex-King's Cross	60889	G. W. Carpenter	Log included
2	1953	Nov.	Trains Illustrated	422	King's Cross-Doncaster	20th Sept. 1953	"Plant Centenarian"	990,251	J. E. L. Skelton	Log included
3					Doncaster-King's Cross	27th Sept. 1953	"Plant Centenarian"	990,251	P. W. B. Semmens	Log included
4			Railway World	242	Doncaster-King's Cross	27th Sept. 1953	"Plant Centenarian"	990,251	O. S. Nock	
5				249	King's Cross-Doncaster	20th Sept. 1953	"Plant Centenarian"	990,251	W. J. Reynolds	
6	1954	Mar.	Railway World	50	Grantham-King's Cross	1st Aug. 1953	9.16 a.m. Grantham-King's Cross	60916	G. W. Carpenter	
7		June	Trains Illustrated	224	King's Cross-Darlington	16th Oct. 1953	"Tees-Tyne Pullman"	60066	R. B. Meadows	
8					Leeds-King's Cross	5th Jan. 1954	9.50 a.m. Leeds-King's Cross	60007	R. A. H. Weight	
9		Nov.	Trains Illustrated	458	York-King's Cross	19th July 1954	"Elizabethan"	60024	G. W. Goslin	Further comments–Trains Illustrated, April 1955
10	1955	Mar.	Railway Magazine	184	York-King's Cross	19th July 1954	"Elizabethan"	60024	G. W. Goslin	Log included. Further comments, Railway Magazine, July 1955, p. 484

Ref No	Year	Month	Magazine	Page	Section	Date of Run	Train	Locomotive	Recorder	Comments
11	1955	June	Railway World	135	King's Cross-York-King's Cross	3rd April 1955	Westminster Bank Railway Society Special	60103	–	
12		Dec.	Trains Illustrated	494	York-Tollerton	1st Sept. 1955	"Elizabethan"	60033	R. I. Nelson	
13	1956	Apr.	Railway World	85	Grantham-London		"Flying Scotsman"	60015	P. J. Lynch	
14					Grantham-London		"Flying Scotsman"	60008	P. J. Lynch	
15	1957	Jan.	Railway World	2	Peterborough-Grantham	7th Aug. 1956	"Elizabethan"	60004	M. G. Langdon	Log included
16					Peterborough-Grantham	20th Oct. 1956	1.5 p.m. ex-King's Cross	60157	N. Harvey	Log included
17					Tollerton-King's Cross	8th Aug. 1956	"Elizabethan"	60011	M. G. Langdon	Log included
18					King's Cross-Newcastle	5th Nov. 1956	"Talisman"	60026	–	
19					King's Cross-Newcastle	9th Nov. 1956	"Talisman"	60025	W. Robertson	New Barnet Bomb Incident Guard's times included
20			Trains Illustrated	52	King's Cross-Newcastle	5th Nov. 1956	"Talisman"	60026	–	
21		Jan.	Trains Illustrated		King's Cross-Newcastle	9th Nov. 1956	"Talisman"	60025	–	Guard's times included. New Barnet Bomb Incident–corrections published in Trains Illustrated, March 1957 p. 165
22		Apr.	Railway Magazine	266	Grantham-King's Cross	–	"Flying Scotsman"	60015	P. [illegible] Coster	
23		June	Journal of the Stephenson Locomotive Society	181	King's Cross-Grantham	–	"Northumbrian"	60032	N. Harvey	

Ref No	Year	Month	Magazine	Page	Section	Date of Run	Train	Locomotive	Recorder	Comments
24	1957	June			King's Cross-Doncaster	–	"Yorkshire Pullman"	60007	N. Harvey	
25					King's Cross-York	–	"Tees-Tyne Pullman"	60034	N. Harvey	
26		Aug.	Trains Illustrated	412	King's Cross-Newcastle	9th Nov. 1956	"Talisman"	60025	W. Robertson	Log included. New Barnet Bomb Incident
27	1958	Feb.	Journal of the Stephenson Locomotive Society	43	King's Cross-Newcastle	5th Nov. 1957	"Fair Maid"	60003	A. J. Boston	
28		Apr.	Journal of the Stephenson Locomotive Society	110	King's Cross-Darlington	6th Jan. 1958	"Fair Maid"	60158	–	
29		June	Railway World	154	King's Cross-Newcastle	–	"Talisman"	60013	N. Harvey	
30		Oct.	Trains Illustrated	540	Peterborough-Newcastle	30th May 1958	"Flying Scotsman"	60869	N. Harvey	After failure of No. 60157 at Peterbourgh
31	1959	Jan.	Journal of the Stephenson Locomotive Society	21	King's Cross-Newcastle	5th Nov. 1957	"Fair Maid"	60003	A. J. Boston	
32					Darlington-Hitchin	26th June 1958	5.5 p.m. Newcastle-King's Cross	60033	–	
33			Railway World	3	Grantham-Peterborough	10th Oct. 1958	"Flying Scotsman"	60033	D. F. Howard	Log included
34		Feb.	Railway World	64	King's Cross-Grantham	9th March 1957	1.5 p.m. King's Cross-Bradford	60055	–	Log included

Ref No	Year	Month	Magazine	Page	Section	Date of Run	Train	Locomotive	Recorder	Comments
35	1959	Feb.			Grantham-Peterborough	17th Aug. 1957	8.10 a.m. Newcastle-King's Cross	60157	–	
36					King's Cross-Grantham	13th Oct. 1958	9 a.m. ex-King's Cross	D207	D. F. Howard	Train incorrectly referred to as "Flying Scotsman"
37			Trains Illustrated	105	King's Cross-Newcastle	5th Nov. 1957	"Fair Maid"	60003	A. J. Boston	
38		May	Journal of the Stephenson Locomotive Society	149	Peterborough-Grantham	28th Feb. 1959	8.20 a.m. King's Cross-Doncaster	"Deltic"	P. G. Barlow H. G. Ellison	Log included
39			Railway World	285	Newcastle-King's Cross	16th Nov. 1955	"Tees-Tyne Pullman"	60007	G. Petit	
40					Darlington-York	–	11.55 a.m. Newcastle-King's Cross	60034		Log included
41					Darlington-York	–	5.5 p.m. Newcastle-King's Cross	60033	D. F. Howard	Log included. 35 minutes for 44 miles
42					King's Cross-Peterborough	30th Mar. 1957	"Heart of Midlothian"	60007		Log included
43					Peterborough-Grantham	28th Feb. 1959	8.20 a.m. King's Cross-Doncaster	"Deltic"	P. G. Barlow H. G. Ellison	For further details, see No. 54
44			Trains Illustrated	242	King's Cross-Grantham	21st Feb. 1959	8.20 a.m. King's Cross-Doncaster	"Deltic"	M. G. Langdon	Log included
45					King's Cross-Grantham-King's Cross	5th Mar. 1959	Test run	"Deltic"	C. J. Allen	Log included. Braking tests

Ref No	Year	Month	Magazine	Page	Section	Date of Run	Train	Locomotive	Recorder	Comments
46	1959	June	Journal of the Stephenson Locomotive Society	190	King's Cross-King Edward Bridge	16th Mar. 1959	Test run	"Deltic"	–	
47					Harringay-King Edward Bridge	18th Mar. 1959	Test run	"Deltic"	–	
48					Newcastle-Hornsey	19th Mar. 1959	Test run	"Deltic"	–	
49					Huntingdon-Stevenage	15th Apr. 1959	Test run	"Deltic"	–	100 m.p.h for P.W. Inspectors
50					King's Cross-Grantham-King's Cross	5th Mar. 1959	Test run	"Deltic"	–	Brake tests
51		July	Journal of the Stephenson Locomotive Society	200	King's Cross-Doncaster-King's Cross	23rd May 1959	S.L.S "Golden Jubilee Special"	60007	–	Logs included
52			Railway World	362	King's Cross-Newcastle	14th Aug. 1957	"Flying Scotsman"	60156	K. H. Leech	
53				371	King's Cross-King Edward Bridge	16th Mar. 1959	Test run	"Deltic"	–	Partial log included
54					King's Cross-Doncaster	28th Feb. 1959	8.20 a.m. King's Cross-Doncaster	"Deltic"	P. G. Barlow H. G. Ellison	Log included
55					Harringay-King Edward Bridge	18th Mar. 1959	Test run	"Deltic"	–	
56					King Edward Bridge-Hatfield	19th Mar. 1959	Test run	"Deltic"	–	
57					Doncaster-Ferme Park	21st Mar. 1959	Test run	"Deltic"	–	Minerl wagons and dynamometer car
58			Trains Illustrated	26	King's Cross-Doncaster King's Cross	23rd May 1959	S.L.S "Golden Jubilee Special"	60007	C. J. Allen	Log included

Ref No	Year	Month	Magazine	Page	Section	Date of Run	Train	Locomotive	Recorder	Comments
59	1959	Aug.	Railway World	422	King's Cross-Doncaster-King's Cross	23rd May 1959	S.L.S "Golden Jubilee Special"	60007	N. Harvey	Logs included
60		Nov.	Railway World	570	King's Cross-Durham	30th June 1959	3.10 p.m. King's Cross-Newcastle	60026	J. Child	Partial log included
61					Tollerton-King's Cross	7th July 1959	"Elizabethan"	60027	G. Petit	Last trip
62	1960	Jan.	Journal of the Stephenson Locomotive Society	36	King's Cross-Newcastle	15th May 1959	"Flying Scotsman"	60007	N. Harvey	
63					York-Peterborough	30th May 1959	"Northumbrian"	60007	A. J. Boston	
64					York-Darlington	–	"Tees-Tyne Pullman"	60015	–	
65					Darlington-King's Cross	–	5.5 p.m. Newcastle-King's Cross	60033	–	35 mins. for Darlington-York section
66			Railway World	5	Darlington-King's Cross	1st July 1959	"Tees-Tyne Pullman"	D208	N. Harvey	Log included
67		May	Railway World	131	King's Cross-Doncaster	27th Apr. 1957	"Yorkshire Pullman"	60133	N. Harvey	Log included
68					Peterborough-Grantham	20th Oct. 1956	1.5 p.m. ex-King's Cross	60157	N. Harvey	Log included
69					Grantham-Essendine	16th Feb. 1957	"Flying Scotsman"	60157	N. Harvey	Log included
70					Granthan-Stoke	–	–	"Deltic"	J .F. Clay	Log included
71					Darlington-York	15th Aug. 1957	8 a.m. Newcastle-King's Cross	60156	N. Harvey	Log included
72					Darlington-York	17th Aug. 1957	8.10 a.m. Newcastle-King's Cross	60156	N. Harvey	Log included

Ref No	Year	Month	Magazine	Page	Section	Date of Run	Train	Locomotive	Recorder	Comments
73	1961	Aug.	Railway World	251	King's Cross-Peterborough	30th May 1958	"Flying Scotsman"	60157	N. Harvey	Locomotive failed at Peterborough
74	1962	Apr.	Railway World	111	Leeds-Wakefield	17th Sept. 1956	9.53 a.m. Leeds-King's Cross	60008	N. Harvey	
75					Leeds-Wakefield	28th Apr. 1957	10.23 a.m. Leeds-King's Cross	60015	N. Harvey	
76					Leeds-Wakefield	30th Apr. 1958	10 a.m. Leeds-King's Cross	60800	N. Harvey	
77	1963	Feb.	Railway World	65	Darlington-York	–	5.5 p.m. Newcastle-King's Cross	60033	D. F. Howard	35 min. for 44.1 miles. Log included
78	1964	Jan.	Railway World	3	King's Cross-Grantham	3rd Mar. 1953	"Northumbrian"	60010	F. Mayes	
79		Feb.	Railway World	62	King's Cross-Newcastle	30th May 1958	"Flying Scotsman"	60157/60869	N. Harvey	Log included, Peterborough-Newcastle. Locomotive failed at Peterborough.

In addition, further references will be found in the following books:
1956. British Railways in Action-0. S. Nock (Nelson).
1957. On Engines in Britain and France-P. Ransome-Wallis (Ian Allan)
1962. British Pacific Locomotives-C. J. Allen (Ian Allan)

Locomotives and Locomotive Classes

Index